WHY
JESUS?

WHY JESUS?

REDISCOVERING HIS
TRUTH IN AN AGE OF MASS
MARKETED SPIRITUALITY

RAVI ZACHARIAS

New York   Boston   Nashville

Scripture quotations noted KJV are from the King James Version of the Holy Bible.

Scripture quotations noted NASB are from the New American Standard Bible®. Copyright © 1960, 1962, 1963, 1968, 1971, 1972, 1973, 1975, 1977, 1995 by The Lockman Foundation. Used by permission.

Scripture quotations noted NIV are from The Holy Bible, New International Version® NIV®. Copyright © 1973, 1978, 1984, 2011 by Biblica, Inc.™ Used by permission. All rights reserved worldwide.

Scripture quotations noted NKJV are from the New King James Version. Copyright © 1979, 1980, 1982, Thomas Nelson, Inc., Publishers.

FaithWords
Hachette Book Group
237 Park Avenue
New York, NY 10017
www.faithwords.com

FaithWords is a division of Hachette Book Group, Inc.
The FaithWords name and logo are trademarks of Hachette Book Group, Inc.

The Hachette Speakers Bureau provides a wide range of authors for speaking events. To find out more, go to www.hachettespeakersbureau.com or call (866) 376-6591.

The publisher is not responsible for websites (or their content) that are not owned by the publisher.

Printed in the United States of America

First Edition: January 2012
10 9 8 7 6 5 4 3 2 1

LCCN: 2011943610
ISBN: 978-0-892-96319-5

To my first grandson,

Jude Kumar McNeil.

His name says it all—

He is a gift from our Lord

and the twin ethnic heritages he represents.

CONTENTS

Acknowledgments   IX

Introduction   XI

CHAPTER 1.   Movie Making or Soul Making   I

CHAPTER 2.   How the West Was Lost Through Its Gains   21

CHAPTER 3.   Exhaling the Old, Inhaling the New   45

CHAPTER 4.   From Oprah to Chopra   61

CHAPTER 5.   The Religion of Quantum   83

CHAPTER 6.   Go West, Young Man   95

CHAPTER 7.   The Three Gurus   115

CHAPTER 8.   Smiling Your Way Through Puzzles   133

CHAPTER 9.   Do You Really Want to Live?   151

CHAPTER 10.   The Ties That Bind   161

CHAPTER 11.   The Search for Jesus   181

CHAPTER 12.   Reshaping Jesus to Suit Our Prejudices   197

CHAPTER 13.   The Greatest of All   227

CHAPTER 14.   False Assumptions and Magnificent Truths   249

Appendix: Suggested Bibliography on the Authority of the Scriptures   273

Notes   275

Acknowledgments

Anyone who has ever accomplished anything knows there is very little one can do without enormous support and help from others. In fact, that help may come from the most unexpected places. I write thousands of miles away from home, far from the distractions of other responsibilities, so that I may focus on the job at hand. So first I would like to thank those who have given up so much time with me to free me to do a project like this—my family, my colleagues, my friends. In fact, they have done much to cheer me on from a distance. My thanks to all I meet while traveling, some of whose names I do not know, who take the time to talk and interact with me. To the team that takes care of my back to minimize my pain during protracted hours of writing, my deepest gratitude. Without you all, I could not do this.

Finally, I want to thank the four who work behind the scenes: Wolgemuth & Associates, my agents, are also my friends; the efforts of Joey Paul of FaithWords, whose diligent pursuit helped me sharpen the focus of this book, cannot be gainsaid. Joey is a unique man. I wish there were more like him in this world. Also Danielle DuRant, my hardworking research assistant, who reminds me of what I said where and helps me say it better; Margie, my wife, who is a night owl when it comes to working on manuscripts. She gave up many nights of sleep to do the editorial work. I can't thank her enough.

But all is not said: As a teen without meaning in my life, I found Jesus as my Lord, Savior, and the shepherd of my soul. Little did I know then how much his message of love and forgiveness would change everything for me. This book is a defense of who he is and of why his name is still above every name.

INTRODUCTION

I had just walked through one of the newest shopping malls in New Delhi. It is one of those globalized reproductions where you see the same stores whether you are in Hong Kong, Paris, Tokyo, or New York. What's in a name? A lot of money, depending on whose name it is. But you can also walk into shops in Bangkok or Jakarta and find, in popular jargon, a "knockoff version" of the brand name that looks identical to the original. If it is a Rolex you are looking for, the shopkeeper will tell the person who is wearing an original one, "You'd better put yours in your pocket, because when you place it side by side with my fake one you won't be able to tell the difference." The replicas are so identical to the real ones that only an expert can tell the difference. When, out of curiosity, I asked one salesperson how they were even able to manufacture these, he reprimanded me, saying that his fakes were genuine fakes and not the fake fakes that the man around the corner sold. When I asked the man of the "genuine fakes" if his genuine fakes would fail within a little while, he looked me in the eye and said, "So will you in a few years."

Not only was there the genuine/fake market in this mall, there was the exotic touch to the way products were promoted. The health food stores advertised revolutionary magical slimming and wellness products from America, Switzerland, and points west. I couldn't help but think of the wellness magazines I have seen in the West, all of which advertise revolutionary products from the East: the juices of Tibetan berries, "age-old" remedies from India, China, Japan, and Indonesia; from the jungles of the Amazon to the mountains of Kashmir, they offer myriad cures. What a world we are living in! The more foreign-sounding a word, the more mystique we attribute to it and endue it with powers to bring about nirvana.

Who doesn't want to be well? Who doesn't want a life free from stress? Who, deep in his or her heart, doesn't want to know God, if he really exists? So the wellness industry and the spiritual centers are thriving, each offering their own version of bliss.

Recently, Deepak Chopra went to Thailand to be ordained as a Buddhist monk, and, according to an article I read in India, Julia Roberts has become a Hindu. She and her family go to a Hindu temple every now and then, to chant and repeat certain sounds that are supposed to help her gain peace. I wonder if Roberts and Chopra realize that Buddha was born a Hindu and turned his back on some of Hinduism's fundamental teachings in order to begin his own pilgrimage and discover a new path. At least in Buddha's defense we can say his was a lifelong pursuit. In Chopra's case, he was a monk for a week.

This book is about the deep, irrepressible spiritual hungers we all have. We long both for an escape from the world around us and for solace within us. Our world extracts too much from us. Where does one find replenishment and ultimate meaning, especially in a world that mass-markets numerous paths to truth? At every turn we are offered special words, sounds, discoveries…genuine fakes, fake fakes…and everything else that is today subsumed under the sweeping category of "spirituality." Just as sin has gone out of vogue and evil has remained a legitimate category, though limited, religion has gone out of vogue while spirituality remains a valid pursuit.

Over years of careful research and reflection I have given deep, detailed, and extended thought to this subject. More than forty years and numerous countries and conversations later, I have some thoughts to offer that I trust the reader will pay careful attention to. I genuinely and passionately care about this search.

In spiritual matters, too, there is the genuine, the genuine fake, and the fake fake. Tired, in the West, of what C. S. Lewis called "the same old thing," and having become accustomed to abundance and the bliss of multiple choice, we have now a spiritual supermarket before us from which we may choose whatever form of spirituality we fancy. We think we can follow whichever path we want and still end up with something meaningful. It all boils down to branding and appearance. Questions of truth are hinted at but seldom asked. Life is lived with a smorgasbord of sounds and chants.

Spirituality is writ large in the West as gurus come and go. Perhaps a primary reason for this spread of alternative spiritualities and a key to unlocking much of this puzzle for us is our means of communication today. Cultural shifts do not happen in one giant step. How is it that a culture that once frowned upon certain sexual practices now frowns upon those who frown upon them? How is it that from the normal use of language in public broadcasting and in public discourse, so well tempered that even mild deviations were viewed as serious infractions, we now experience on a daily basis entertainment that has moved from the genius of humor to the crassness of shock and vulgarity? Why is it that the more perverse the story, the greater the audience it draws on television or at the theater? Why do people create false scenarios in order to have their own "reality" shows?

Who are these icons created by the media of the visual whose belief in some form of spirituality seems real, even if they are made-up for the sell? Has all this happened because our taboos were wrong or is it that, in a very real sense, we have pushed the Replay button on the saga of Eden and can now look, touch, and taste anything we wish to because *we* have become gods, determining for ourselves what is right and what is wrong?

There is no greater force in cultivating tastes, legitimizing beliefs, and achieving mass impact than our capacity for visual communication. It is hard to even remember how we lived before its inception. At the same time, it is hard to imagine a culture more gullible than that of America today, priding itself on being a culture that is willing to absorb anything indiscriminately.

Two personalities that typify what we have in the spiritual smorgasbord before us today are Oprah Winfrey and Deepak Chopra. And if they represent two ends of the spectrum, there are hosts of others in between. Their success has demonstrated how easily an idea can be marketed, reshaped, repackaged, and taken at face value by a generation that not only fails to ask the right questions, but doesn't care enough about truth to even *think* the right questions. Combine the power of the camera and the power of the Internet with the hungers deep within, and you have a ready mix of spiritual time and space in different dimensions.

This thing we now call "spirituality" has itself evolved as a term over the last few years. People will say that they're not "into" religion but they are "into" spirituality. That in itself is a sociological phenomenon. And just as existentialists don't like to be categorized, neither do the advocates of the New Spirituality. Because so much is encompassed by that term, to deal with it in a simplistic manner is unfair to any reader. So, instead, I have looked at the most popular forms of the New Spirituality and then at the marketing of this vast new field. Then I have gone further and looked at those religions and exponents that actually provided the underlying worldviews from which these popular forms of spirituality have emerged.

Finally, I have looked at what it is about the message of Jesus Christ that, if properly understood, still offers the beauty, the power, and the only hope of any future for mankind. So much of the fake has overtaken the depth and breadth of his teaching. He said that he came to give us water to drink that would quench our deepest thirsts. Yet the superficiality with which his message has been presented and manipulated by the media has obscured if not destroyed his message. One ought never to judge a philosophy by its abuse. Yet that is what the message of Jesus has suffered. The same manipulations attend the "new" spiritual movements, but for a different purpose. Should our pursuit be to abuse the message, or should it be to discover what is actually being claimed by these belief systems and test these claims for authenticity? At their core, the worldviews behind these new spiritual movements are completely different from that of Jesus.

There are four key elements that come to the fore in a study of these systems and beliefs. The first is the combination of *truth* and *relevance*: How do I know that what I believe is true, and is what I believe in any way relevant to my day-to-day life? The danger here is that we often mistake relevance for truth and make truth so academic that it seems to have become irrelevant. Either we become so rigid and dispassionate about truth that we forget to filter it down to the level of our emotions, or we place such stress on "feeling good" that we forget to ask the basic question of whether what we believe is based in truth.

But there is a second combination, and that is of *reason* and *faith*. Every worldview has to bring together reason and faith.

Some admit to both, and some like to pretend they have both in the proper order. The naturalist is too proud to admit that a heavy dose of faith is required in order to believe as he or she does. And the religious person can often become smug and say, "I really don't care what you *say*, my faith is the most important thing to me." I have often put it this way: God has put enough into this world to make faith in him a most reasonable thing; but he has left enough out to make it impossible to live by reason alone.

I was born in Chennai, in the south of India, and raised in Delhi, in the North. My ancestors came from the highest caste of the Hindu priesthood, the Nambudiris and the Nairs, from Kerala. Several generations ago, as far as we know, one of them heard the message of Jesus from some German-Swiss missionaries and became a devout follower of Christ. She was ostracized, expelled from her community and family, and paid dearly for her newfound faith. Her descendant was my grandmother, who married into the Zacharias family, which had also been converted from Hinduism several generations back.

However, generations later this newfound faith had become true in name only because, unlike every other religion, being born into a Christian home does not make one a Christian; it is the specific decision on the part of every person to follow Christ that makes that person a Christian. It took my generation, asking the hard questions about belief, to once again study the message of Jesus and respond to its simplicity and sublimity. I became a Christian while on a bed of attempted suicide at the age of seventeen when I cried out to God in prayer, "Lord Jesus, if you are who you claim to be, reveal yourself to me and take me out of my desperate situation and I will leave no stone unturned in my pursuit of truth." Five days later I walked out of that hospital room a brand-new man, and I have never looked back. Jesus Christ does not only change what you do, he changes what you want to do.

But here is something important: One cannot just grasp the finger of an experience of a moment and assume, therefore, that one has grabbed the fist of reality. I have followed through on my promise to pursue truth and have devoted my life to the study and understanding of all the major religions and systems of belief in the world. It was the right and proper thing to do. Jesus makes an amazing statement. He not only claims to be unique and to have the power to transform anyone who comes to him, but the Bible says that we are "made complete" in him (Colossians 2:10 NASB). What does that mean? I hope that in the pages to follow you will stay with me on this journey to find truth and relevance, faith and reason, and discover that when we have Jesus, we have life. All other hungers for spirituality are a reflection of why it is that he offers himself as the Way, the Truth, and the Life.

Even if you disagree with me, please stay the course. Honesty of intent and thinking seriously about the content will make the difference between the genuine and the spurious. Coming to the right conclusion on a matter such as this will define eternity. You may be surprised what your spiritual hungers and God's self-disclosure might bring to you. At the point of his conversion C. S. Lewis said, "I thought I had come to a place. I found out I had come to a person." That's what this book is about: examining the places we wish to be and those we should walk away from until we find the Person for whom we are looking.

CHAPTER I

MOVIE MAKING OR SOUL MAKING

It's a Dream World

From the first moment of the movie *Inception*, you are taken through enough mysteries and plots strung together that you are not sure whether you are watching the movie or the movie is watching you. You feel yourself trying to determine whether you are dreaming that you are awake or are awake and dreaming. You begin to question whether you understand reality at all or if reality has conned you, and a series of mind games follows: Is consciousness a cause or an effect? Are we human beings eternal entities given a quantity of time to exist or are we time-laden bodies pretending to be eternal? In short, in the complex mix of the drama, the biggest struggle is whether you, the watcher, are the ultimate dreamer or merely the dream.

Ironically, the unavoidable reality in this brilliant production is that dreaming or awake, the lead characters display their infinite capacity for human depravity. The schemes that wreak devastation—wholesale slaughter, explosions, killing, everything in the news that clutters our daily lives—are the staple of this movie, whether the characters are in a state of slumber or awake. One thing has to be said for Hollywood: there are some real geniuses behind the levels to which they can carry the imagination.

The plot of *Inception* is built on the idea that a person can infiltrate another individual's mind through their dreams and steal that person's subconscious thoughts and plans. The extractors of the information that is gained through the dreams and their victims sleep in close proximity to one another, linked by a device called the "Dream Share," which administers a sedative that allows them to share the dream jointly. Interestingly, pain experienced in the dream world is real, and if one awakes in the middle of the dream, death will result from the abrupt crossing of consciousnesses. So one must remain in a state of sleep and endure the pain in order to accomplish the extraction. The sedation has to last. So in this depraved reality, if you are the extractor you must remain asleep, enduring someone else's pain, until you can extract the information you want. That's about it.

The lead character carries a little spinning top called a "totem" that either spins unceasingly or topples, allowing him to determine whether he is dreaming or awake, respectively. Odd, isn't it, that even in the wanderings of our imaginations we still want to know the difference between fantasy and reality by implanting a world within a world to separate the realities? No human emotion is missing from *Inception*: family longings, children at play, the usual array of surreal underworld figures and big-business shenanigans and the angst of marital strains all form the tapestry of the story.

The overall mission in this film is to secretly implant an

idea that will topple a business adversary. Just trying to figure out what is going on is enough to keep your attention as you are swept into the story with its gripping motif of how the power of an idea planted in the mind can change an individual and in fact, rearrange reality when it is given motivation and direction. The web that is being spun becomes even more complex, delving into deeper and deeper levels of the subconscious with proportionate ramifications. Just enough of the supernatural is included to tantalize the viewer with a world beyond the physical, and the producers have created a psychological terrain and breadth of imagination that would have made Freud look sophomoric.

Intriguing about this mix is how its creators concoct a mesmerizing blend of mutually exclusive worldviews. But in the world of moviemaking the irrational and the rational work hand in hand to create worldviews that, in the end, endow a human being with divine powers. That seems always to be the desired result, and the means are harnessed to accomplish that end.

Interestingly, the same man who brought us this movie spectacular also brought us *The Dark Knight*, which was really Batman made postmodern. In that movie, award-winning actor Heath Ledger played the sinister role of the Joker with near satanic powers. Once again, you walked away from the movie thinking it was "just a movie." But was it? One can write a whole book on some of the lines in that story. You can't seem to escape the question of whether that was all there was to it…just a movie.

In the real world, devoid of pretense, when the news of Heath Ledger's sudden and mysterious drug-related death at the age of twenty-nine hit the news, the question being bandied about was whether his portrayal of the Joker had so overtaken his thinking that he couldn't break free from the script of Batman. According to his co-actors and friends, Ledger ended up possessed by the Joker and unable to break free from the character, even away from the set. He so immersed himself into the thought processes of the character he was playing that the dividing line between imagination and being imagined, from acting to becoming one with the character, was erased. The sinister won the day and the Joker was no longer a phantom character, but was embodied away from the set with dire real-life consequences.

It's Just a Story

Is it possible to read a story and not enter into it; to write a story and not become part of the script?

When I was writing my first book, my family and I were living in Cambridge, England. Our young son, who was just nine years old at the time, decided to write a book as well. So every evening after school, he would get out his pad of paper and start dreaming his plot. Needless to say, every second page was filled with some kind of crisis. One day, I came to the table where I had my material all set up and I saw him seated there as well, pen in hand, pad in front of him, the weight of the world apparently on him as tears ran down his face. I immediately put aside all I was thinking of and asked him what on earth the matter was.

"I know it, I just know it," he said between sobs.

"Know what?" I asked gently.

"I just know the dog is going to die."

I had to pause to process what he was talking about and realized that the world of make-believe and his make-believe characters had taken over his own will to believe. It was amazing to see in his eyes the sense of inevitability from which he wanted to escape but couldn't, even though it was in his power to do so. Frankly, I didn't know whether to break him out of the role of storyteller or let him know that when you write a story, it tends to take on a life all its own. Such is the immense power of the imagination when it intersects with reality. This is actually how cultures are shaped.

It is one thing for this to happen in the mind of a nine-year-old who enters the world of make-believe; quite another for it to happen in the mind of an actor employed in the billion-dollar industry of sophisticated storytelling, the biggest imagination-controlling business in the world today. If Heath Ledger couldn't break free from the story, being close to the script and knowing he was just acting, how can the audience break free from the story when they don't know what is going on behind the scenes?

Watching a movie with my mother-in-law is worthy of a script all its own. She sits there almost in a trance, watching every move, and often she will call out to the character, "Watch out, there's someone hiding behind the door!" I have a lot of fun reminding her that actually the actor knows better than she does that there is someone behind the door and that he is going to get mugged, and the only reason he appears to be unaware of it is that the director has told him to look that way. Not only that, he has practiced this a few times before it looks real enough for the director. Perhaps she has a greater grasp of the imagination; and it is true that there is fun in drama, even if it ushers us into the surreal and then traps us there.

The important point I am making is worthy of repetition. If the actors themselves, aware that they are playing roles, are unable to break free from the media and the message, how is it possible for the viewer to be freed from the stranglehold of the imagination? In fact, we go even one step further than crossing the line between the imagination and reality by deifying the actors. And movies become narratives played out by gods.

What we are witnessing, at the very least, is that the propensity within us to blur the lines between what is real and what is imagined has been deliberately taken advantage of by fiction writers and especially movies. Stories can alter one's way of viewing things. The playwright or author is no longer writing the play or story. The play or story is writing the playwright or author. And, in turn, the playwright and the play rewrite our own stories. This is the real world of our time. The world of entertainment has become the most powerful means of propaganda, and the audience is unaware of how much it is being acted upon and manipulated, paying for it not only in cash but in having its dreams stolen.

It's a Growing World After All

What Disney World is for fun and for children in their small world, the intrigue of the movie and media world is now for adults, encouraging us to believe what is most often make-believe.

I bring these thoughts regarding the deliberate overlap between imagination and reality to the beginning of our journey through the minefield of conflicting worldviews to help us find the truth about life's greatest quest. Why is there so much of the supernatural in story lines today, and why do those assumptions so often promote a worldview that tries to make the human divine? And why is that not possible without including our fascination with evil within the human story? In a strange way, is not the marring of beauty now the force of entertainment? Is not the spiritual always irrepressible in its power to tell a story? What is it about us that we constantly seek answers? What lies beneath the physical? In country music it is always about a broken vow; in the world of stories it is invariably about a broken world. Where do we go to be mended? Has Christianity had its say and been rejected in the West? Are old answers passé?

Certainly old answers once deemed doctrinaire and dogmatic seem totally irrelevant today. Why are we always on a quest for the spiritual without categories? Why do we always find ourselves at odds on matters of the sacred? It is a terrifying indictment of our existence that, unable to solve our problems in the phenomenal world, we now dig deep into dream states and, with the aid of technology, leave audiences in a dream world of their own. The visual has, in fact, distorted the spiritual rather than clarify it. How easy it is to forget that behind these story lines are storytellers who are often themselves in knots in their own private worlds. Have we been trapped by a means that has engineered the ends? Are there now manipulators at work who have grasped the ends and means better than any preacher ever has? These stories are not just tales for the imagination; they are entire bodies of belief that are reshaping society beyond recognition, doctrines dressed up as entertainment.

How else does one explain the tragic self-destruction of actor Charlie Sheen, a news item for millions to watch and be entertained by? He himself made the incredible statement that his producers have broken their contract with him because he was living in reality like the loose-living, "anything goes" character in his very popular TV sitcom. When he translated his values from the show to reality, they broke ties with him. Is it that we think by watching his meltdown we can change the ending? How else does one watch comedians humor their way out of embarrassing and frankly immoral situations?

The message is massaged into the subconscious by media that make the undesirable attractive and the good appear boring and flat, while shattered lives look intriguing and full of the divine. Worldviews are being smuggled in by the power of the lens, far beyond what any evangelist could have done. *Inception* reminded me of the aphorism of the famed Chinese philosopher Lao Tse: "If, when I am sleeping, I am a man dreaming I am a butterfly, how do I know that when I am awake I am not a butterfly dreaming that I am a man?"

It's a Science

If the person promoting the fantasy is incapable of defending it and wishes to be taken seriously, then it becomes clever to inject into the argument a dose of the final authority—science. What novelists were to existentialism and deconstructionists were to postmodernism, pseudoscience or selective science has become to the postmodern spiritual quest. This is quite ironic. At its core, postmodernism is a philosophy of inexactitudes. But in an effort to find credence, it goes to the exact sciences. The wiggled-in entry point is generally the branch of science called quantum physics so that it can seem to hold on to the worlds of the empirical and the uncertain at the same time.

Marilyn Ferguson, one of the earliest voices to announce "the Age of Aquarius," opined in the early days of what is now branded broadly the New Age movement that "the brain's calculations do not require our conscious effort, only our attention and our openness to let the information through. Although the brain absorbs universes of information, little is admitted into normal consciousness."[1]

With that no-man's land of comprehension one is supposed to buy into a whole metaphysic of religion. Just think of that line: "The brain's calculations do not require our conscious effort." She is telling us something of our susceptibility to belief even though we might not be willing to believe. And so the abnormal is now normal in entertainment, because the normal is treated as subnormal in the world of the media. That, I can assure you, is consciously done.

Scientist Stephen Hawking espouses a "multiverse" theory, meaning that ours is not the only universe there is; there may be an infinite number of universes out there. He does not need God to explain the universe. Gravity does that. So while Richard Dawkins, an atheist, espouses that this show on earth is the only show in town, Hawking suggests that though our show may be the only show in town, there may be other towns, perhaps many of them. And one day, supposedly, we will discover those other towns or, more to the point, we will be found to be just one of many.

In a strange way, the New Spirituality may comfortably cling to both positions—this town that we know and the make-believe towns that are made by science to look real. What Hawking proposes with his "physics," the arts had already implied in its metaphysics. In a made-to-order spirituality, the multiverse theory may also be positioned as being inside us, not just outside. In a not-so-subtle way, we are beginning to believe that we are inhabited by a multiverse within us.

Coming to terms with what is happening, then, we have a multiverse within us, immersed in the pluriverse around us, in which we are pursuing an imaginary universe that will unite us. And all this is done in dark theaters or in the privacy of our own homes, giving us the illusion of being entertained while we are actually being indoctrinated by ideas that are deliberately planted within us.

This is truly to have our cake and eat it, too. It makes for a charming story, but the spoiler is that our depravity gets in the way. Everyone knows that Karl Marx said that religion is the opiate of the people. But very few go on to finish what he said next; that it is the sigh of the oppressed and the illusory sun that revolves around man *as long as man doesn't revolve around himself.* The New Spirituality has solved that dilemma. We have found a religion that has helped us to revolve around ourselves, and once we have believed that the spiritual imagination needs no boundaries because we are gods, everything becomes plausible and nothing needs justification. We are now in the precarious situation where science has given us the tools—and possibly the imperative—to convey fiction, and fiction has the persuasive power of science. This is the New Spirituality.

One major news network carries the distinctive tagline "Go Beyond Borders." There is a pun intended. But when crossing borders worldviews often collide, and on that, there is a strange silence. When Deepak Chopra (a household name to many in the spirituality movement of our time) was on a program with scientist Richard Dawkins, he tried to smuggle some terminology of quantum physics into his argument. Dawkins, rather puzzled, asked him what his spiritual theory had to do with quantum. Chopra tried to explain his position by saying, "Well, well… it's a metaphor." "A metaphor?" countered Dawkins, looking even more puzzled. It could have been a comedy routine, but it wasn't. It is one thing for Deepak Chopra to impress the popular audience with scientifically rich terms, but when pushed by a rigorously pure scientist, all of a sudden his science becomes a metaphor…whatever that means! Chopra looked like a little boy caught with his hand in the cookie jar. But gurus can get away with saying nothing if they cloak it in ponderous terminology.

It's Superman

By the visual media and a selective if not perverted use of science, new consciousness patterns were introduced into the West just four decades ago when Transcendental Meditation (TM) made its first foray onto Western soil. The lead voices at that time caught the West on the turn culturally, and the result was a fork in the road in Western spirituality. As innocuous as it seemed then, it has redefined spirituality for Western culture so that a whole new way of thinking about ultimate reality has emerged. The Eastern gurus arrived in large numbers, using terminology that sounded scientific but, when challenged, became "just metaphors." I will deal with three of these gurus and their specific teachings later.

These meditation experts offered a systematized teaching that could plumb the depths of the subconscious and enumerate several states of consciousness. And while scientists talked of dimensions far beyond the three we know, spiritualists jumped into the narrative with a meditation technique that was actually more of a psychological theory of the spirit, though it was asserted as an exact science. Starting from the crassness of the material world, their theories led to a spiritual journey that progressed through different stages of meditation to a state of dreamless sleep and, ultimately, to attaining a transcending sense of cosmic consciousness where the pilgrim became one with the universe. The biggest challenge, then, was to make what was momentary, normative: to breathe one's way into a relaxed consciousness.

To be sure, we were told again and again that TM was not a religion; it was merely what sages have taught for centuries, nothing more than a method to awaken the dormant divinity within each one of us. It was continually reemphasized that one did not have to change their religion in order to participate in this spirituality. The magical potion in these meditative techniques was not a spinning top, as in *Inception*, but the taming of the spinning mind. And as a culture, we entered the brave new world of self where everything is viewed through individual, tailor-made lenses. At the same time that we were on the cusp of technological advances, our high-paced lives and stress were tearing us apart inside. How and where could we experience both technology and spirituality? The best of Western technological advances combined with the best of Eastern ancient divinizing techniques made for the inception of a *nirvanic* world where we could become the new *avatars*.

Back to the Future

The meditative techniques that were introduced to the West four decades ago were a hybrid of automation and stagnation: If only this spiritual secret could be transmitted through the utterance of some words of empowerment by a teacher who has already attained this *nirvanic* bliss, what peace would ensue individually and cosmically! There was a time in the West—not so long ago—when words like *mantra*, *chakra*, *tantra*, *moksha*, and *nirvana* needed explanation. They are still not generally understood, even by most of those who use them regularly, but they make for an intellectual veneer in a subculture. The ensuing patent wars that have emerged over which theory or guru owns the rights to yoga are a bizarre twist in these spiritual schemes that are purported to release stress and induce peace.

One medical practitioner with an avocation in spiritual apologetics for Hinduism is on a crusade "to give credit where credit is due," insisting that the world owes a debt to Hinduism for these techniques. Meanwhile, Deepak Chopra, also a medical practitioner whose primary practice is writing on spiritual themes, challenges that claim and declares that yoga, among other practices, is part of a universal religion and not the private possession of just one: *Sanatan Dharma*, he brands it…the "Eternal Religion"…essential and pure spirituality that goes beyond any "ism." The inescapable conclusion of all this is that whether meditating or awake, ancient or new, depravity is the constant. Stay tuned! We will fight one another verbally or legally for the right to preach a stress-free life, and do so with material means for material gains, all for the glories of a nonmaterial transcendence.

I was pondering the other day how much in our lives has to do with boxes: We give gifts in boxes, we buy our food in boxes, we drive in boxes, we live in boxes, we sleep in boxes, and we ultimately leave this world in a box. But this brand of spirituality hates to be boxed in by absolutes, so the edges of reason are erased and spirituality oozes into another realm like a vapor or a cloud. As boundaries have been erased our world has changed, and the means by which we now share this world are not necessarily that far removed from planting ideas in a mind that is half asleep. The resulting inability or even desire to reason and think through an idea logically is demonstrated by one-liners such as "I'm not into 'isms.'"

Existentialists don't want to be boxed into an "ism" either; nor do postmodernists. The person who isn't into "isms" gives himself the liberty to conveniently dismiss anything he doesn't like or agree with as an "ism," which by his definition does not deserve to be taken seriously, while his own beliefs are defended against being considered an "ism." Giving yourself the privilege of destroying other positions while parking your own position in an unidentifiable location is a form of linguistic terrorism.

In the world of non-isms, you are introduced to terminology that seems to have magic powers. You make an appointment for a massage and are told that they will work on your *chakras* so that you will reach the *tantric* stage and ultimately *nirvana*. I shall resist further comment on this right now. This form of spiritual communication has unfortunately hijacked reality and holds truth hostage, never to be released until one is willing to pay the price of relativism. Couched in jellylike terminology, reality reshapes itself, and rather than being a constant, it can become whatever you want it to be. But like the actors who still have to leave the set and live in the real world, we all now have to return from the escape of a story to the harsh questions of our private worlds.

Where can we find reality the way it was meant to be? Allowing ourselves to be beguiled by foreign terms is not consolation for reality. The greatest and most notable casualty of our times in which we are inundated with spiritual terminology is, unquestionably, *truth*. As Malcolm Muggeridge would have stated it, "The lie is stuck like a fishbone in the throat of the microphone."

I would add that today it is not so much the microphone as the camera and the vocabulary of the verbal magician.

Some years ago I sat in as a visitor on a trial in London at the Old Bailey. It was the trial of a man accused of raping two minor girls. I was there for the opening arguments, watching from the gallery. I remember the defense lawyer's plea so clearly. He looked intently into the faces of the two minor girls separately and said to each of them, "I am interested in only one thing: one thing and nothing more—the truth. Do you understand me?" he asked. "All I want is the truth. If you have the answers, give them to me. If you don't know the answers, tell me you don't know. I want the truth. That's all."

Here is my question: If the truth is so important in one isolated courtroom case, how much more important is it in the search for the spiritual answers to our deepest hungers?

"The most valuable thing in the world is the truth," said Winston Churchill. "The most powerful weapon in the world is the truth," said Andrei Sakharov, the man who gave the Soviets the atomic bomb. "God is Truth and Truth is God," said Mahatma Gandhi. From its value, to its power, to its deification, even as an abstract category truth becomes the final question in any conflict. Yet, again and again we find ourselves uncertain as to what truth means and why it matters. "What is truth?" asked Pontius Pilate impatiently…and walked away, without waiting for an answer. The irony is that he was standing in front of the one Person who, as the personification and embodiment of Truth, could have given him the answer.

In the musical play by Andrew Lloyd Webber *The Phantom of the Opera*, the Phantom sings a beautiful piece titled "The Music of the Night." One of the lines intimates that under the cover of darkness it is easy to pretend that the truth is what each one of us wants it to be. When there is no light held to our version of truth to call our bluff, we confuse what *is* with what we think *ought* to be, and infuse "the ought" with our own ideas to make it what we *want* it to be. Truth is that foundational reality we often resist but that, ultimately, we cannot escape. Nothing is so destructive as running from the truth, even as we know it will always outdistance us.

Tragically, we seem to be at a time in our cultural history when we no longer care about this question whatsoever. Seduced by terminology carried by a media that distorts, we willingly, it seems, buy into a lie. From the news to the weather to advertising to entertainment, we are sold *feelings*, not truth. I have often pondered the vast terrain of uncertainties that surround us: *mystery—* we love mysteries and are held in their grip; *manipulation—*we dabble with the mind and find it fascinating; *money—*we all fear it, yet we all live immersed in it; *more—*we all spend most of our lives either earning it or desiring it, hardwired, it seems, to keep adding to what we have already accumulated. When mystery, the manipulation of the mind, and the accumulation of wealth are offered to us all tied up in one neat package, our dreams are being tapped into and we have become the dream-givers, having our dreams taken from us. Add to this the dimension of music or chanting, and we have the beat to which we can lull ourselves into other *consciousnesses.*

Mystery, the manipulation of the mind, the desire for money and accumulation of wealth, music—what a recipe for feeling! One practitioner of Ayurvedic medicine sums it up by saying that you can create your own universe out of desire; that when you empty your mind and focus on the thing you want, the distance between you and your desire disappears, your brain cells rejuvenate, and you become open to all possibilities.

The truth is that if you repeat this kind of self-inducement often enough, you begin not only to believe it, but to smile in pity on those who don't. You begin to feel a sense of security in a world that has become like jelly because you don't really have to make sense of it all. It is somewhat like being a college student who doesn't have to be an earning member of the family or lead an orderly life because he has not yet finished his preparations for life. A disheveled room and appearance are acceptable in a college student…after all, that's a license that dorm life gives you.

Such is the vocabulary and narrative of the New Spirituality, which has leveraged and thrived on a privatized logic while claiming the ultimate strength of philosophy wedded to science. But how did we get here? How did we reach such an incredible way of reasoning? Who stole the fire of reason from us?

As an easterner, raised in the East, I see such irony in all this. A short time ago I was asked to address a small group of the entertainment elite in the East. They sat listening with courtesy and concentration as I reminded them that they were the icons of our time, the envy of the masses, while they themselves knew that inside each of them was a big vacuum. By the end of the talk, some were in tears and after the talk there was a lineup of these successful people, asking for time alone and the opportunity to open up the depths of their own struggles. I admired their candor and transparency.

As I left that setting, I thought to myself, *Why are we always beguiled by something foreign?* In the West, Eastern mysticism is "in"—chants, sounds, and practices with foreign words have made an appeal of culture-shifting proportions—while in the East, where these very same techniques have been tried for centuries, many are disillusioned and are seeking solace somewhere else. Before me the entertainment elite of the East gave their full attention to a talk on "Why Jesus Is the Ultimate Fulfillment," while in the West, entertainers are looking toward the East for their answers.

The movies of the East have been played out in an artificial dream world interwoven with the spiritual long enough. The lyrics of their music often speak of disappointment. The setting for a very popular song in the Hindi language is a man standing in front of a sage, asking his advice. He sings that he has been to the holy river and to the holy sites, but his heart is still searching for fulfillment. It is not gold or silver that he is seeking; it is the fulfillment of his soul.

Pilgrims go to the sacred sites of India by the millions, in search of inner liberation. The devout of every religion embark on spiritual journeys in the hope of finding God. Thus, in the final analysis, it is actually to God himself that we go, asking, "Where is the answer?" That's the irony, as I see it.

In the 1960s there was a song made famous by Tom Jones titled "The Green, Green Grass of Home." Hearing it for the first time is a thrill that dies by the last verse. The song describes the thrill of touching the green, green grass of home and seeing loved ones long missed. But as the story progresses, we get to the last verse.

Yes, those who know the song know the ending. The singer is on death row, and the morning brings the harsh reality of his last steps to the grave, a different green, green grass than that with which the song begins.

We all have yearnings and longings. We all dream of hope

and peace. We all long to align our hearts with ultimate reality. We need to be grateful for at least one thing that the New Spiritualists have done: They have awakened us to a place of our need. We all search for deep fulfillment and yearn for answers that are satisfying at the level of our feelings, not just at the philosophical level of truth and logic. Is there somewhere that the two existences align? Stay with me as we endeavor to broach this subject in the pages ahead and find some life-transforming answers.

CHAPTER 2

HOW THE WEST WAS LOST THROUGH ITS GAINS

Barely twenty years after trying to reshape the world in the horrific aftermath of the Second World War, America was caught in a war of her own making from which she has not recovered. In the backdrop was the Civil Rights movement, guilt over the past, cultural blunders, and spiritual hungers. And in the foreground was a brewing rebellion as the young questioned why they were being sent into a war in Vietnam that they felt was unnecessary and ultimately unwinnable. It was the perfect storm for the overthrow of what had been believed and held inviolable for generations.

This was also a time of forging new horizons, nationally. The landing on the moon did not merely happen; the nation actually *watched* it happen on the new television sets in our own living rooms. And this same new medium allowed America's military enemy to win because they were able to harness it and make it serve their advantage more than it served those who had developed it. The medium of viewing at home made the war cabinet room not a single location in some subterranean setting where war strategy was determined. Rather, every household was able to watch the carpet-bombing by the B-52s. Every home was able to witness the psychological breakdown of the nation's troops. The pictures of war that could be seen and experienced at home through television changed the war from one fought just on the battlefield and brought it into each home. The burning of draft cards and the uprising from within the nation made the Vietnam War a very personal thing. More than fifty thousand individual lives were ultimately lost. And the nation returned from the war with its soul in a body bag.

The camera had won the battle of seeing and believing. The world, and America in particular, was foundationally transformed. The zeal of the young, combined with the material means that their parents had fought to give them and the invasiveness of the medium of television, made for a powerful overthrow of the reigning worldview.

There were really several wars going on. Politically, though the administration that supposedly brought "peace with honor" had inherited the war, it has been forced to carry the blame for it ever since. Conservatism became the pariah of political verbiage, and "politically correct" became synonymous with anti-traditional values. It was really the absolutizing of relativism, the new anti-values value. The Cold War was at its grimmest and weapons of intimidation and destruction were piling up, with each superpower living in fear of the other.

The battle was carried into the universities, whose own academic experts were flaying America, and the intelligentsia hit hard at political demagoguery, as they called it. At the same time, the race struggle was reaching conflagration points on many fronts. Watts became synonymous with rioting. And all this was reflected in the arts as rock stars changed the mathematical rules of music and discord became entertainment. Noise became deafened to reason. Woodstock became the stage for selling propriety in exchange for public nudity. Sexual mores were questioned as the gender exploitations of the past came home to roost. In all of these areas of debate there was just one identifiable winner.

At the time, most people failed to understand the power of the media to change their views and reshape their thinking. Instead of viewing the world *through* the medium of television, they allowed the medium to define the world for them. A new purveyor of truth and relevance was in the making, one that has triumphed over all and is here to stay. And from now on, whatever our view on any issue, not just war or a particular war, we cannot get away from the assault of the visual even if we don't watch television, because of its impact on the way the rest of society makes its judgments.

There is a war raging. It is the battle for thought and belief through a weapon of mass deconstruction. In that battle, it is not firepower we need to fear as much as it is electronic power. From the conscious to the subconscious we are in its grip. From wars in different lands to battles for moral acceptability, the television set has won the day. I stress this because I believe that almost none of the New Spiritualities would be so pervasive if it were not for the genius and built-in distortion of television. It reinforces what we *want* to believe, and if what we *want* to believe is what we are *told* to believe through the medium, no amount of logic or argument can shake that conviction. Whichever way you want to look at it, television—and now viral media—is the shaper of everything we think and believe.

Life's Dim Windows

William Blake long ago warned us about the vulnerability of the eye when he said:

> This life's five windows of the soul
> Distorts the Heavens from pole to pole,
> And leads you to believe a lie
> When you see with, not thro' the eye.[1]

We are intended to see *through* the eye, *with* the conscience. Instead, the visual media, especially television and movies, manipulates us into seeing *with* the eye, devoid of the conscience, whose role it is to place parameters around what we see. The supremacy of the eye-gate makes it easy to strain at a gnat and swallow a camel.

Seeing is believing, it is said. But by seeing something only in its narrow sense, one may miss the big picture and believe something that is actually not true. And that belief, even though it may be false, may become the generator of culture and national mood.

What is it about television and movies that makes them both attractive and dangerous? In so many ways, television is truly a fantastic medium. Which of us who watched the first landing on the moon can ever forget the awe-inspiring sight? How incredible it is that we can sit at home and watch some of the greatest performers, as if they were in our own living rooms! The experience of being able to watch a great sporting event or national and world event such as a royal wedding or the funeral of a great leader or a national memorial service is a memory that lasts forever. It allows the imagination to soar and gives wings to dreams. The imagination is one of the most vulnerable, though fascinating, faculties that we humans have. Nothing better describes the beauty and vulnerability of the human imagination than the song written and sung by John Lennon years ago, "Imagine." He wanted us to imagine no heaven, no hell, no countries, and no religion. No, he said, he was not a dreamer, just offering possibilities.

Anyone who has heard the song cannot help but stop and hum the tune as they read these words, and even hear Lennon's voice in the words. It's a beautiful, haunting melody...especially after sitting through the daily news and wondering when all the strife will end. When you think about it, why did he need all those descriptions about an ideal world? Why not just one or two lines? A world without killing and all of us living as one—that's the dream, isn't it? Who can take issue with that? And nothing could have been more instrumental in killing the dream than the senseless killing of Lennon himself at the hands of an assassin. English journalist Steve Turner writes of Lennon's brief struggle with Christianity, a struggle that his wife, Yoko, strongly influenced him against and toward magical stones and astrology instead.[2]

Isn't it interesting that no astrologer was able to warn him and protect him from that fateful day? Just because Lennon could *imagine* such a world doesn't mean that it exists, or that there is any chance of it existing. Just because he *wanted* to believe in such a world didn't make it real, even for him. And here is the contradiction: He imagined a pure world without any ultimate reason for life and destiny. He amputated accountability but wished for a world of responsibility. That's the privilege of music...it doesn't have to justify its flawed reasoning.

Fame, fortune, and adulation are generally based on measurements that serve only to disfigure reality and make the imagination king over common sense. Common sense ought to tell us that there is no guarantee that a person with a gifted voice and musical genius is any better a person than someone who cannot sing or write music. Common sense ought to tell us that a world without heaven or hell in the future generally leads to one or the other in this world. But a gifted voice and an errant imagination can angle a lie to fit into the worldview one wants to believe.

It has been said that at first art imitates life. Then, life imitates art. Finally, life finds the very reason for its existence in the arts. This visual medium of television was catapulted into our private living space via electronic advances and we understood its power very little. I believe that this medium was a key means by which the truth came to be seen as a lie.

The Displacement of "It Is Written"

Throughout the history of man, communication from one person to another had been primarily oral. The faithful transmission of tradition was key and human beings could rightly have been called Homo rhetoricus. Language was the medium. Story was the form. When in 1456 the Gutenberg press was invented, a print culture was set in place. Texts and contexts were in focus. Ideas could be distilled, disseminated, argued, spread, and debated. Still, it was language and concept that carried the day.

In 1839, a key advance was made in communication: Photography was discovered. Within four decades, in 1873, transformation in mass communication took a giant step. And when it was discovered that light could be converted to electrical impulses, transmitted over a distance, and then reconverted into light, the age of television dawned.

When one studies the viewing habits of the young and considers the thousands of hours spent unthinkingly in front of a TV screen or iPhone, it is easy to see why the power of abstract reasoning has died since the advent of television and, in the words of Jacques Ellul, we are living with the humiliation of the word. The loss of reading has also reduced the individual's capacity to write. "Enlightenment" has a whole new meaning now, each person in front of his or her own screen deciding for himself what is truth and what is fancy. No longer does one have to leave his palace to see poverty, disease, old age, and death, and meditate on its meaning under a tree as Buddha did. Death, disease, old age, and suffering are all visible on the televisions in our own living rooms or on handheld devices in our own cars.

One can turn on a television station and "meditate" using the direct-dial numbers that are given. Some advertisers even promise a worry-free life after just a fifteen-minute call. The end result is spirituality without dogma, religion without God, argument without substance, rationalization without rationality, and tranquillity by transfer of funds from the seeker's bank account to the company that makes the best offer of nirvana, at the same time producing dogmatism about relativism in matters of ultimate meaning.

I mentioned in the introduction that Deepak Chopra, the Western-marketed, Eastern proponent of the New Spirituality, visited Thailand to become a monk for a week. On his website there are pictures of him, clean-shaven, a begging bowl in his hand, sleeping on the floor of a temple. When I mentioned this to an Indian friend, he wondered aloud if Chopra would have done this had there been no photo op to tell the story. Curious, that that was his first response. Perhaps the cynicism that has been bred through the caricatures of reality that are created by the visual is what makes the nighttime stand-up comedians on television so popular.

After reading the article, I went to the leading computer mall in Bangkok, where I happened to be while writing, to buy some accessories for my laptop. I had to wait my turn, because two monks were talking to the salesman, buying their own hardware for who knows what.

First, we had a monk for a week; then, we have computers for saffron-clothed ascetics. I can't imagine a greater contradiction than monks at a computer store, nor a greater manipulation of spirituality than becoming a monk for a week, with publicity to boot. One may as well be married for a week and think one now knows everything there is to know about marriage. I'm sure the Buddha would have had some thoughts on Chopra's exploits. And on his fellow ascetics buying computers.

Electronic dissemination became the progenitor of the computer, and now the visual has gone viral with each person having his own network. One police beating or one errant act anywhere in the world can be viewed by millions within minutes. Not too long ago a student in the United States was covertly filmed by a roommate while engaging in a private act, and within minutes thousands were watching it on their cell phones. The young man could not live with the shame of the world watching his private conduct and committed suicide.

While television and movies became the means and the microchip was making its entry, the very substance of our culture was at risk. First to fall was our values. What we treasured and what we revered became expendable and profaned. There was a new way of popularizing rebellion against age-old values. Humor became vulgar. Sensuality was mass-marketed, and that which we thought should be private now became public. How else could a late-night talk show host have humored his way through a public disclosure of his duplicitous life other than by skillfully using the medium to his advantage? The normally immoral became the brilliantly creative. Television triumphed again.

The Eye Is the Lamp

Jesus made a very profound remark about the eye. He said that our eye must be "single" because the eye is the lamp of the body (Matthew 6:22 KJV). "If then the light that is in you is darkness, how great is the darkness!" he said (6:23 NASB). I cannot think of a more powerful metaphor for the imagination than the metaphor of light. Pretense and distortion are at the heart of a world without any light. That is why the light emanating from the TV screen, or better still reflecting off the screen, must be examined to see whether what is being revealed is truth or a distortion of the truth. Where is the light of reality in a setting where everything is staged?

Four words that are easy to grasp capture the medium of television: *induction*, *seduction*, *deduction*, and *reduction*. Take a good look at those four words, and it is easy to see how we have found ourselves playing mind games in a world of images, running counter to truth and redemption.

A Problematic Induction

The Latin word for *induction* literally means "to lead to." Inductive reasoning moves from the particular to the general or from the individual to the universal. Induction is simply a process that leads from something or some assertion to an inference for something else. It starts with particular truths. New Age Spirituality runs amok by displacing inductive reasoning and replacing it with a personalized mystical revelation as the sufficient if not sole basis for universal truth: Person A found enlightenment while meditating; person B found enlightenment while meditating; therefore, silence and meditation are the answer for all humanity. No matter how much it is denied, this kind of thinking surfaces in key assumptions. This is an invalid basis for establishing universal truths because it fundamentally ignores the contradictory conclusions that others have come to in the same process. It is not a valid means of truth testing. The correspondence and coherence tests for truth are discussed in the closing chapter.

In a cartoon I saw some time ago, a man dressed in a tuxedo lay apparently dead on the floor, surrounded by a host of other men, also in black tuxedos. One tuxedo-clad man is saying to another, "Where does one begin when something like this happens at a Butlers' Convention?"

If intuition is the only test for truth, to say "The butler did it" doesn't help.

No court of law can function in such mystical fog as exists in the New Spirituality. Consider, for example, the famed Sri Sri Ravi Shankar, one of the most influential gurus today. Based in Bangalore, India, his charming smile, flowing locks of hair, and pithy one-liners have made him the person to know and to quote.

By the way, it is fascinating to consider how one even gains such titles. Normally, one would use one titular name, "Sri," which actually means to diffuse light and implies respect, reverence, or even lordship, as it was used by Bhagwan Sri Rajnesh. He was content with only one Sri in his name because he placed Bhagwan (meaning "God") before the Sri: How can one exceed that? But for Ravi Shankar, one Sri is not enough. In effect his name means, "the Revered Revered, Ravi Shankar." But even that is not enough for him, and now his title is Poojya Sri Sri Ravi Shankar ("poojya" connotes the idea of "His Worship"), so what we actually have is "His Worship, the Twice-Revered Ravi Shankar."

Ravi Shankar's take on truth is that there are two ways of knowing: through logical understanding, which comes from intellectual analysis and for which there must be empirical proof...even though that proof may not stand for long; and the knowing that comes from intuition or through deep meditation, for which you need offer no proof to support its claim to truth. The latter, he says, is more reliable. If you meditate long enough, he says, you will recognize the connection that has always existed between all religions, even today. And when through meditation and intuition you have recognized that all religions are connected to every other religion, it's quite reasonable to see, in that light, that Jesus lived in India for twelve years and returned to Israel in a saffron robe...or as a Hindu holy man.

His essay ends with these words:

Jesus is the only way. Jesus is love. Jesus has many names. He is Buddha, he is Krishna, and he is you. Your name also belongs to Jesus. Do you really think that your name is yours? Jesus is the Son of God. He inherits what belongs to God. Do you inherit what belongs to God? Then you belong to Jesus. Isn't it? What do you say?[3]

But that is not all. He has to add in a sarcastic footnote that there was a group of people in America who believed that the world would end on a certain day in 1994. They gathered in their churches on that day, but "obviously nothing happened," he says. "All fears and anxieties are caused by believing wrong things. You need that guru to tell you what is right and what is wrong."[4] His prescription is that meditation, yoga, and a guru will help you distinguish truth from nonsense.

This is amazing stuff! How does one respond to assertions that are so flatly induced with false premises and deductions and then given to the masses as "truth"? There is something extraordinary going on here. When any statement is made concerning the oneness of all religions, either meditation, intuition, or textual extrapolations are used. The differing doctrines of each religion are always left unaddressed. But when the mystics are questioned, they resort to falsifying other systems by switching to induction (e.g., "These misguided people went to a church expecting the end of the world, but obviously it didn't happen"). According to his own argument, how can he say they were misguided if their "intuitive awareness" guided by a guru—or minister—impelled them in this direction?

Even those who maintain that meditative extrapolation is a sufficient basis for defending their belief system smuggle in an inductive approach when they need it to attack someone else's system of belief. They use inductive reasoning to assert charges of falsehood against a counterperspective, while a mystical argument is enough to defend their personal belief. Logical consistency is a consideration only when they are uneasy with someone else's perspective; experiential relevance is all that is needed to justify their own perspective. The same rules are not applied both ways.

This method of reasoning underlies the teachings and writings of all the advocates of the New Spirituality. According to them, truth is discovered in silence or in a sudden burst or gradual arrival of insight. Bringing into question Jesus' statements about truth, they force you into a "Hobson's choice"[5] dilemma: There is no choice but to accept a pantheistic Jesus. There is no other option.

This is a false way of induction. It leads to beliefs based on falsehoods, such as that Jesus lived in India for twelve years and returned in a saffron robe. Isn't it interesting that it was not some incarnation of Krishna who went to Jerusalem and came back wearing a crucifix? Imagination and meditation are not secure ways on which to build a worldview that reflects reality. They may make for a beatific smile but not for a philosophical alternative to truth. A worldview tested by truth will inform imagination and meditation, *not the other way around*. That is why the rigorous way of testing truth has always been through logical consistency, empirical adequacy, and experiential relevance.

Seeing *with* the eye alone, induction can easily be manipulated. As academic as they seem, the basic laws of logic are few. I shall not go into them now. However, when those laws are applied to any system of thought, it is easy to see whether the statements and/or arguments are true or false or purely speculative. This is especially important with systems of thought that make numerous assertions. Here, let me just suggest that viewing a story that has been staged and scripted does not make the story true and is not the most solid ground for truth. In the business of television, where even the weather report has to be dressed up, to say nothing of the news itself, how can one legitimately engage in inductive reasoning? A false induction is serious and can be tested.

Beginning with a problematic induction, television takes us to the next step.

The Dangerous Seduction

In early March 2011, Japan was rocked by a deadly combination of an earthquake followed by a tsunami. Through the wonderful gift of communication, it was immediately brought to the world's attention. Many of every age bracket responded to what had happened, and the human spirit came to the fore with help and rescue. That was the positive side of the visual medium of television. We didn't just read or hear about the devastation, we *saw* it and were able to feel the tragedy to a certain degree. Just today, when I met a Japanese man in the elevator, I placed my heart on my chest and said, "I am so sorry for what your country is going through." He bowed in response and said, "Thank you." The breadth of the calamity brought every human being into a compassionate posture.

There was, therefore, something very strange in the response to the tragedy of one television personality, Gilbert Gottfried, the former voice of the duck in the Aflac Insurance Company commercials. He is a highly paid and skilled comic actor. But a few days after the tsunami hit, he tweeted ten jokes about the Japanese tragedy, one being that in Japan people don't go to the beaches, the beaches come to them; another, not to worry if you lost your Japanese girlfriend, another one would soon wash up on shore. It absolutely strains credulity that anyone could find anything humorous in one of the greatest tragedies of modern times, the full extent of which has still not been fully realized. The outrage against him was immediate, the vast majority focusing their incredulity on the fact that he would say such things in the face of the instant dissemination of any communication in our day.

But my thoughts were different. What, I ask, was this man even *thinking* to write such things, regardless of who would have picked it up? Is such tragedy a subject for humor? Is this his ready wit? Is this his way of trying to bring some lightness into a heavy situation? I don't think so. I really think the camera does things to a person and seduces him into believing that it's all about him; that somehow his is a persona that transcends the usual boundaries for ordinary people. It is precisely the same pitfall that needs to be avoided by professional athletes on the screen for whom life has been reduced to a game and the game has been elevated to life. That is the power of the camera. I feel sorry for Mr. Gottfried. He lost his lucrative contract over a pathetic blunder. He can no longer be taken seriously because he failed to see the seriousness of life and death. The reason he gave for his comments was that he is a humorist and that making jokes is his calling. But he didn't know boundaries.

How much more serious is the impact of the visual media for those who are dealing with issues that concern the souls of people! No one ought to be more mindful of this seduction than those who deal with spiritual matters. Though the mass media began its onslaught upon the Christian faith and the academy gave it sophistication, it would not have been that easy to discredit the faith of millions in this country except for the fact that American Christianity itself bought into the gimmickry of television. And that is what gave the attackers their legitimacy. The message became nothing more than glitz and glamour. Being seen through the lens of a camera became the mission.

Study the lives of those in Christian ministry who fell into this trap. Two in particular come to mind, Jimmy Swaggart and Jim Bakker, who, according to Google, is "best known as the disgraced PTL TV host." Look at what happened to them personally, and it becomes evident that the medium massaged them into a false sense of their own preeminence and status until they collapsed under the weight of their own fame. Both became victims, seduced and hoisted ultimately on their own petard. They were the Heath Ledgers of American evangelicalism.

No, there is no reason to celebrate, nor is there reason to mock any of these personalities. We all are vulnerable to the seduction of fame. It could have happened to any one of us in the same situation, standing before the cameras and lights, recognized by millions around the world, with millions of dollars in our bank accounts by virtue of self-seduction. It was *Inception* in real life. The pain was real, and when they awoke from the dream it was to realize that the real person who was there at the beginning had died.

I recall that I was on my way to do my early morning workout routine when the story broke, years ago, of what had happened to the PTL television network. I remember at the time thinking that this piece of news was going to permanently change the way the gospel would be seen and then ridiculed. Common sense could have told us this was going to happen sooner or later. I couldn't help but think of how Jesus was pressured by his followers to become a king, to change stones into bread, to use God for his own ends. Jesus resisted the temptation of self-aggrandizement—and for him who was God of the very God, it would have been legitimate—but some of his followers haven't.

The cost was in more than the loss of the message. The economics of it demanded that the better part of the *PTL Club* program be spent in generating money to pay for the airtime, rather than in any real ministry. The scene at the temple when Jesus walked in and overturned the tables of the money changers comes to mind again and again. This is America in the age of television. Everything is made for sales.

Prayer was no longer sufficient in this portrayal of Christianity; tears had to flow to make it real, while in the background, telephone volunteers were viewed taking calls and pledges. The simple truisms of the gospel were so often repeated and used for impure reasons that they became lines for derision even though they are true: Jesus died for your sins; Jesus is coming again; you must be born again; come to Jesus; give your heart to Jesus. Bumper stickers like "Honk If You Love Jesus" abounded. Just like John Lennon and "Imagine," you can hear the lines in your mind, and even the way some of them pronounced and stressed the syllables. It was not just "God"; it was "Gaw-dah." I know people who even now can do a perfect imitation of the way these one-liners were thundered by TV preachers.

The gullible swallowed this distortion of the gospel unquestioningly. The skeptic was given fodder for his ridicule. Christianity was denuded and the walls of traditional belief came crashing down. The message of Christ was sold out to the medium of television, and in the ensuing vacuum, politics were mocked, conservatism became suspect, *fundamentalism* became a bad word, and long-held and sacred values were overthrown. *Liberty, equality*, and *fraternity* were redefined to mean "autonomy," "relativism," and "fragmentation." The gospel of Jesus Christ was made synonymous with the methods that had devalued the truth, and people began to search elsewhere for answers. The miracle is that in spite of everything, some were touched and some lives were actually changed. But by and large, the medium seduced the user. The programming and simplistic message that was promoted with sophisticated techniques made the whole message of Christ appear as a lie, taken seriously by very few "thinking" people.

The same television screen that had a hand in the ridicule of the truth became the means of promoting a different belief and a different hero. And the same mix of mindless belief and razzmatazz that appeal in the promotion of the New Spirituality will meet with the same result, some day. Believe me, I see it and can see through it. The same shenanigans are at work.

At first blush, the New Spirituality provided a welcomed escape and was hailed as a needed relief from the dogmatism and clichés that branded Christianity as "Western" and invasive to our private lives. As the generation gap widened, the young wanted something they could call spiritual, as their forefathers had had, but that provided a new way of sacred thought that would allow them to escape the restrictions of the past. It had to be an egalitarian, all-inclusive, nonjudgmental, non-Western way of looking at things. There should no longer be a dominant faith in the West. Culture and Christianity were both examined and found wanting. The old way of belief was expelled and the New Spirituality made its entrance.

When Critics Fail

Until this time in our history, our faith, our convictions, and our basis for decision making in the West were implicitly or explicitly provided by the Judeo-Christian worldview. That is not by any stretch to say that America was a Christian nation. Certainly not. But the Judeo-Christian worldview provided the essential definitions for the founding of America, beginning with the conviction expressed by our founders that at its core life is sacred and that our legitimate rights as human beings have been endowed to us by our Creator. Which other worldview could provide that categorical statement? Naturalism? Pantheism? Islam? No Islamic nation in the world operates with a belief in the inalienable right of liberty. Naturalism does not acknowledge a Creator who could endow us with inalienable rights. And pantheism, with its karmic bequest, does not see us as being created equal; instead, pantheism assumes that we are born to a life of karmic repayment until the debt is paid. Please understand that this is not a reference to the caste system. This refers to the fact that according to pantheism, my present station is at a level determined by a previous life and is something that those who promote the New Spirituality conveniently ignore.

The critics of Christianity often missed the mark in this quest for spirituality that came to be called New Age. Within the New Ager's mind, there was obviously some legitimacy for his New Spirituality. But the critic of the status quo did not readily sense the error in New Age thinking that lay much deeper than was evident on the surface. There were really three layers to their thinking. Some realized only the most superficial layer; others were able to comprehend the middle layer of New Age thought. Few grasped the most meaningful substratum of New Age thinking.

On the surface New Age thinking was simply a reflection of the distrust many had in the old ways and a conviction that they were being oppressed. The young were tired of being told how to think, how to feel, how to love. Why should they listen to a generation that had dragged its young into a conflict for which the very reasons were so blurred? So, along with the eviction of conservative politics, the eviction of the religious worldview was not far behind. They were tired of preachers who moralized and of church people who, at their core, were no better than anybody else. They were tired of the pursuit of materialism they saw in Western culture, often seeing it as the plunder of older traditions. Ivy League professors left their posts and smoked pot, instead. Some went on spiritual pilgrimages.

But there was more to it than just disaffection. As the American military reached its zenith and technological advances created dizzying changes in the world, there were deeply felt resentments and a strange irony in the rejection of our own values. "What makes us think we are better than anyone else?" was their entreaty, and the West became the target of attack by the young from within the West itself and, yes, from the intellectual liberals who felt that the West had succeeded on the backs of weaker nations. All of a sudden causes were addressed that became aligned with New Age and New Spirituality.

There are those who insist that New Age and New Spirituality are not identical. That may be so in terms of their building blocks, but it is not so in their epistemological starting points. From the environment to the institutions of government, learning, religion, and the family, a new day of revolutionary thinking began. The irony lay in the fact that it was the same technological knowledge that made possible both the advances that were being seen as detrimental to human potential and their alternatives.

There were layers beneath layers in this cultural and religious revolution. Sexual liberation, gender conflicts, and abortion rights all hit the fan at the same time. Someone has said,

"Any stigma can lick a good dogma." For several reasons, church and state were both called into question, and anything that argued for coherence in moral reasoning was deemed oppressive and was generally placed in the lap of Christendom at large.

I will never forget a particular scene that ought to have signaled to me, as a young man, what was happening. I was a newcomer to Christ. A friend of mine, who was the president of our youth group at church, caught everyone off guard when he let it be known that he was "gay," a new meaning for the word at that time. For the youth at the infancy of that movement, processing it was a challenge, including the one with that disposition. But we were friends and we would sit late into the night talking about these things. Who determines right and wrong? Isn't love the only thing that counts? he would say. Why does it matter to anybody else what my private life is like? I turned these questions back on him, and his answers were no more convincing than the ones he was attacking. There was no rancor, no anger, but a deep struggle that I sensed but found hard to process and express, as I listened. It was truly turning the world upside down.

When word of his lifestyle got back to the church leaders, he was summoned by the board of elders to face some serious questioning. As I recall being in the room, also serving on the youth committee, the very setting was symbolic. The silence as he entered the room was quite pronounced. The leadership were all dressed in dark suits, while he sat in his casual attire and defended his position and his practice. He smiled his way through the meeting. They grimaced under the strain. I little knew then how the setting itself portended the future and represented the backstage of life. There were no harsh words. There was no condemnation, which one might have expected. But it was obvious that he felt, *This is me against the church*. Naturally, he was relieved of his responsibilities as a leader among the youth. It was fascinating to see how he used the religious terminology and doctrines of Christianity that he had learned at Bible college to defend his new lifestyle and choices. He still saw himself as a "Christian"... he just didn't see himself as a "churchman" anymore.

What none of the leaders or, for that matter, he himself knew was the heartbreak that awaited him. I befriended his partner as well, even though culturally and in belief we were worlds apart. I spent hours listening to their emotionally hard-hitting responses to traditional morality. Until the fateful Saturday morning that I received a call from his partner. The call caught me by surprise, as I realized that something life-threatening was happening. I dashed off and drove the several miles to their apartment, but when I knocked on the door there was no response. The door was unlocked, so I opened it and found a scene I will never forget. It appeared as though the house had been ravaged the night before. Broken bottles of liquor and clothes were strewn all over the place and there was leftover food on the floor and on the furniture. I walked in carefully, feeling that I was entering a crime scene. Frankly, I was afraid. I heard a groaning sound from upstairs and ran up to find the partner in a stupor. I called for help and he was taken to the hospital, his last journey in this life, as it turned out. The power of an idea had overtaken his life and left it in shambles.

This, I dare suggest, is the substrata of all that lies beneath: One simply cannot live without boundaries. The question is, whose boundaries? This was what the self-appointed critics of established society didn't quite know how to deal with: If we are going to dismantle the boundaries set by society, which boundaries are we going to promote? For we cannot live as a society without boundaries. These cultural revolutionists never paused to think of our infinite capacity for destruction. Anti-absolutist thinkers seldom come to terms with the fact that freedom is not destroyed only by its retraction; it is devastated by its abuse.

The three layers that made up the rebellion against the status quo of Western society were, first, the disillusionment with materialism and the status quo; second, the shallowness and, at times, hypocrisy of the Church, or of those who claimed to be Christians; and third, and perhaps most compelling, a desire for liberation from all restraint, especially in matters of sexuality. Those rebelling wanted the foundations of society replaced and a new foundation of their own choosing established. But the foundation they wanted was actually the absence of any foundation. They wanted no point of reference for values, except one's self.

Restlessness in the soul, disillusion with a commercialized Christianity, and a hunger for free expression came together to find a new way. In the high-speed descent into a profane culture, they tried to reexamine why anyone had ever bought into the sacred anyway, and a New Age dawned with a new way of discovering or defining the "sacred."

CHAPTER 3

Exhaling the Old, Inhaling the New

The Dawn

In a November 2, 2008, article in the *Los Angeles Times*, staff writer Elaine Woo reported on the death of Marilyn Ferguson, the author of the 1980 best seller *The Aquarian Conspiracy*. Ferguson had died on October 19 of that year, at the age of seventy. She was described as "a galvanizing influence on participants in scores of alternative groups that coalesced as the New Age movement."[1]

From the extreme focus on rationalism came a balancing response of empiricism. From the displacement of personal value in empiricism came the tidal wave of existentialism that championed individual will, passion, and choice. From the nihilism that came hand in hand with existentialism, postmodernism was waiting to be born. Existentialism had harnessed the arts and wanted to tell philosophy in a story. But stories required an author, and the subjects of the stories reacted against the author and claimed their right to reinterpret the story as it seemed right to them. The likes of Michel Foucault, Jacques Derrida, and others framed the world of postmodernism and deconstruction. While these terms merit a rigorous philosophical analysis, the resulting authority was clearly the individual, and the reader claimed authority over the author.

The tale would go something like this:

In the beginning, God.

God spoke. But that was a long time ago.

We wanted certainty—now.

For this, only Reason and Rationalism would do.

But that was not enough. We wanted to "test."

So we went into the senses and found the empirical.

But that's not what we meant by testing. We really meant "feeling."

So we found a way to generate feeling into the picture.

Truth was framed into a scene.

But the scene was left open to interpretation. Scenes are not absolute.

So the story was told as an art form.

But the reader still didn't like it, because he was not the author.

So he read the story while he sat in a reconstructed and deconstructed cubicle to make of the story whatever he wished.

But what does one do with the long reach of the empirical?

The best way was to find a blend between the empirical and the satirical and end up with God again.

The only difference was that God could not be the storyteller.

We still needed God.

So we became God.

That's precisely what the counterculture wanted. Postmodernism engendered a philosophical stance devoid of truth, meaning, and certainty. In literature, texts were deconstructed to fit the mind-set of the reader, not the writer. Foucault's own foray into a sensually driven lifestyle that ultimately took his life was based on his aphorism that there were no boundaries. There were no absolutes.

While on the one hand those in the counterculture movement openly debunked American individualism, on the other hand, they brought in its place the individualism of a subculture with the underlying theme that it was all "in you and me." Ferguson was one of the lead voices coalescing this collection of individuals, and she harnessed the popular theme of human potential. Her monthly newsletter, *Brain/Mind Bulletin*, won a great readership and became the catalyst for new ideas in spirituality that were a mix of science, albeit an inexact one, with ancient texts of spiritual voices, which in turn, would engender "new discoveries in neuroscience and psychology." The writer of her obituary goes on to state: "That work led her to discern that a massive 'cultural realignment' was occurring, a conspiracy in the root sense of disparate forces all breathing together to produce personal and social change."[2]

The Aquarian Conspiracy was the first comprehensive analysis to be written of the seemingly disparate efforts that fed the movement—from the scientific world, experiments with biofeedback, altered states of consciousness, and alternative birthing centers; from the political world, experiments in "creative" government; and from the religious world, a Christian evangelist who seemed to be promoting forms of meditation more familiar to the East—all coming together to break from traditional mainstream Western practices and beliefs.

Ferguson's message was optimistic: "After a dark, violent age, the Piscean, we are entering a millennium of love and light—in the words of the popular song 'The Age of Aquarius,' the time of 'the mind's true liberation.'"[3] By her definition, Aquarians were people who sought to "leave the prison of our condition-ing, to love, to turn homeward. To conspire with each other and for each other."[4] Numerous publications exist today that were birthed and made popular by this category of thinking.

The *Los Angeles Times* also recorded some who disagreed with her positions, finding her views simplistic. In the journal *Science Books & Films*, R. C. Bealer wrote that Ferguson offered the "hyperbole of the 'positive' thinking huckster."[5] Bealer's questioning of Ferguson was the same as Dawkins's puzzlement by Chopra's use of *quantum* as a metaphor for his brand of spiritu-ality. By embracing alternative religions, Ferguson was accused of undermining Christianity. As her ideas gained followers and moved more toward the center of society, she was considered a trailblazer, and her work became the classic explanation of the New Age standard ideals and goals.

Has "spirituality" become such a vacuous term that like Humpty Dumpty one can assemble it to mean whatever one chooses to make it mean? But let me not move too far ahead of the argument here. Let me take a step back and then several steps forward to see what all this spirituality is about anyway. While its path may have been along political-cultural-religious lines, the destination to which the spiritual masters of today want us to head is clearly defined, rising above politics, religion, and culture. So let us give it the best representation and see where it leads to and where it leads from.

High Noon

Elizabeth Lesser is the co-founder and senior adviser of the Omega Institute in Rhinebeck, New York. Prior to taking that responsibility, she was a midwife and childbirth educator. It is not without design that the front and back cover endorsements of her book *The New American Spirituality* are from medical doctors. The back cover suggests that her book will take us through four landscapes of our spiritual journey: the mind (the root of stress and anxiety); the heart (the root of grief and pain); the body (the root of the fear of aging and of death); and the soul (from which come meaning and mystery).

To help us in our understanding of that spiritual landscape, new definitions are forthcoming in the book. It is interesting that she doesn't even begin to define spirituality until page 30 in her book, in a chapter titled, "What Is Spirituality?" After several paragraphs of telling us what spirituality is not—not religion, sentimentality, cynicism, or narcissism—a definition is finally broached. She certainly doesn't define it as synonymous with New Age Spirituality. In her terms, not all spiritualities are created equal. The spirituality she is speaking of is an attitude of fearlessness toward life, of adventure; a search for the truth about existence. It is, as Buddhism describes, "a tranquil abiding."

Quoting from Buddhist texts, Hindu texts, Sufi texts, and so on, Lesser offers a cornucopia of spiritual thought until you have to wonder whether she is engaged in pursuing truth or in a mix of ideals, being careful not to broach what else each of these sages has said that would negate what the others have said. Then comes the prescriptive moment in the book. This is an extensive quote, but it must be given because it is vintage New Spirituality:

> Sit quietly right where you are, and close your eyes. Feel yourself breathing. Follow the breath on its journey into and out of your body. Sit feeling yourself breathe for a few minutes. Place your hand over your heart and feel

the warmth of your hand connect with the steady beat of your heart. Then put your hand or fingertips lightly on the spot in the center of your rib cage, to the right of your physical heart. It is the spot you can feel when you are startled and draw your breath sharply inward. Move your hand gently, and breathe slowly and softly into that spot until you are focusing intently on what many traditions call the spiritual heart or the heart center.

Imagine that the spot you are touching is the top of a deep, deep well. Follow your breath on a journey into the spacious interior of your own heart. Breathe slowly in and out. Let yourself be pulled ever more deeply into the well of your heart. As you meet thoughts and emotions on the journey, do not push them away. They are part of you, but not all of you. Greet what you find and move on, ever deeper into the well of your spiritual heart…

Welcome whatever you discover, without judgment, as part of yourself, but not all of yourself. Sit in this state, letting yourself be pulled by your longing into the well of your heart, observing your breath, for as long as you feel comfortable and then slowly remove your hand, return to normal breathing, and open your eyes.[6]

The metaphysical roots and the means of discovery of the not-so-new New Spirituality are acknowledged: The Westernized Eastern spirituality that Elizabeth Lesser writes about has all been tried and done before. But she is very clear about how important it is to even know what to call it. Referencing her own book, she says that she shies away from the label of "new American Spirituality" because it is often confused with "New Age" which, she says, implies such things as crystals and UFOs and elevator music.[7]

This problem of what to call the New Spirituality is resolved in the spring 2000 issue of *Spirituality and Health* magazine:

> In our times [it] seems best described as "21st-Century Spirituality."...It contains the nature-centered traditions of the original peoples of the Americas. It is part science, which has underscored, for most of the 20th century, our unspoken collective philosophy. It respects both a mistrust of heavy-handed authority, and the willing surrender to a greater power. It draws from the religious teachings of the past: the biblical traditions, the spiritual roots of Africa, the meditative schools of Asia, and other diverse mythic and religious worldviews. And it draws from our own times, from the wisdom of psychology, democracy, and feminism.[8]

Why such a sweeping epistemology that seems to include everything would feel the need to distance itself from crystals, UFOs, and elevator music is intriguing. We shall let that be. Lesser's own spiritual journey is sad while, in her words, triumphant. But if you get past the story line, you can see that the very things she resists constantly surface. I shall get to more of this later. But she is representative of the ideas and so I take her at her word.

In the end, she sums up the difference between the "Old Spirituality" and the "New Spirituality" according to her understanding of ideas of authority, the path to God, spirituality, truth and the sacred in each:

1. AUTHORITY: In the "old" spirituality authority is held by the church; in the "new" spirituality the individual worshipper has authority to determine what is best for him or her.
2. SPIRITUALITY: In the old spirituality God and the way to worship have already been defined and the worshipper just follows the rules; in the new spirituality the worshipper defines spirituality for him- or herself.
3. THE PATH TO GOD: In the old spirituality there is only one way to God, all else is wrong; in the new spirituality there are unlimited paths or combinations of paths one can follow...you can string a necklace all of your own making.
4. SACRED: In the old spirituality parts of yourself are considered evil (the body, ego, emotions) and must be denied, transcended, or sublimated; in the new spirituality anything goes.
5. TRUTH: In the old spirituality truth is knowable and constant, leading to the same answers at every stage of life; in the new spirituality you never quite arrive at the truth as it is constantly changing to accommodate your growth.

With the safety net she has provided for determining truth, who can ever fall? Only those who believe in the exclusive nature of truth. So there is exclusivity implicit, cleverly disguised as accommodation.

As a result of this excursion into an embrace of everything except metaphysics (and crystals, UFOs, and elevator music), walk into a health food store that promotes this philosophy and look at what is advertised by the business cards of persons with the following specialties that are on display and for the taking:

Mystery School Instructor, Clairvoyant
Archetypes, Cartomancier, Astrologer
Numerologist, Medium, Healer
Shaman, Angel Therapy Practitioner, Empath
Clairvoyant, Channel, Kabbalist, Hypnotherapist
Medical Intuitive, Tarot, Reiki Master

I remember walking on the streets of Kuala Lumpur, Malaysia, some time ago, and seeing a man sitting on the side of the road with a parrot in a cage. Beside him were about twenty or thirty little books no bigger than the size of a child's hand, laid out on the sidewalk side by side. I stood nearby and watched. A woman came and sat in front of him, with her sari draped over her head so that she wouldn't be recognized. After he spoke to her for a few minutes, he opened the birdcage, took the bird on his hand, and placed it in front of the little books. The parrot waited a few moments and then picked up one of the books and gave it to the fortune-teller. The man opened the book and began to read to her. She kept nodding, clearly happy with the book selected. She reached into a side pouch draped over her waist, paid him for his services, and walked away. The man sat there, continuing to call to people as they walked by, until the next customer was landed. He even looked in my direction, paid me a compliment, and invited me to be his next client. He should have known, being a fortune-teller, that I would turn down his kind offer.

The evangelist from the Old Spirituality pleaded with his audiences to "invite Jesus into your heart"; the apostles of the

New Spirituality tell you to invite yourself into your heart, to feel your own breath. We might well conclude that Narcissus may have been on to something. But if inviting yourself into your own heart doesn't help, there is a host of "Mystery Instructors" who will find the right formula for you. The Oracle at Delphi has come to life again.

Is life a tale told by an idiot or are we being idiotized? Is there truth in religion or is religion a free-fall zone where each one designs his or her own parachute to feel most comfortable? Has man really "come of age" and are the skeptics right? Is it time to turn the lights out at temples, mosques, and churches? If there is truth in these matters, we had better find it before the world is sent into a dream world turned nightmare.

But let me come back to the core of my concern. Anyone who promises utopia through mass communication and mass dissemination simply has run afoul of the facts. Several years ago, Ted Turner, the media mogul, made a statement that now seems almost laughable, except that it is sad. He presented his own "Ten Voluntary Initiatives," although he did add the caveat that people of this age shouldn't be told to do anything. They are suggestions, all of which have to do with the environment, and the tenth is to support the United Nations and its efforts to collectively improve the conditions of the planet. "One way to get this going, believe it or not, is TV. I believe mass communication has helped make us all closer together than we have ever been."[9] I wonder if Mr. Turner still believes that.

I remain firmly convinced that changes do not take place overnight. It is the old story of placing a frog in a kettle of cold water and gradually bringing it to a boil, so that it doesn't know when to jump out as the water temperature rises to a boiling death.

Yes, I am a Christian. I am persuaded that the whole teaching of Jesus stands unique in all of the world's religions. I am persuaded that his analysis of the human condition is the most real and empirically verifiable. I am also certain that if we fail to come to terms with what he said and taught, we will put all of humanity at risk. You must make up your own mind. But after four decades of traveling around the world and listening to some of the leading exponents of the human situation, disappointments, and potential, what I am writing now I write with the deepest conviction that whether it is heeded or not, it has to be said.

I am a lover of the world's cultures. I see beauty and drawbacks in all of them. No one culture has all the right ways of doing things. Having been raised in the East and having lived in the West for the past forty years, I have lived and learned much from both. In my veins flows Indian blood. In my language, I am comfortable in both Hindi and English. I must confess that in my culinary delights I am prejudiced toward Indian cuisine, which stands uniquely exotic above all others. (You could question that, but when more than a billion people stand with me in that opinion, at worst it would come in a close second if numerical factors were weighed.)

There is a strange twist in this fascination in the West with the East and with Eastern spirituality. When a westerner is attracted to Eastern spirituality, the East claims credit for having had the answers all along. But should an easterner be attracted to Christianity, it is seen in the East as a betrayal of one's culture. Ask any Christian from India and you will find that to be true.

But God Finds a Bridge

Some years ago, as a young speaker I was addressing a rather small audience in New Brunswick, Canada. During the evening, my hosts invited another Indian gentleman to join us for dinner, a schoolteacher. In the 1970s the Indian population in Canada was very sparse. So anyone who knew two people from India took it upon themselves to make certain that the two should meet. Such are the vagaries of human friendships. He came from a Hindu background and when he met me for dinner, he was extremely hostile. He believed I had betrayed my culture by becoming a Christian and somehow made the assumption that the purpose in my meeting him was to convert him to Christianity. To say that it was an uncomfortable evening was to put it mildly.

I listened and assured him that whatever prompted the host's invitation, I was as much a guest as he and that he was under no obligation to attend the evening talk later that evening. It was entirely his choice. He did attend. He did listen. He left without saying anything.

Several years went by before I received a call from him. He was in a hospital in Toronto and asked if I would come to visit him. I knew that the hospital he was in specialized in cancer treatment. When I walked into the room at the hospital, I quickly apologized to the occupant for being in the wrong room and stepped out again. But he corrected me and called me by name. It was, indeed, he, but he had been reduced to a shadow of himself and tears flooded my eyes. He gave me a hug and told me not to feel bad for him and then began to tell me that during the twisting path he had followed after we met, he had come to know and enjoy a relationship with Jesus, the same Jesus he had so shunned at our first meeting. He had learned what it meant to walk with God while still cherishing the culture of his birth and to find peace and hope in his innermost being. As we talked and finally bade each other good-bye, it was a fitting parting. God was with him, and he knew what true spirituality was about.

Why Jesus? What difference does it make what you believe? Is truth really even knowable? Could it be that postmodern spirituality is really the expression of a universal hunger rather than an answer to anything? What are the deep-seated questions that drive the quest for spirituality? Why is it that in the West we seem to have discarded the message of Christ, while in the East they have begun to realize that he is the one they are looking for? I have just one plea as we proceed: Let us consider these things frankly and honestly, without the rancor or bitterness that too often clouds the vision and makes truth the casualty.

In my college days, I read an essay in which the writer stated that one ought always to be grateful to those who made you try harder. I mention this because I have to commend the New Spiritualists for setting the bar high for us by awakening us to the questions of life's purpose and forcing us to take the journey of life earnestly, and perhaps consider seriously what we have always taken for granted. As a philosopher and follower of Jesus Christ, I cannot ignore the New Spirituality; I have to ask myself whether the worldview being espoused really has the answers people claim to be looking for or the package that is presented is more substantive than its content. Are they pointing to a disease without giving a real cure?

One thing the promoters of New Spirituality have unintentionally done with certainty is to illustrate the truth of C. S. Lewis's statement that each of us as a human being does not *have* a soul; each of us *is* a soul. We each *have* a body. That is the paradigm from which I want to respond to the New Spirituality and demonstrate that everything the New Spiritualists say they are seeking is actually found in Jesus. No, not the Jesus of popular television marketing. Not the Jesus of the New Ager's imagination. And not the Jesus of all talk and no walk, who is heard but never seen. The Jesus I am talking about is the Ultimate Reality who became flesh to bring us grace and truth that we might become the children of God.

Our destiny is in a relationship to a person, not in a pilgrimage to a place. Our purpose is in communion with the living God, not in union with an impersonal idea or nameless Higher Power: Such categorization is intellectual cowardice. Access to an abstract power gives you no one to be grateful to in times of blessing and no one to question and receive comfort from in times of sorrow. The world was made for the body. The body was made for the soul. And the soul was made for God. Not everything is actually as it is marketed to be, good or bad.

Hinduism uses the term "*leela*" to describe its story. The very word means a "play" or a "drama." So as the wheels of fortune have turned from texts to pretexts to contexts, we have arrived at a time in human history when science claims to be the ultimate authority for everything, and if science can't quite explain everything just yet, it is on the verge of a theory. We are at a time when postmodernism defies certainty, truth, and meaning; when spiritualism dabbles in quantum theory; and when randomness has become the order of the day. Isn't it ironic that at the same time, the world is on the edge of financial bankruptcy because we have conducted our financial affairs in a random fashion, as if there are no absolutes? Every serious-minded person needs to ask the questions of spiritual truth honestly. The game shows and showmanship in the marketplace may tantalize for a while. But truth will triumph in the end. The daunting questions represented by this New Spirituality, so obscured and propelled by the media, will not go unanswered.

I remember a statement made by the president of the ill-fated PTL. Commenting on the icons they had become in the eyes of the masses and the material success that oozed from their gains in wealth and fame, he said, "We became less than what we were meant to be." That statement is profound.

The New Spirituality represents this same tragedy. In promising sublimity and divinity to each of us, its proponents have actually made us less than we were meant to be. God alone knows how to humble us without humiliating us and how to exalt us without flattering us. And how he effects this is the grand truth of the Christian message.

CHAPTER 4

FROM OPRAH TO CHOPRA

From a problematic induction to an inescapable seduction, we move to an inevitable reduction and, finally, to a false deduction. Two of the biggest names associated with the New Spirituality reflect this very well. It will be worth our while to see a "Pilgrim's Digress" here…how one starts out with a belief, pursues her dream aided by the values of that belief, attains the dream by capturing a medium for her gifts, lifts the power of those gifts to dizzying heights, is seduced by that very power, begins to market a belief different from that which brought her to those heights, and finally shapes that belief into making herself the object of the viewer's belief. I might put it the following way:

First, the innocent is attracted to climb a mountain. Then the innocent draws others into her orbit to keep her company as she climbs. Then she seduces the others into believing that she has attained a higher status than the mountain and now has a transcendent perspective. Finally, she makes it look as if all along, the mountain should have tried to scale her heights but it couldn't, because it is not the mountain that created the climber but the climber that created the mountain and everything around it is the climber's creation. Now when others come to the mountain, it is to find that the mountain actually leads to her.

Through these two personalities that exemplify the New Spirituality, we see the perils of the New Spirituality made to look glamorous and a pseudoscience wedded to a mystical vocabulary that results in absurd deductions. I have chosen Oprah Winfrey and Deepak Chopra to illustrate what I am saying. One reveals to us the slow but sure grip of being made an icon by a seduced populous and the inevitable devolution of a belief. The other shows the flawed induction of this New Spirituality, and the predetermined conclusions that defy both reason and observation. If they both represent two sparkling lights in this astral spectrum, there are hosts of others that also shine. Their beliefs and means of communication have shown how an idea can be taken and marketed, reshaped, and repackaged until it is taken at face value by a generation that has failed to ask the right questions. There is no spinning top here to tell them whether they are dreaming or awake.

The breadth of thinking ranges from the genuine to the fake to the fake fake and the genuine fake (I hope you read the introduction). You are told in smooth-flowing tones that you have an "ageless" body and a "timeless" mind, when you know full well that your body is aging and that your mind is still swallowed up by time. But if you keep repeating the mantra with your eyes shut and your mind emptied of anything meaningful, you will float through the various degrees of the mystical overriding the rational. That notwithstanding, both Oprah and Chopra show us something very profound in the process. Allow me to take you on this brief journey to show the digression they have followed.

For one, life began in poverty and has ended up in incredible wealth. For the other, life began in the East and has ended up in the West. For one, the definitions started with "You are nothing until you make yourself something." For the other, it was "No matter what you make of yourself, at the core you are really nothing"…or everything, depending on your science or religion. For one, common sense and brutal reality are transformed into a rags-to-riches show-and-tell on the wings of telegenic strength. For the other, "quantum cosmology" and esoteric terminology provide the double-edged strength of two escape doors whenever questions are put to either; there is always a default position to the other when fault is found with one. The two things both Oprah and Chopra have in common are wealth and spiritual talk. Wealth is concrete, usable, power-leveraging, and the cause of mass envy. But the spiritual is the intangible, soul-appealing, sometimes foreign phraseology made marketable in one-liners and aphorisms that have the world eating ideas out of their hands.

What do I have in common with them? Very little, and very much at the same time. I, too, was born in the East and now live in the West. I, too, was raised in a small home and shared a small room with four other siblings. Just twenty-five yards away from where I lived, a family of eight lived in a shack made out of mud and cow dung. Poverty was writ large in a culture such as that. I grew up with spiritual talk all around me. I went to a school where the prescribed postures, breathing, and chants were part of assembly each day. I lived in a neighborhood where the silence of the dawn hours was regularly broken by voluminous chants in Sanskrit that wafted through the walls. The land of my birth is a country of complexities. You have both extreme wealth and extreme want. You have the ancient and the modern existing side by side. You live with dogma and myth. The ivory tower of the academy and the scourge of illiteracy exist a few feet apart.

But I have come to a conclusion radically different from those of Oprah Winfrey and Deepak Chopra. I have looked into their ideas and their impact and wondered aloud if they have pondered long enough the reasons for their success. Is it not odd that both knew the impact of some form of Christianity in their upbringing? Is it not odd that both have made their fortunes in a country where the impact of the gospel made possible freedom to the enslaved and liberty to pursue one's dreams? Is it not odd that the spirituality one touts still holds captive millions who are told that they are born inferior at their core? Is there an elephant in the room? Are they so enamored with their own statures that they are missing the fact that something larger than they are is struggling to make itself visible?

To their credit, they have in effect revealed the "unpaid bills" of Christendom. People yearn for the mystical and the relational. But at the cost of truth and reality? The vortex that suctions a person down the funnel of falsehood is that people are enamored by material success and want to know how they can get a piece of the pie. As Tevye in the musical *Fiddler on the Roof* would say, "When you're rich, they think you really know."

From Orpah to Oprah—Making Television and Being Remade by It

"The reason I wanted to be a white kid is that I never saw little white kids get whippings."[1]

With these words, Oprah summarizes some of her early struggles as a child. Born on January 29, 1954, in Kosciusko, Mississippi, and named *Oprah* because her mother misspelled Orpah from the Bible, this child was destined to become a cultic figure and a household name. In these days when the names of "stars" are given to children, her mother had no idea she was naming a star. Who knows, maybe "Orpah" would just not have made it: Cary Grant's birth name was Archibald Alexander Leach…it doesn't have the same iconic ring to it as Cary Grant. That aside, not only was Oprah to become a household name, she was in effect to become the point of reference for terms and phrases such as "the Oprah effect," "Oprahfication," and "She Oprah'ed it out of me"…new words in cultural jargon. One writer says, "She's not just working with the languages out there; she's helping to create those languages."

In a remarkable way, Oprah has embodied her own storied life. She interviewed the famous people who made her famous. She then went on to interview people who became famous because of her. We really don't know them except through the sound bites of their interviews with her, which can be all of about forty minutes of give-and-take. But we think we know them. Oprah, interestingly, is also only known to us from the sound bites in which she handles her guests and periodically reveals her own inner hurts. "She's like the one friend you trust," said a fan, waiting in line to see her show. "You stick with a girlfriend like that, you know."[2]

Being regularly seen by many on a television screen insidiously imparts a sense of trust. That is why advertisers use familiar screen personalities. The Earl of Shaftesbury once remarked that if the pope were married, he would know that he is not infallible. If we lived close to these television personalities, we would see them very differently from the cosmetic way in which we see them as "stars."

While we were in the makeup room being dabbed and readied for a television program, a friend quipped, "This is what you call preparing the body for viewing." That's about it…making the dead *seem* alive, the old *look* young, decay *look* fresh. Can real bonds be forged through such a medium or is it part of the charade? One critic rightly calls this "intimacy at a distance." The orchestrated informal, interactive style of the talk show encourages the audience to have a sense of intimacy with the host. The host's conversational style of speech, direct gaze at the camera, and the sense of intimacy between the host and the audience give the viewers the feeling that they are part of the conversation they are watching take place before them. One viewer is reported to have said, "Oprah is me. We're both black, we're both the same age, we treat people the same way. That could be me." Even Oprah's choice of "I'm Every Woman" by Whitney Houston as her show's theme song is no accident.[3]

It's hard to know someone when there is no "authorized" biography. One wonders how well someone can be known even through an authorized version. But there are glimpses we get of Oprah that convey the shaping strands of her life. More to the point, her fans find her appealing because she reflects their inner hungers to escape the hard knocks of life and find someone who "cares." Oprah credits her grandmother Hattie Mae for giving her a start that made it possible for her to pursue her values. But one gets a mixed story here. "My grandmother whipped me with switches. You go and pull a little limb off a tree and you bring it in. It's what Richard Pryor described as the loneliest walk of your life—to get your own switch. Amazing, isn't it?"[4] She goes on to say that our prisons are full of men who as young men "had the living hell beat out of them."[5] The beatings that today would be considered child abuse, she says, form her memories for the early years.

I can relate. Speaking personally, in the culture and times in which I was raised, beatings and thrashings were common fare.

And I mean thrashings. It was and still is a system of values that thrived on imparting fear and shame. If fear could not be leveraged, shame would be. If neither worked, suicide became the option.

Beyond these beatings and the poverty (they had outhouses…something you never forget, she has said), Oprah's life seems to have been fraught with twists and turns to find some solid footing somewhere. Her early years were immersed in instability. At the age of six, she left her grandmother's home and moved to Milwaukee to live with her mother, Vernita Lee, who worked as a cleaning woman and supplemented her income with welfare. After first grade, she went to live with her father and stepmother, but that was short-lived, and before long she was returned to her mother. Gleaning through her comments, you discover several shaping influences.

The principal feature of her early life was fragmentation… where nothing is the way it is supposed to be and a child is forced to grow up all too soon. She describes her own birth as the result of a "one-night stand." No one would label herself that way without struggling to justify her existence as either an accident or design: If life becomes a protracted misery, then the accident takes primary place; if it turns out to be a Cinderella story, then design surfaces, in spite of the pain. But this is where spiritual depth determines whether she would see the details of her life as luck or providence, the result of personal perseverance or grace. I think, for Oprah, there are shades of all these, at least in the early years. Though sometimes others can see us better than we are able to see ourselves, it is the hazard of life that others can also mistakenly see us as greater than we really are…or less than we really are.

Oprah's own admission is that she remembers her home

being smaller than it actually is. Funny, in my memories my home and neighborhood are much bigger than they actually are. When I returned to India for the first time after years of being gone, I wondered why I remembered those small rooms as being quite large. Was it because I didn't know any better? When Charles Dickens returned to his hometown and remarked that his city had changed, someone responded that it had not changed nearly as much as he had.

Oprah has the distinct trait of remaking herself many times over. From the glamour of fitting into a smaller pair of jeans to forcing an interest in particular themes so as to keep the show going, the power of a lens is incredible. This, audiences seldom ponder. As I read snippets of her own assessment of her life and career there are several unmistakable conclusions that can be rightly drawn.

Oprah was and is almost unstoppable—determined, hard-working, driven, a keen exponent of her medium (television), knowing precisely where her audience is. In fact, she knows them better than they will ever know her. With determination and skill she has combined her grit, gained in spite of the fragmentation of her life, with an intuitive strength of knowing what to serve up to her worshipping audiences. She has pursued every opportunity toward her goal, and when opportunities seemed to disappear, she created them. She understood the medium and wrested it to her advantage.

The fragmentation was a drawback, but she has used her wounds and hurts to her advantage. These, I have no doubt, have conditioned her thinking, and she has drawn from them at the precise moment of maximum impact. There are two ways to use a wound: either as a stepping-stone by looking beyond it, or as an exploitative thing to be leveraged for gain. I shall leave the individual to decide which is what. A little child in the arms of a beggar can elicit pity. But if the child is exploited for the purpose of material gain, there is a thin line between pity and seduction, or even deception. Any confession that paints the subject as a victim, and at the same time as a survivor, will draw a large following. Her personal stories of repeated molestation at the hands of relatives and friends opened the door of this harsh memory for large numbers of women.

Some of these experiences she has revealed in her shows; others have been dragged into the public eye without her desire to see them made public. Her first experience at being molested happened, she says, when at nine years of age she was left alone for the day with her nineteen-year-old cousin. When she was fourteen, she was molested by an uncle. Her pain has been shared by many women who have found an echo for their own pain in her voice. When the subject comes up, tears flow and those who have never experienced that trauma can still feel the weight that is being borne by those who have. The emotional scars make for desolation and rejection by the self, of the self. This is the self no little girl would choose. In this, Oprah has to be seen as a trailblazer, instrumental in unifying the public revulsion for such actions.

But then came a bombshell from a completely different source. In March 1990 Oprah's half sister betrayed a deep family secret to the *National Enquirer*, saying that when Oprah was fourteen years old she gave birth to an illegitimate child. In Oprah's words, "That experience was the most emotional, confusing, and traumatic of my young life." One can only imagine the double-edged pain felt by a public figure who is betrayed in this way, when deep hurts that never leave you are turned into public wounds to be exploited.

Oprah talks about this subject quite extensively…the resulting fears, the promiscuity, the silence that was bought by the perpetrators. The most distressing thing about this story to me is not even addressed; that it is possible for no one in the family to know that a nine-year-old has been molested when it is a family member who is responsible; that no one asks, "Who?" "When?" "Where?" Is it the unwritten law in a family that has experienced this to ask no questions, lest one hears what they don't want to hear, or risks being exposed for their own crimes? Such victimizers have learned to run from reality themselves and do not consider that they are criminals and could stop the crime.

There were other forces at work in shaping her life. Moving from home to home, repeatedly packing her bags and living sometimes with her grandmother, sometimes with her mother, sometimes with her father…the transitory feeling of being constantly uprooted was always present. Life has a way of compelling the "homeless mind" to either surrender or persevere. Oprah chose the latter, and she credits her father with pointing her in the right direction. "His love of learning showed me the way. Reading gave me hope. For me it was just the open door."[6]

One writer offers several reasons for "why Oprah is a compelling and successful spiritual teacher."[7] These speak clearly to her success and take nothing away from her; in order to be the success she is, she has had to exhibit extraordinary and sustained skill. I believe they are an accurate assessment of Oprah and of her story and explain why she is so admired and loved. Below is my take on the reasons offered:

- First, she is very human…people are able to connect with her as a real person. This is an icon but one that is "in the flesh." This combination of "being up there yet down here" is probably her greatest appeal.

- Oprah is familiar with suffering and wants to do something about it. Here again, I see that she is a reflector of people's anguish. They, too, can come to a show almost unknown, yet be known. These traits I believe point to something very striking as a human need.

- Oprah is a name that now signifies "community." Whereas authors trigger discussions in book clubs where the writer provides the ideas that shape the discussion, Oprah *becomes* the idea that shapes the discussion.

- As a pioneer, she has encouraged self-examination but has done so without cheapening people or exploiting others.

- Oprah is a firm believer in gratitude.

- Her speech is easy to understand. She engages with simple concepts, plainly spoken.

- Oprah is a great listener. As she interviews, she gives the impression that she is completely engrossed in what the person is saying and carries that discussion to bring in the audience.

- She has a contagious generosity that encourages people to give and to care.

- Forgiveness has been a key part of her own life. She has had to learn to forgive. Oprah is a promoter of goodness and honest living.

As one makes their way down this list, one begins to see that these were not values cradled in a vacuum. I am not sure that

I necessarily agree with this blanket assessment, because it all needs explanation. Many seriously take issue with whether all that has happened in Oprah's life has been as stated and without exploitation. Nonetheless, that is how she is portrayed. That is the persona that is believed to be the real thing. But what we must pay heed to is that even if this is not who she really is, this is what people are looking for...a person who cares, who listens, a person in whom people see reflected their deeply cherished hopes and longings. We are guilty of living contradictory lives, but we can still recognize what really matters deep within. It almost sounds like something you would hear at church: As Paul said in Romans 7:16 and 18, "I do what I do not want to do...For I have the desire to do what is good, but I cannot carry it out" (NIV).

Oprah had a church upbringing. Her spiritual heritage included music, drama, Sunday school, and, most of all, storytelling. She is a master storyteller. She embodies what she does. She talks to people about people. She feels what she wants people to feel. She wants authenticity to be normal and common. That's what comes through. At least, that is what her admirers say about her. Any famous person will always have their detractors. Even as I write this, an unauthorized biography by Kitty Kelley has just been released. The unfolding story is quite remarkable.

In the content of her programs, she sometimes comes extremely close to the truths of her upbringing and then suddenly drowns them in a sea of postmodern reality. Even though her life was fragmented, I strongly suspect there were those in her family background who prayed for her, those who asked Jesus to take care of her and who, as church members, withstood their own pain because the gospel gave the possibility of hope to them. Fatalism would have been easy. But dependence upon

God is that sixth sense that somehow holds on to the last sprig of support. I shall return to this. For now, I simply wish to underscore a backdrop of pain and disappointment. Yet I strongly suspect there existed lines of the gospel that kept in check those in whose charge she was raised.

That is one side of the story. To be a victim and rise above it is to one's extraordinary credit. Until the program changes you. That is the fearsome side of god-makers.

The Person Who Conditioned Others

Journalism is classified within our minds into certain categories. I had to smile when Tiger Woods gave his first interview after his tragic fall from grace. One of the press reporters audaciously asked him, "How could you lie to so many for so long?" That, coming from a journalist, had to be the most ironic thing I had heard for a long time. But whether we like it or not, the media news is part theater and part information. Journalism that is crude or provocative is branded "tabloid." There is a long list in this category. But if we can do the same thing with recognized personalities, we call it a talk show. Strange thing, this hero worship of ours.

Just reading a list of the programs featured by Oprah leaves one thoroughly perplexed by the power of an individual who, though clearly indulging in shock television, is passionately defended by her fans who don't see her that way. Her interviews on sexual matters have often gone beyond the pale, and leave one questioning the true motives here. One of her biographies gives a word-by-word description of perversions that were the subjects of some of her programs, viewed by millions. In one instance, she interviewed a transsexual quadriplegic whose boyfriend's sperm was inserted into her sister. The quadriplegic became the biological aunt/uncle and also adopted the child. When Oprah was strongly criticized for the program she said, "[Meeting the child] was just a moving thing. I thought, 'This child will grow up with more love than most children.' Before, I was one of those people who thought all homosexuals or anything like that were going to burn in hell because the Scriptures said it."[8]

Quite clever, isn't it...turning a story of criticism into a heroic one? Jeff Jarvis, the former television critic, wrote to her after one terribly explicit show, saying,

Oprah, you can't act as if you don't bear considerable responsibility for this. You brought sex to afternoon TV. Now I don't think you should be fined for that and I don't think you should be taken off the air for that; I just don't watch you. But you're doing nothing different from Howard Stern—except getting away with it. So cut your holier-than-thou disapproval of sex on the rest of TV. You are the Queen of Trash.[9]

This is where we are today. We locked Jim Bakker of PTL behind bars for years because he defrauded people of money. But there is no similar law against the seductive power of stories that actually exploit people. This is the postmodern version of the freak shows of years gone by. But here is the crucial step in impact: Once you have gained a following of such magnitude; once you can do no wrong by virtue of the adulation you receive; once you are one of the richest people in the world and can buy the companies that sponsor you; once you have a magical impact on the minds of people…is it not a short step to playing god in the minds of your followers?

But every human god-maker needs a god while playing god. Fame and success alone do not satisfy. Spirituality was truly the next step. You can't make people feel good just by telling stories. You have to be drawn into the story itself and become a hero or heroine in that story. And so…the spiritual side of Oprah's programming. Mystics, spiritual masters, all are in the lineup to give the viewer the feeling that she who has become all but deified in their eyes can now make each viewer just like them. What better way to do good than to make each person listening feel good while the spiritual master is instantly made rich just by being interviewed and the host becomes the pathway to hope and peace in the process? This is a win-win-win situation: The host, the guest, and the audience benefit…to say nothing of the advertiser and the station.

This is the free market at work, and the best win out. It is a long way from the wanderings of a Buddha or the sacrifice of the Son of God, but it has eye appeal in a time in history when gullibility is king and riches control appetite.

The Long Journey from God to Self-Exaltation

Along the way while Oprah was being made and making herself, her spiritual metamorphosis was taking place. Take note of Oprah's spiritual journey.

In high school, she wrote in the yearbook of her friend Gary Holt, "You have showed me more by your actions, by the way you live from day to day, that there is truly One Way, Jesus Christ!

And that without Him taking control, without Him running the whole show, life is just an endless go-round with no meaning."[10]

During a "look-back" show twenty-two years later, Oprah invited Gary Holt on her show. But it didn't turn out the way either he or she expected. As he saw her surrounded by her entourage of beauticians, production team, and other assistants he asked why she was doing all this. "Because I want to bring truth to the world," she said. Gary paused, took the yearbook out of his bag, and showed her what she had written two decades earlier. She added a few pleasantries and wrote further, "God is still King!"[11]

Changes may come in small increments, but they come indeed. The erudite know how to best talk their way out of their unattractive transformations.

There is another telling passage about her spiritual journey. When she joined an A.M.E. church in 1976, Oprah was described as a "preacher woman" fervently committed to Jesus Christ, having also memorized books of the Bible. She was strong in her faith and in calling people to live consistently with those truths found in the Bible. "I was raised to not question God. It's a sin… But I started to think for myself…and that's when I really started, in my mid-twenties, my own journey towards my spirituality, my spiritual self," Oprah has said.[12]

In picking the moment of change, she references a sermon she heard from her pastor, Rev. John Richard Bryant, on the text that says God is a jealous God (Exodus 20:5):

I was just sitting there thinking for the first time after being raised Baptist…church, church, church, Sunday, Sunday, Sunday…I thought, "Now why would God, who is omnipotent, who has everything, who was able to create me and raise the sun every morning, why would that God be jealous of anything that I have to say? Or be threatened by a question that I would have to ask?"[13]

Really, Oprah! This is what started it all? Do you really want us to believe that all of a sudden, after preaching the truths of the Bible for years and memorizing whole books of the Bible, you didn't like this God you had been following?

If this renunciation of God is true, either she didn't understand what the text meant and what she had believed all her life or she was deliberately looking for a way out to choose *this* reason for rejecting the faith of her childhood and youth. Often when we are struggling with how best to say we no longer believe what we once did, it is easiest to find one idea and either warp it or take it out of context and make ourselves heroes for being willing to renounce the unacceptable. I cannot help but be reminded of my friend in the last chapter. But the journey down the lane of the mystical, bolstered by a heavy dose of self-confidence and spiritual jargon, made Oprah the spirituality queen of the talk shows. The God she grew up believing in may have no longer been there, but there was an awful lot of spiritual talk. Redefining terms is the best way to smuggle in hungers while remaining autonomous. We all know this trick well.

Strange esoteric beliefs were waiting for acceptance. It is a long way from quoting the Bible to her fascination with *The Secret* by Rhonda Byrne. Beyond even that is what she has declared her second-favorite book, after the Bible: Gary Zukav's *The Seat of the Soul*. Authors such as Eckhart Tolle (*The Power of Now*), John Gray (*Men Are from Mars, Women Are from Venus*), Iyanla Vanzant (*Acts of Faith*), and Sarah Ban Breathnach (*Simple Abundance*) caused her to become verbose about their spiritual insights.

Dr. Phil was catapulted to fame as a regular feature on her show. These were branded "Change Your Life" shows. She ended that series with an astonishing segment called "Remembering Your Spirit," which was introduced with New Age music in the background as she said, "I am defined by the world as a talk show host, but I know that I am much more. I am spirit connected to the greater spirit."[14]

She has ascended into ethereal ranks and the mountain now bows to her. For this little kid, for whom so much had gone wrong so early, to reach these plateaus is miraculous in people's eyes. She has turned stones into bread and gained all the kingdoms of this world.

Early in her success, she told a friend that it was all God's plan and doing for her.[15] But in an ironic shift, as the years went by and a relative asked her why she embellished stories about her childhood so much until they became lies she said, "Because that is what people want to hear." The *visual media* had done its work. One is tempted to pun on the word, hence, I italicize it.

The seduction was complete. The lie is what people want, so why get hung up on the truth? All she wanted in the beginning was the truth. Now, if this is true, a lie is acceptable because that is what the audience wants to hear. Only very recently, she discovered she had a half sister. If anything needed to be a private moment, one would think that the first meeting of siblings would be it. No, not for a performer. The cameras were positioned so that the tears could flow for the viewers, garnering more publicity. Something so manufactured ought to be seen through, but astonishingly it is just regarded as even greater evidence of her greatness and another cause for applause. This life's dim window of the soul has beguiled the soul once again.

Truth and authenticity are easy casualties before the power of the lens. Between Deepak Chopra's co-opting of quantum terminology to support his version of spirituality, Oprah's capacity with telegenic splendor to blur the lines between fact and fancy, and the empty rhetoric of televangelists with their perfect coiffures and elaborate stage sets that are inversely proportional to the substance of what they are saying, we will never be able to roll back the clock. But maybe we can find a true point of reference for time. Between the ancient and the postmodern there may not be much of a difference except in the inferences we have drawn.

Having said all that, if I had the opportunity to talk to Oprah one-on-one, I would have some questions for her. Those questions I shall pose and attempt to answer myself in the pages to come. How can someone this accomplished and clear in her speech draw near to things spiritual yet remain muddied in her spiritual thinking? That, to me, is the bottom line of a life that has been so successful and so shaped by the influence of converging and conflicting views.

Here are some of the questions I would initially ask:

1. Why is the spiritual side of life so important and what do you personally think the true spiritual experience is?
2. If forgiveness is such a key aspect of your thinking, who is it that ultimately forgives the very motives and intents of the human heart?
3. Gratitude without a person to be grateful to is an incomplete thought. As G. K. Chesterton said, "If a child has Santa Claus to thank for putting candy in his stocking, have I nobody to thank for putting two feet in mine?" To whom are you ultimately grateful?

4. When you use the term "God," to what or whom do you refer? Is it not important to be right in your thinking about God?

5. You are a good listener. That is a good trait. Do you believe God listens to your prayers when you pray?

6. What are your thoughts on the nature of sin?

7. What do you believe ultimately about individual human destiny?

8. Do you believe success has made you happy or is there something greater than that?

9. You are a great believer in values: What is the source of those values?

10. What do you think is the purpose of life?

11. Who do you believe yourself to be?

12. Who do you think Jesus is?

I believe the answers to these questions will tell me not what she believes, but *why* she believes it.

That said, it was quite amazing to hear her closing words at the end of the last taping of *The Oprah Winfrey Show*, the end of this phase of her career. I do not think for a moment that this is a farewell. I think it is a fork in the road. And how could one blame her? With the kind of following she has and the power that comes with that, it will be hard to escape the camera. But her closing comments may well be the twin shades of her spirituality. That she gave God the glory for her success and mentioned Jesus and "the Alpha and the Omega" did not escape discussion everywhere.

Ultimately, only God knows a person's heart. As I see it, deep inside her is that childlike faith and the memory of all that has happened to bring her this far. But the tug of the camera and of

the Spirit of the Age, and a desire to make spiritual truth acces-
sible and not dogmatic, may well have led her to say things that
she thought would draw people closer to decency in their inner
lives, even if she didn't fully believe those things herself. Who
knows? But that is precisely the game that can be played under
the lights. Farewells bring out emotions that cannot suppress
some beliefs. But with time and fame, the line between trusting
God and playing God can easily be erased. When we are at the
peak of success we may lead other people to believe that we are
God. When we say good-bye, we know we are not.

CHAPTER 5

THE RELIGION OF QUANTUM

A More Educated Icon

Deepak Chopra is in effect the spiritual counselor for and a household name to millions. He was born in Delhi in 1946 or 1947 (depending on the source). He is a graduate of the All India Institute of Medical Sciences (1968) and a former leader of Maharishi Mahesh Yogi's Transcendental Meditation and Ayurvedic Medicine programs.

His own trek to his present position is quite interesting. His early love, first for literature and then for journalism, was replaced by the study of medicine. He moved to the United States around 1970, where he interned at a hospital in New Jersey before relocating to Boston and establishing his own practice in endocrinology. In 1985 he was appointed chief of staff at New England Memorial Hospital. As time went by he became disenchanted with traditional medicine, which he thought was too dependent on drugs, and having come under the influence of Maharishi Mahesh Yogi's teaching, Chopra resigned his position at the hospital and co-founded Maharishi Ayur-Veda Products

International, Inc. (MAPI), with Maharishi Mahesh Yogi, a powerful practitioner of Ayurveda.

MAPI offered a line of herbal supplements, teas, oils, and incense, as well as other products relevant to the business of wellness from the Ayurvedic perspective. As the Maharishi's representative, Chopra became the head of a Lancaster, Massachusetts, Ayurveda Health Center, the first of four such centers in America. His Western education and career as a doctor in a respected Western medical facility gave legitimacy to *Ayurveda* (a Sanskrit word that means "knowledge of life") for many who were initially skeptical, and the clinics grew quickly, especially once it was known that such celebrities as Elizabeth Taylor, fashion designer Donna Karan, and the investment banker Michael Milken were clients.

Though his first several books met with a mixed critical and popular reception, *Ageless Body, Timeless Mind,* published in 1993, sold more than a million copies and suddenly, with his blend of medicine and spirituality enhanced with a sprinkling of scientific terms, Chopra was becoming the premier Eastern name in an increasing Western fascination with all things Eastern.

By the mid-1990s he founded the Chopra Center for Well Being in La Jolla, California. Now himself an international celebrity in demand for speaking and lecturing, his subsequent books were very well received by a public that had been expertly primed. And in spite of the many articles written by well-qualified medical practitioners and scientists who have questioned and even openly ridiculed Chopra's statements, whatever he says continues to be accepted unquestioningly by his large following, to the extent that one cannot help but wonder at their gullibility.

But do not be deceived: Deepak Chopra is not just promoting

Eastern medicines; he is a shrewd businessman who has prof-
ited greatly from the new spirituality combined with his brand
of gimmickry. His following statement succinctly sums up his
belief in wellness:

> Quantum healing is healing the bodymind from a quan-
> tum level. That means from a level which is not mani-
> fest at a sensory level. Our bodies ultimately are fields
> of information, intelligence and energy. Quantum heal-
> ing involves a shift in the fields of energy information,
> so as to bring about a correction in an idea that has
> gone wrong. So quantum healing involves healing one
> mode of consciousness, mind, to bring about changes in
> another mode of consciousness, body.[1]

I'm sure that was helpful. It was a medical doctor who
once told me how upset he was with his doctor's diagnosis of
the strange pains and sensations he was having in his right leg.
The treating doctor said to him, "It's a seventy-year-old leg, you
know." After a moment of reflection my friend said, "I know. But
the left leg is a seventy-year-old leg, too. Why is the right one
hurting and the left one not?"

By changing the information on one level of consciousness,
we can heal the other areas of consciousness. Each recipient
mutters the same terms and concepts and assumes that the listener now fully understands this cure. While millions in his and
my homeland live in huge deprivation, the center at La Jolla is
here to promote quantum healing for the wealthy. But there is
no reason to complain or to feel "taken." Beneath all the trappings, what he is actually arguing for is very clear to anyone who

is willing to see it. We shall get to that shortly, and I will raise my personal philosophical challenges to his system at that point.

Along the way of his association with TM (Transcendental Meditation) and then his own independent enterprise, there were reports of some issues of disagreement that signaled what the tensions were actually about. The origins of some of his teachings and writings were challenged in the law courts. I have provided links for those who wish to study this further. Frankly, I am more interested right now in the substance of what he is teaching than in who was right and who was wrong in court, or who promoted it first. But it does reveal the "not-so-pristine" reality that lies behind the scenes. All the talk of peaceful splendor and nirvanic pursuits masks the usual bouts of infighting, lawsuits, and competition. It is interesting, don't you think, that a God who describes his sacrificial love for each of us as a jealous love merits rejection, but demagogues jealous of one another's successes who engage in outrage and lawsuits are considered decent and peaceful.

More serious, for the moment at least, is the very purpose behind Chopra's supposedly scientific terminology: to falsely assert a connection between quantum physics and "consciousness." Among his claims are those stating that "quantum healing" can defeat the aging process, that the mind may be healed by harmonizing or balancing the "quantum mechanical body," and that by localizing your awareness on the source of your pain, you can direct healing to begin because, according to him, the body naturally sends healing energy in the direction you are giving your attention. Or, as he also says, you make happy molecules by having happy thoughts. As one writer states, "This 'quantum mysticism' has no basis in physics or biology and represents a leap of the metaphysical imagination."[2]

This same writer goes on to counter and challenge this

supposed blend of science and mysticism. He traces Chopra's teachings to the popular publication of Fritjof Capra's *The Tao of Physics: An Exploration of the Parallels Between Modern Physics and Eastern Mysticism* (1975), and describes Capra's attempt in that book to connect ancient religions and modern physics as "an abysmal failure."[3] According to him, it is this that has influenced Chopra and other New Age energy medicine advocates to claim that quantum physics proves the reality of everything from chi and prana to ESP, despite the denial of most physicists. Notwithstanding the claims of Chopra and others that the mind can control diseases like cancer, the evidence from scientific studies says otherwise. It is true that there is scientific evidence that optimists live longer than pessimists, but it is not necessary to bring in quantum physics to explain why.

Chopra and others of his ilk claim that modern physics validates ancient Hindu metaphysics, a claim that is vehemently rejected by serious scientists who insist that there is no connection between the discoveries of modern physics and the metaphysical claims of Ayurveda. In fact, physicist Heinz R. Pagels, author of *The Cosmic Code: Quantum Physics as the Language of Nature*, goes so far as to say, "No qualified physicist that I know would claim to find such a connection without knowingly committing fraud."[4]

Physicists like Dr. Pagels deny any connection between modern physics and Chopra's "field of consciousness," asserting that his claim that large numbers of people meditating can reduce crime or avert war by creating a "unified field of consciousness"[5] is pure foolishness and that the presentation of physics that so willfully distorts scientific truth in support of these ideas can only be seen as a deliberate intention to deceive those who don't know better.

According to Chopra, the state of your health is a matter of personal choice: By taking your pulse, he can identify your *dosha* and whether or not it is out of balance. He can cure your allergies by addressing your digestive problems; reverse or prevent cataracts by rinsing your eyes with a mixture of spit from brushing your teeth, tongue scrapings, and water; and reverse or retard aging by redirecting the way your body "metabolizes" time. And, of course, he also promotes aroma therapy based on Ayurvedic metaphysical physiology and sells the oils and spices needed.

When it comes right down to it, what he and other "alternative" healers are really selling to the gullible is hope for healing and the hope of living forever. But it is a hope based on mysticism, imagination, and good marketing skills rather than on science.

Here, I cannot resist a personal word on two experiences within our own family that I have recounted elsewhere. When I was a young lad, I remember how much my father suffered from asthma. He was advised by an Ayurvedic doctor to go to the city of Hyderabad three years in a row at a certain time of the year. He would have to rise before dawn and stand in a line with others also waiting for treatment. At the first blush of dawn, a priest would place a small minnow with a concoction of spices into the mouth of the sick person and they would be cured of whichever disease was ailing them. Combining the astrological chart with nature's herbs and the administration of a priest would bring about the cure.

It is important to know that my father was not some kind of gullible ignoramus. He had studied at Nottingham University in England and was a deputy secretary in the Home Ministry of the government of India. I remember him often saying, as he struggled to breathe in the midst of an asthma attack, that he would never wish his ailment on his worst enemy. The intensity of his respiratory struggle sent him to a city more than a thousand miles away for three years in a row. Did it cure him? It made not one whit of difference. When he came to Canada in his mid-fifties, the identification of his particular allergies and the cleaner air rid him of his asthmatic condition once and for all. I remember him saying that so simple a corrective for so deep a malady was denied him by years of other methods that did nothing for him.

My closest friend growing up in India was the son of a homeopathic doctor and the strictest vegetarian who often scolded me for not being likewise. In his early fifties, he suffered a massive heart attack and died. His father died young as well.

I tell these stories to warn people that medicine is multifaceted. To make either Ayurveda or homeopathic or Western-style medicine, often called allopathic medicine, the cure-all is ludicrous and just plain contrary to facts. Each has their distinctive place. What disservice these propagators of metaphysical medicine perform in an effort to peddle their philosophy! They play god and make gods while denying us our essential humanity. They take the pragmatic and make it the total view. They take the ancient and make it the better view. This comes perilously close to deception and distortion. Keep these philosophies for what they are and let the truth seeker discover whether the ideas behind them are coherent or incoherent.[6]

In fact, I can speak from the perspective of my own search for wellness as a result of serious back injuries that have left me living with an incredible degree of pain. On my travels to India I have tried numerous medicinal cures to relieve the pain. Nothing is so all-encompassing within the mind of a person who is in pain than the desire to alleviate it. I have been told by medical practitioners that the greater challenge in pain management is the emotional toll that the pain exacts. I have tried the non-invasive and therapeutic methods, which include an evaluation where they talk about the Vata, Pitta, Kapha, and so on, followed by a prescription for massage and diet. The meditative side of these treatments I do not need. My ancestors left those practices when they became followers of Jesus Christ. But I did undertake the massage treatments with the oils, just to mitigate the pain.

There is a dangerous half-truth to the claims of Ayurvedic medicine. Some of the Ayurvedic oils do work; some of it is just plain psychological game-playing. That is as kindly stated as I can afford. The real truth is that I have seen doctors who practice Eastern medicine desperate themselves to get to the West to be treated with Western medicine when faced by their own debilitating disease. I have seen massage therapists who spend their lives using those oils, only to find no relief themselves when they are injured or fatigued from overusing their muscles. This is the plain and simple truth.

There can sometimes be palliative benefits to several of these methods, without the invasiveness of some Western medicine. But any positive effect on my skeletal and genetic problems for me personally has just been a pipe dream. The same is true for many others I know. Without the care of doctors here in the West or those in the East who are highly trained in Western medicine, I would not be walking at this point. As with everything, there is a balance. By all means collect the wisdom of the ages, but there is far more to be gained from using the wisdom of the present, as well.

Unfortunately, the lure of money and power, the influence of the media, and the struggle of the human heart make us pursue these things and, in the end, quarrel over who has the rights to the cure while the heart and mind are severed from ultimate truth. What is the driving force behind these searches? The answer is in one word: *pain*. Whether it is the emotional pain of someone like Oprah or the physical pain that comes with illnesses, it is pain that stalks us and drives us in this search for spirituality. The simplistic solutions of Deepak Chopra cannot stand against the lofty and deep teachings of Jesus Christ. However well-intentioned people like Chopra may be, the claims that are made in those wellness centers and the costs incurred for whatever is offered there leave one incredulous. When one begins with a problematic induction, through an inescapable seduction, there is an inevitable reduction and ultimately a false deduction. Here is Chopra's deduction about the who and what of humanity:

> Success in life could be defined as the continued expansion of happiness and the progressive realization of worthy goals...Even with the experience of all these things, we will remain unfulfilled unless we nurture *the seeds of divinity* inside us. In reality, we are divinity in disguise, and the gods and goddesses in embryo that are contained within us seek to be fully materialized.[7] (Italics mine)

Chopra says that he wrote part one of his thoughts on success in his book *Creating Affluence: Wealth Consciousness in the Field of All Possibilities*. Now in *The Seven Spiritual Laws of Success* he is revealing the guidelines that underlie all success. Why do I think I have heard such language before? Is this not a different version of the prosperity gospel? Evidently, the prosperity gospel is not restricted to televangelists; rather, the same goal is now being offered in a different path. What does the old adage say?

"Fool me once…" You know the rest of it. The only difference between the two is that the televangelists misrepresented divinity; this group goes one better and tells us we *are* divinity.

As I am writing this book, India has just won the world cup in cricket, a beautiful game. I love the game. But here is one writer commenting on the victorious Indian team: "These boys in blue are not just boys. They are men. They are not just demigods. They are Gods." How fascinating that he has forgotten that some of the gods in the Pakistani cricket team were disqualified from playing because they were charged with match-fixing in other tournaments. So we have gods aplenty that are here today and gone tomorrow. Yet these are the same voices that during earthquakes and natural catastrophes want to know where God is.

It is easy to see how and why entertainment icons and these spiritual gurus and celebrities have come together. One thinks they are gods and the other tells them they are right; and what's more, the rest of us are gods, as well. The words of Reinhold Niebuhr come to mind: "No amount of evidence to the contrary seems to shake man's grand opinion of himself."

I remember reading of a businessman who had gone to Las Vegas to find something there that would satisfy and fulfill him. He took his own life in his hotel room and left a one-line note that said, "Here, there are no answers." For the ultimate hungers of the human heart, all the terminology, all the wellness claims, and all the supposedly scientific terminology only leave you with the deep conviction that "here, there are no answers." I shall let Deepak Chopra have the last word:

I in fact don't believe in the existence of time. That's one thing I have to tell you, and the other is that I don't take myself or what I am doing seriously.

I don't believe in anything supernatural.

Hope is a sign of despair.

Cynicism is a risk factor for sudden death from premature heart disease.[8]

Clever...but what a way to build an empire.

It is something to watch a person in the making and see how they end up seeing themselves. It is equally fascinating that just because a person carries some credentials in the field of health, we accept as equally authoritative his pronouncements in philosophy. The successful marketing of a product is often mistaken as the substance of the product. Both health and philosophy deal with the spiritual, but, unwittingly, they make it evident that the greatest disease of life is of the heart, as Jesus described it.

Whether in competition in business dealings or in the big business that spirituality has become, Jesus' words ring true. The heart of humanity is pride, greed, and lust...insisting on having our way. We do not have the seeds of divinity. That is the ultimate seduction. Apart from a Savior, we just play to the stands. Only in his answers will we find the ultimate hope for the human heart. That is the pursuit of this book.

CHAPTER 6

꩜

GO WEST, YOUNG MAN

There is a tongue-in-cheek saying in the Hindi language: "*desi murghi pardesi chaal.*" It sarcastically refers to a local person who returns from abroad and puts on airs as if he is now above the locals. It literally translates, "a local chicken with a foreign walk." Much of the New Spirituality that we witness in the West is the reverse of this saying; it is a foreign chicken with a local walk. No unkindness is intended here, but it amazes us from the East to see this hybrid so brilliantly marketed and accepted in the West. I like to call it "Weastern" Spirituality because of the genius in combining Western materialism and Eastern spirituality.

Years ago, the ultimate attainment of Eastern spirituality was represented by bony "sadhus," or holy men, who walked the dusty miles every day and found shelter at night in a "dharamsala," or inn. You can still see them along the highway from Delhi to Mathura, their staffs in their hands and a bundle draped over one shoulder. They get their meager daily meal of rice and lentils from anyone willing to share his food with them, and engage in conversation with anyone willing to listen as they expound on the benefits to the soul of not living for the body. Following a ceremonial bath and their time of puja and bhajans (their hymn singing), they settle in for the night on a cement floor.

Eastern spirituality is represented quite differently in America today. Those whose books are most quoted and make the *New York Times* best-seller lists, the frontline figures in the movement, are generally at the head of very wealthy empires. No excessive attachment to detachment is in evidence. Though our clothes these days may bear the label "Made in China," there is no doubt that the new form of spirituality is "Made in India." There is both an explanation for it and yet a lack of explanation when I ponder "Weasternism." In the earlier part of the last century, missionary E. Stanley Jones's best-known book was titled *The Christ of the Indian Road*. It will not be long before a publication emerges titled *Krishna of the American Road*. Better yet, *Dharma of the American Road*.

There is actually some very serious vitriol in the continuous debates between Indian practitioners on this. Deepak Chopra likes to imagine his religion as disentangled from Hinduism and instead calls it "Sanatan Dharma," or the "Eternal Religion." But some Hindu apologists are not happy with this disavowal of Hinduism. I suspect I know why he does not want that tag of Hinduism on what he is teaching: By disavowing the tag he can retain his beliefs, and a very gullible American audience is not able to see what is really at work here. Besides, it conveniently frees him from having to defend anything in that system of belief that is embarrassing. But the thinking of Chopra and of others like him, such as Eckhart Tolle, is generally built upon the work of at least one of the great exponents of this pantheistic thought. "Three Gurus Who Changed the Face of Spirituality in the West" is the title of a very recent article in the *Huffington Post* written by Philip Goldberg, the author of *American Veda*. The title says it all.

Home Is Where the Heart Is

So goes the familiar truism. But the mind has to come to terms with what the heart believes. This is a difficult section for me to write, because it is so close to home. As I have already stated, it is sad that whenever somebody like me questions the main ideas of the dominant religion that is woven into the culture of my birth, they run the risk of being seen as a traitor. A traitor to what, I ask? If my disbelief of the religion that shaped my culture is such a terrible thing, why are westerners being encouraged to become traitors to the West and to the worldview that has shaped the West? Why is it that a westerner moving toward the East in his or her thinking is doing a good thing, but the reverse is a betrayal? The tirade against Chopra by Aseem Shukla, a urologist by profession, from the University of Minnesota and of the Hindu American Foundation, is over Chopra's resistance to call his brand of spirituality by its rightful name, which Shukla insists is Hinduism. If this is a demonstration of the kind of castigation one faces for believing the same thing but calling it something different, imagine the hostility toward a fellow countryman who doesn't believe the same thing.

Some time ago, a noted Indian historian by the name of S. D. Jha wrote an article in one of India's leading newspapers on the pre-Vedic and early Vedic practice of meat and beef consumption. He mustered a wealth of Sanskrit scholars, linguists, and historians of religion to show that this was indeed so, not only, I might add, of Hindu priests, but also of the Buddha himself. Mr. Jha is a highly respected and qualified historian. The vitriol the article engendered and the hate mail he received was beyond belief.

Is it not possible to be honest in what one says without being seen as attacking one's roots? Is it not possible to expose a falsehood and still love one's culture of birth? I am an Indian through and through…by birth, by love, by admiration for all that this great culture has poured into my soul. In India we have the term "*dharti kay admi.*" It means "a person of the soil." I am of Indian soil. But I have to ask questions where absolute truth is claimed, in order to be able to find reasonable answers. On that, the great sages of India agree. That is what I am trying to do here and, out of my love for both India and the West, demonstrate that the metaphysics that has changed Western spirituality is based on a flawed epistemology.

Some years ago, when the former Soviet Union was still in the grip of the Cold War, I happened to be visiting there with some friends. After we had finished lunch one day, the waitress politely intoned, "Would you like any dessert?"

"Yes, we would," we answered. "What do you have?"

"Ice cream," came the sweet reply.

We waited. It was soon evident that nothing further was coming. "Then we'll have ice cream," we said.

"What flavor would you like?" she asked.

"What flavors do you have?" we inquired.

"Vanilla," came the polite answer.

We waited. We stared at one another. That was it. We concluded that she really only wanted to know if we would like vanilla ice cream for dessert but asked us with the charming grace of making us feel that it was the dessert of our choice, among myriad options.

That is precisely the sweet talk of contemporary "Weastern" Spirituality. "Choose the religion of your choice…as long as you include our fundamentals. If not, we'll call you a fundamentalist." Chopra never hesitates to use that description in a pejorative way for those who take the Bible as God's Word. The purveyors of this New Spirituality are brilliant at playing the game to appear very generous while being actually very defining. This is the same game relativism plays: You are told there are no absolutes, but if you run afoul of the relativist, the castigation that follows knows no boundaries and the bigotry vented knows no limits. Chopra wants us to believe that this New Spirituality is not dogmatic and is all-accommodating. But the truth is that its foundation is in the Hindu/pantheistic worldview and the implications of Vedic teaching are at its root. On that there is no equivocation.

Every chapter of Chopra's *Seven Spiritual Laws of Success* begins with a quote from either the Hindu scriptures or a pantheist. The last quote is from Einstein, and that completes his scenario of pantheism wedded to science. Dr. Aseem Shukla rightly takes Chopra to task for playing games with words. Here is how he states it in their serial exchange in the *Washington Post*:

[Deepak] Chopra is the perfect emissary to fire a salvo against my assertion that delinking Hinduism from its celebrated contributions to contemporary spiritual dialogue—yoga, meditation, Ayurvedic healing, the science of self-realization—renders a rich tradition barren and unrecognizable to its adherents...

A prolific writer and gifted communicator, Chopra is perhaps the most prominent exponent of the art of "How to Deconstruct, Repackage and Sell Hindu Philosophy Without Calling it Hindu!"...

The contention that yoga's foundation is "in consciousness alone," thereby preceding Hinduism, is a sad demonstration of the extent Chopra and other Hindu

philosophical profiteers will go to disassociate themselves from Hinduism…Hinduism and yoga are inextricably intertwined, and the dedicated practice of yoga is
absolutely a Hindu practice…Hinduism, being avowedly
pluralistic, requires no membership, affiliation or oath of
loyalty to borrow, and yes, benefit, from its sacred wisdom…Frustratingly, also, Chopra takes the disingenu-
ous path of impugning a "fundamentalist" agenda to my
contentions…But the guilt of plagiarism carries no stat-
ute of limitations, and Hindus are wise to the machinations of the pretenders.[1]

The back and forth between Chopra and Shukla makes for
a fascinating exposé of the hostility between them. There are
no beatific smiles on display here, no enlightened meditational
peace; just plain polysyllabic vitriol. I find it fascinating that
Shukla, verbose and rich in philosophical terminology, naively
or tendentiously calls Hinduism "avowedly pluralistic" when
all the fundamentals of Hinduism are in clear contradiction to
the fundamentals of monotheistic religions. All Hindu scholars
like to perpetrate this illusion of pluralism within Hinduism.
But borrow any of their views, and they will doggedly demand
that you identify this "avowedly pluralistic" thought as uniquely
theirs. It is quite humorous, actually…the old story of "all yours
is mine and all mine is mine."

Regardless of whether or not we agree on our worldviews, it
is necessary that we learn to live peaceably with our differences.
Swami Vivekananda used to say, "Not just tolerance but acceptance." It is a noble intent, but I ask what exactly we are to accept,
the belief or the person? I would like to add that tolerance of the

belief is the gracious thing to do; acceptance of the person is the loving thing to do. But loving a belief that violates the starting point of your own belief is the hypocritical thing to do.

In the end truth will triumph, whether we like it or not. To sound grand and magnanimous by saying, "I accept all religions," is actually to either violate them all or violate reason, or both. We all have a right to proclaim what we believe about ultimate things. But that does not mean that everything we believe is right. The thinking person must honestly weigh the evidence and come to the right conclusion. To force anyone to believe matters of transcendent truth is to violate the very nature of those truths. Chopra is not reticent to refer to "empty churches" and the unmet needs of the American seeker after truth. I can tell him the same thing about thousands of Indian youth and businesspeople, those in the arts and leaders in India who come to ask questions about the gospel because their spiritual hungers are not met in the metaphysics of pantheism and the so-called Sanatan Dharma.

It is ironic that the fastest-growing church in the world today is in China. They have had their share of ancient teachers and pantheistic sages. They had atheism forced down their throats by the iron will of a demagogue. In fact, having burned their seminaries and banned gatherings in churches, the Communist leaders were certain that religion in general and Christianity in particular were forever expunged from the Chinese memory. Now, they are turning to Jesus Christ in China literally by the millions. I have spoken there and met with some of their scholars. A Christian professor teaching in one of the most prestigious universities there told me that one of his colleagues made an astounding comment to him: "Whatever you want to say about communism, you can be thankful for one thing; it left the soul empty and that is what makes it possible for you to find students who listen eagerly when you talk about Jesus Christ to them."

So why Jesus and not anyone else? What are the reasons? Before we get to that, let me turn back to those shapers of the modern Western spirituality that is based in the pantheistic worldview of the East. Again, let me say that Christianity is neither Eastern nor Western. It is the worldview behind it that is different from these other religions.

Keeping Up with the Joneses

E. Stanley Jones was born near Baltimore, Maryland, in 1884. After studying both theology and law and holding a professorship in the United States, he became a missionary to India. He dearly loved the Indian people and became a close personal friend of Mahatma Gandhi. His conversations with Gandhi, recorded in one of his books, became an inspiration to Dr. Martin Luther King Jr. Jones is considered a trailblazer in India for his enormous effort to give Christianity an Eastern face; not to *make* it Eastern as much as to return it to its Eastern roots without distorting it. It seems that once anything is seen as being "Americanized," it is castigated by those who don't like America or think America philosophically sophomoric. To reverse the process and remove the prejudice is very difficult to do.

In Europe, Christianity was abused when it was used for political power; in America it has been abused by using it for economic power. And today it is abused by its detractors who deny its power and remove it from any position of moral authority. These detractors live under the illusion that it is the only belief that claims absolutes. The price paid for these distortions has been enormous. Gandhi roundly criticized the Christianity he saw practiced around him and advised E. Stanley Jones that if the message of Christianity were to make any inroads into India, it would have to look more like Jesus than like his followers. That is, I am afraid, a very legitimate criticism to this very day, and not only in India. I would be very curious to have heard his thoughts on how Eastern spirituality has been marketed and demonstrated in the West. What many "consumers" of Eastern spirituality in the West have missed is that many of the same methods of distortion that were used to promote Western spirituality are being used to peddle Eastern spirituality.

The list of massage treatments and the offerings in Chopra's center makes the faith healers in "the old country" look like novices. As a skeptical friend of mine used to say, "There are big bucks in the God racket." Check out Chopra's wellness center and ask yourself honestly whether or not this is commercialization at its height, all in the name of wellness and consciousness. Pardon the pun, but the emperor has no clothes, and few are willing to expose it for what it is. These may be strong words, but that is the legitimate response to claims that are empirically so extreme.

The challenge to E. Stanley Jones was immense as he faced a religious culture whose views of the gospel had become so distorted from the reality of Jesus and his teachings. But Jones succeeded. His gentle personality, his life, and his lifestyle won the admiration of all. The challenge, as I said, was immense because he did not have the advantage of mass visual communication. However, I strongly suspect that if he had, the dangers would have been proportionate. His appeal was both to the outcasts and, because he was from the West and well learned, to the Indian intellectual as well.

I had the privilege of hearing E. Stanley Jones address an

audience shortly before he died. He spoke for nearly an hour and a half, without a single note in front of him, while Indian intellectuals and government leaders listened in rapt attention. The mystical and spiritual side of the Christian faith was beginning to take root in India because it appealed to the Indian mind-set. Some of the more famous Christian mystics in India were actually two Sikh converts to Christianity and contemporaries of E. Stanley Jones, Sadhu Sundar Singh and Bakht Singh. Converts from Sikhism are rare. But both Sundar Singh and Bakht Singh had made a profound commitment to Jesus after their earlier years of hostility to the Christian message.

Christianity first came to India under the teaching of the apostle Thomas. Numerous Indian scholars support the view that Thomas first landed on the southwestern shores of Kerala, India, and that he had a powerful impact on the priests of India. Kerala is often considered the intellectual bastion of India's Vedic teaching. The best-known Indian philosopher, Shankaracharya, came from Kerala. Ayurvedic medicine is at its best in Kerala. I strongly suspect that the oils that Deepak Chopra uses in his wellness centers are brought from there. It was to Kerala that Thomas first went and then to Tamil Nadu on the southeastern coast.

After the conversion of seven priests in that region and of a woman of nobility, Thomas was assassinated while he was praying. How ironic that the man who would not put his trust in Christ until he had seen and felt the nail holes in his hands and the spear hole in his side was ultimately speared to death himself! A fascinating history of Thomas's activities in India is chronicled by several writers. Ancient historians such as the Venerable Bede, Clement of Alexandria, and Gregory of Nazianzus, as well as several Indian historians, all make reference to

Thomas in India. The oldest Christian denomination in India today is named after Thomas, the Marthoma Church.

The Christ of the Indian road that E. Stanley Jones presented to India demonstrated that the values and patterns of Jesus' teaching had been forgotten in the Westernizing of Christianity. Christian ideas like meditating on the goodness and grace of God, solitude in prayer, and commitment to community and family are all part of the gospel of Jesus Christ. Jones also penned a remarkable book called *Christ at the Round Table*; he called it such because he wanted to encourage dialogue and open discussion. Jones began several "ashrams," or retreats, in India, places conducive to meditation and prayer where the gospel was the message and Jesus the focus. He did everything to retain the "Indianness" of the expression of faith in Christ without losing the substance of the message.

This is important to note. There were already strands of theism within the wide embrace of Hinduism. The Gita talks more of devotion, worship, the need of a sacrifice, and so on. The famed Indian philosopher Radhakrishnan said, "You can be a Christian, a Muslim, an atheist, and still be a Hindu." Needless to say, he equivocated on the other terms but clearly meant that strands of other faiths could be found in Hinduism. So the message of a supreme, transcendent, personal God was not completely foreign to Indian thought.

By contrast, when Vivekananda and Yogananda brought their teachings to the West, it was to bring a worldview completely different from what America was founded on, a worldview that if taken seriously would completely uproot the basic beliefs of the West about the nature of God, humanity, and human destiny.

If you were to go to India today and ask an average person what India's biggest problem is, the chances are you would be told "corruption." If you were to ask what brings many of them to the West, the chances are you would be told, "To be given a fair chance to succeed." It is not accidental or unconnected that the two major types of institutions started by Christian missionaries in India were schools and hospitals. I am writing this portion of the book in India. It is interesting to see the hospitals and dispensaries crowded with patients who are being treated with Western medicines by doctors who are Western-trained.

Chopra himself studied in a school started by missionaries. This is true of most of the prominent philosophers in India. In fact, the *Statesman*, which was India's first newspaper and is still in existence today, was started by the British missionary William Carey (1761–1834) as a voice for the Indian people in British India. The fight to eradicate the practice of *suttee*, in which a widow was expected to commit suicide by throwing herself on the funeral pyre of her husband, was spearheaded by William Carey in partnership with a famous Indian by the name of Raja Ram Mohan Roy.

I have often wondered if people like Chopra and Shukla who talk so much about the Vedic quest and argue over whether to credit Hinduism or something that preceded it for their beliefs ever pause to realize that the belief in the equal value of every life is a bequest only of the Christian faith. The accepted inequality of life and the lifelong struggle over power in the East is a bequest of the stratified caste system that haunts Eastern worldviews either explicitly or implicitly. This is why Gandhi himself took issue with some Vedic teachings. I know Hindu apologists don't like to bring up things like this. This is the kind of doctrine that I suspect Chopra is avoiding having to defend by giving his belief a name other than Hinduism. Shukla, just by the stroke of a pen—referring to the "*perceived* social ills" of Hinduism—

likes to do away with the critique rather than seeing it for what it is, instead criticizing those who have criticized any negative aspects of Hinduism.

But when millions live under the heel of this belief, what does he expect? Why have millions of members of the "lower caste" left Hinduism to find value in another faith? Maybe, Vedic apologists have forgotten that Gautama Buddha also rejected Vedic authority and the caste system, leaving his palace and his place of privilege in search of another truth. Tragically, I cannot help but wonder if we have now abandoned truth to return to the palace, and rather than sitting alone under a tree waiting for enlightenment, we gravitate to mass entertainment under lights that cater to mass ignorance.

The Nirvanic Quest

In one of his books, E. Stanley Jones writes about the challenge of facing hard questions. To every spiritual claim, he said, there are three challenges: (1) Is it new? (2) Is it true? (3) Is it you?

The struggles of the one versus the many, of permanence and change, of the *I* and the *you* is not new. Greek philosophers also struggled with these ideas and tried to solve them in purely secular terms. The long journey into autonomous spirituality is not really new either. On the question of God, there are only a handful of possibilities. Pantheism, which is the philosophical term that defines the divinity of everything, has tugged at the human heart for centuries. There have been shades of difference, sometimes greater than what appears at the surface and sometimes less. From the various varieties of pantheism—Hinduism, Buddhism, Jainism, and Sikhism—the main idea that the divine permeates all of life, along with its concomitant doctrines of karma and reincarnation, is part of a huge philosophical landscape, which is why it is not easy to put them all under one category. Ideas like yoga and *iso-meditation* are rooted in the same metaphysic. I call it iso-meditation because the idea of meditation is not unique to pantheism, but the idea that the isolated self is all there is, as both the object and the subject of meditation, *is* pantheistic. Let's go back a few centuries and see that it has all been tried and tested before.

A few years ago I was in Athens, Greece, and as my wife and I walked in front of the famed Mars Hill where the apostle Paul delivered his historic message, I remember stopping to look at that historic spot from the main road down below. It is not possible to be in those environs and not take some time to allow your mind to take it all in...the ancient, broken columns of the Parthenon, the winding path that leads to the top of the hill, and the bronze plaque fixed to a large rock, on which is engraved the text of Paul's brilliant address to the Athenians—skeptics, philosophers, pantheists, polytheists, atheists—all gathered to hear him.

This was Athens at its greatest preoccupation...always debating ideas of ultimate significance. Paul himself had been a devout Jew. His dramatic conversion on the Damascus road changed the history of the world. From being a religious fanatic bent on destroying Christianity, he became its greatest exponent, willing to pay with his life to take the gospel to Europe.

The fascinating thing is the initial response his message received in Athens. It was mixed at best, and sparse in impact. As I stared at the hill and we continued our walk down the street to cross at a traffic light, I noticed the name of the road we were walking on: The sign read in Greek, "Dionysius the Areopagite." I immediately stopped and drew my wife's attention to the name. Two thousand years ago, Dionysius the Areopagite was one of two people who responded to Paul's message that are mentioned in the book of Acts, the other being a woman named Damaris. So here we were, almost two thousand years later, standing on a major street in Athens named after a man who had responded to the message of Saint Paul. It is said that Dionysius went on to later become the Bishop of Athens.

Greece was the birthplace of esoteric and soul-defining thinking. A little excursion into that world will help us see that the present-day spirituality is not new but has already been tried, tested, and rejected. It is not even exclusively Eastern. Plato taught that the soul was preexistent and eternal. It was he who gave us the metaphor of the cave: In a cave we can see only the shadow of reality. The essence or the noumenal is known as if through a shadow, not the reality itself. In this state we are restricted to the phenomena and restricted from the "noumena." Somehow, the soul in this cave called time must make its way back to pure essence and ultimately reach that state of divine bliss in order to know its transcendent and original state.

Plotinus, who came after Plato and whose thinking is termed Neoplatonism, climbed the ladder of abstraction even more. God was beyond any definition or description, the "One." This One defies reduction to language—is formless and beyond time, place, intellect, and, yes, the soul. This One is the source of "mind and consciousness," from which emerges the individualized psyche that gives us the hint and link from this transient material world to ultimate thought and mind. By turning inward we, "the ones," can discover the process through which the ultimate One impersonal conscious reality can be attained. This One is the One mind within itself. Pursuing this One through purification, detachment, reflection, and contemplation will ultimately bring liberation and absorption. This is how he worded it:

> The soul is anxious to be free, so that we may attach ourselves to [the One] by the whole of our being; no part of it not touching God. Then it will be possible for the soul to see both God and herself divinely, and she will see herself illumined, full of intelligible light; or rather she will be light itself—pure, unfettered, agile, become a God or rather being a God, and wholly aflame.[2]

When you add to this the manifold debates about the nature of time, the soul, goodness, politics, and matters of permanence and impermanence in traditional Western philosophy, you have all the ingredients needed for a sophisticated spirituality.

Do you remember the other three—Parmenides, Heracleitus, and Cratylus? According to Parmenides, all that is, is. Heracleitus went one better: All that is, is changing; you never step into the same river twice. And Cratylus bettered that: You don't even step into the same river once; not only is the river flowing, but so are you. This means that the you who stepped into the river is in flux and is not the same you who steps out.

The irony of all this thinking is that the *I* and the *you* were sublimated in the mix of metaphysics, as the only way to justify flux and randomness was to find a justification for the mix. On the shoulders of other philosophers, people like Fritjof Capra came along centuries later and in *The Tao of Physics* tried to make all this metaphysics look scientific. Chopra, a latecomer then, appeared on the scene to leverage quantum. And the bigger the egos became as they exposited all this, the more they preached an egoless world.

Once again, take a step back—it is an amazing trail that began with a false lead and spelled a dead end. Dionysius the Areopagite came to know Jesus through the preaching of Paul. Years later, a fragment was found and credited to a man called Dionysius the Areopagite, whose theology sounds very similar to what the mystics were to develop in the years to come. "God talk," he basically said, was more meaningful in negation than affirmation, although he did not completely rule out affirmation. But once the stage was set for this kind of thinking, you can see where it was all headed. He basically played with language and philosophy, and equivocation was the name of the game. One could not even say, "God is good," because God's definition of *good* would be different from ours. Finally, he opined that one had to go beyond Jesus to "the God, perfect and complete" in his transpersonal self: Jesus was only an imperfect revelation of a perfect being. This teaching of Dionysius's was floating around and found ready listeners in the Athens of his day. The Greeks always had a leaning toward putting ultimate definitions in ideas rather than rooting them in the personal.

It is interesting that as research continued it was realized that this Dionysius of Greek philosophy was not Dionysius the Areopagite of Mars Hill; he had just borrowed the name in order that others would take notice of him and read what he was writing…a fitting find for a nonpersonal theology.

This constant free-floating self has been the object of study for the sciences, the mystics, and those who pursue an understanding of our essence. Hence, closer to our time and to the New Spirituality, all of them succeed in muddying the waters when it comes to the self and our essence. Marianne Williamson regales her audiences with lines out of science that she extrapolates into metaphysical pronouncements. She quotes Gary Zukav in describing how the quantum world provides us with the model of "transient forms sparkling in and out of existence." She follows it up with her own quip, saying that though you don't exactly flatter anyone by greeting them with, "Hello, transient form, floating in and out of existence," that's who we really are. The audience laughs. Entertaining speech, trying to make up for a greater vacuum than the quantum world.

I remember as a new Christian walking into a church in Canada and listening to a hymn I had never heard before, a hymn titled "Himself":

> Once it was the blessing, Now it is the Lord;
> Once it was the feeling, Now it is His Word;
> Once His gifts I wanted, Now the Giver own,
> Once I sought for healing, Now Himself alone.[3]

That hymn was written by the well-known churchman and theologian Albert B. Simpson (1843–1919). The first time I heard it I thought to myself, *How profound! How God-centered and how refreshing that the spiritual journey is to move one from focusing on the benefits of belief to the great romance and beauty of knowing the Author and Giver of life!* Heaven, if it means anything, will mean being in the presence of the Ultimate Being, not *being* the ultimate.

Today's spirituality actually would reverse the thoughts to:

> Once it was the Lord, Now it is the blessing;
> Once it was His Word, Now it is the feeling;

Once I knew the Giver, Now the gifts I own;
Once I sought Himself, Now it is the healing and my "self" alone.

Behind the popularizers like Chopra are the real metaphy-sicians of the soul. In the next chapter I shall deal briefly with these three who were the designers of Eastern spirituality gone west.

Chapter 7

The Three Gurus

The Hindu Link

Swami Vivekananda, by far the most prominent and respected name in Vedic thought of recent vintage, was born in Shimla Pally, Calcutta, on January 12, 1863. His actual birth name was Narendranath Dutta. His father, Vishwanath Dutta, was an attorney in Calcutta and had a reputation for being a man with a generous spirit who was quite progressive and liberal in his religious views. His mother was known for her rigorous and disciplined piety and practice. She is supposed to have prayed to Shiva for a son, and according to the legend, saw, in a dream, Shiva rising in the middle of his own meditations to promise her that her prayer for a son would be answered.

There are numerous stories from his life of visions and dreams in which he would see the Buddha; he had a fascination with wandering ascetics and with the life of the meditating monk. He studied the sacred texts of Hinduism and was also well versed in Indian classical music, both vocal and instrumental.

Vivekananda was quite eclectic in his interests and studied a wide range of subjects in philosophy, religion, history, the social sciences, arts, and literature.

Early in his youth, he questioned the validity of the superstitious customs he saw around him and discrimination based on caste. He refused to accept anything without first subjecting it to pragmatic tests for rational proof. When his father moved the family to Raipur in 1877, Vivekananda was more or less home-schooled, as there were no acceptable schools in Raipur, and he enjoyed long discussions on spiritual topics. Adding to his skill in Bengali, he learned Hindi in Raipur and for the first time in his own deliberations, the question of the actual existence of God surfaced. On one occasion, it is said, he went into an ecstatic trance, something that is not uncommon for revered teachers in that culture even today.

After two years in Raipur the family returned to Calcutta, but those two years in Raipur were the most formative for him spiritually, which is why Raipur is often referred to as the spiritual birthplace of Swami Vivekananda. It was in Raipur that Narendranath Dutta became Swami Vivekananda, a teacher to others.

College and Brahmo Samaj

Vivekananda was an inveterate student of religious thought. He made it a point to study Western logic, Western philosophy, and the history of European nations. His research included the writings of David Hume, Immanuel Kant, Johann Gottlieb Fichte, Baruch Spinoza, Georg W. F. Hegel, Arthur Schopenhauer, Auguste Comte, Herbert Spencer, John Stuart Mill, and even Charles Darwin. He became fascinated with the early theorists in evolution and in the works of Herbert Spencer, so much so that he translated Spencer's book *Education* into Bengali and published it.

Alongside his study of Western philosophers, Vivekananda was thoroughly acquainted with the Indian Sanskrit scriptures and with many other writings in his native Bengali tongue. He was considered a prodigy by his professors. Dr. William Hastie, the principal of Scottish Church College, where Vivekananda studied during 1881–1884, described him as a genius, a student the likes of which he had never before encountered even in the European universities in which he had taught.

Vivekananda's initial beliefs were shaped by Brahmo concepts, which are against the worship of idols and include a belief in a formless God. Becoming a Freemason, he was part of a breakaway faction from the Brahmo Samaj led by Keshab Chunder Sen. He was never satisfied with his knowledge of philosophy, and began to wonder if God and religion could be internalized through meditation. He was even known to go about Calcutta asking prominent residents whether they had ever come "face-to-face with God," but he never received an answer that was convincing to him. (One can readily see a blueprint here for Chopra's thinking. I will get deeper into that.)

The major turning point for Vivekananda was his introduction to Ramakrishna Paramahamsa in 1881. The subject of a college literature lecture in college was William Wordsworth's poem "The Excursion" and the poet's affinity to nature-mysticism. In the course of trying to explain the word *trance* in the poem, the professor told his students that if they wanted to really understand the word, they should visit Ramakrishna of Dakshineswar. After his hours of reflection and fascination with the wandering holy men, Vivekananda decided to meet Ramakrishna. It is from this point that we trace the theological views of Vivekananda. About that day, Vivekananda himself later said:

> He looked just like an ordinary man, with nothing remarkable about him. He used the most simple language, and I thought "Can this man be a great teacher?" [I] crept near to him and asked him the question which I had been asking others all my life: "Do you believe in God, Sir?" "Yes," he replied. "Can you prove it, Sir?" "Yes." "How?" "Because I see Him just as I see you here, only in a much intenser sense." That impressed me at once…I began to go to that man, day after day, and I actually saw that religion could be given. One touch, one glance, can change a whole life.[1]

As can be seen, Vivekananda did not initially accept Ramakrishna as his teacher. He was not sympathetic toward Ramakrisha's visions, ecstasies, and dreams, which he considered to be mere figments of the imagination or hallucinations. Also, as a member of Brahmo Samaj, he revolted against Ramakrishna's practice of idol worship and belief in polytheism, in particular his worship of Kali, an especially dark and bloodthirsty goddess in the Hindu pantheon. He often ridiculed Ramakrishna's belief in identity with the Absolute (*Advaitist Vedantism*) as blasphemy and sheer nonsense.

But over the course of the next five years, Vivekananda came to totally accept Ramakrishna as his teacher, and the teacher's beliefs became fully his own as he declared himself ready to renounce everything else in his quest for "God-realization." As he himself said,

The magic touch of the Master…brought a wonderful change over my mind. I was astounded to find that really there was nothing in the universe but God!…Everything I saw appeared to be Brahman…I realized that I must have had a glimpse of the *Advaita* state. Then it struck me that the words of the scriptures were not false. Thenceforth I could not deny the conclusions of the *Advaita* [identity with the Absolute] philosophy.[2]

This belief in identity with the Absolute is at the core of Chopra's philosophy as well. It is the seedbed of the spirituality that the West has imbibed now, albeit without understanding the fuller text or the context. It is a brilliant philosophical move of believing in the divine and of being divine, of reflecting and being the reflector, of being both the subject and the object of one's meditation. We're back to wondering whether we are the dream or the dreamer.

In 1885 Ramakrishna was stricken with throat cancer. There was no Ayurvedic cure here, I'm afraid, and not long afterward, he died. None of his disciplines and pristine practices were able to spare him this terrible ordeal. But during his last days of instruction to Vivekananda, Vivekananda reportedly experienced *Nirvikalpa Samadhi* (a thought- and concept-free bliss), and along with other disciples, he received the ochre monastic robes from Ramakrishna, and became part of the first monastic order of Ramakrishna.

Just before he died, Ramakrishna asked Vivekananda to take care of the other monastic disciples and asked them to accept Vivekananda as their leader. Ramakrishna's condition worsened gradually and he died in the early morning hours of August 16,

1886. According to his disciples, he had reached *Mahasamadhi*, the ultimate attainment of oneness with the Absolute.

Vivekananda was not just a mystic. He was a strong proponent of education and of giving the Indian his rightful place in the world. He protested vigorously against British dominance and encouraged India to develop a more militant mind-set in order to resist the British. Attacking the glorification of poverty and what he felt was an overemphasis on spiritualism on the part of most Indians, he asked why it was necessary for three hundred million people to be sunk in savagery and starvation in order to make it possible for a hundred thousand to reach true spirituality. He was not interested in a God, he said, who would give him eternal bliss in heaven but who could not give him bread here. No, India was to be raised, the poor were to be fed, education was to be made available to all, and the "evil" of priestcraft was to be removed. In short, no priestcraft would mean no social tyranny; more bread would mean more opportunity for everyone.

Vivekananda was aware that his speeches and writings were seditious and wondered why the British never arrested him. He was prepared to go to any length to usher in the revolution he felt was necessary, and at times he even expressed a great longing that he would be arrested and shot; he thought it would be the beginning of the end for British rule in India as news of his death ran through the land like wildfire. It is very clear that though he had renounced the world and become a monk, he could not sit by and watch his country being "raped" by invaders. His immediate task, he felt, was to overthrow British rule. In this attempt he advocated aggression—spiritual, material, and even physical if it became necessary. A study of his correspondence shows that although he was laying the groundwork for a revolution through peaceful means, he was not opposed to using militant methods and was prepared to use force if the need arose. In *Swami Vivekananda, Patriot Prophet*, Bhupendranath Datta writes that after his second tour of the West, Vivekananda told an Indian professor, "What India needs today is a bomb."[3]

From Surendra Nath Sen's private diary we learn that when it was pointed out to Vivekananda that perhaps, instead of aggressive force, he ought to consider the course of "radha" (love) advocated by Chaitanya, he retorted:

Look at this nation and see what has been the outcome of such an attempt! Through the preaching of that love... the whole nation has become effeminate...The whole of Orissa has been turned into a land of cowards; and Bengal, running after the Radha-prema, these past four hundred years, has almost lost all sense of manliness![4]

Arriving at the Parliament of World Religions in Chicago in 1893, he characteristically fired the first volley. His speech on that occasion, from which follows an excerpt, permanently changed religious dialogue in the West:

Brothers and sisters, we who come from the East have sat here on the platform day after day and have been told in a patronizing way that we ought to accept Christianity because Christian nations are the most prosperous. We look about us and we see England, the most prosperous Christian nation in the world, with her foot on the neck of 250,000,000 Asiatics. We look back into history and see that the prosperity began with the invasion of

Mexico. Christianity wins its prosperity by cutting the throats of its fellowmen. At such a price, the Hindu will not have prosperity. I have sat here today and I have heard the height of intolerance. I have heard the creeds of the Moslem applauded when today the Moslem sword is carrying destruction into India. Blood and sword are not for the Hindu, whose religion is based on the laws of love.[5]

"Weastern" Spirituality had arrived. The doors of the West swung wide open for him. If Oprah had been in vogue then, Vivekananda would have been a household name in minutes. Guaranteed. He would have become her guru. I suspect he would have taken the West by a tsunami, not just by storm, if he had had access to television.

Yogananda

The second of the three Gurus is Paramahansa Yogananda. I have already said that the teaching of the New Spirituality in the West is still young and that rancor, divisions, money issues, control, and power will eventually surface. That has already been evidenced in the aftermath of Yogananda's death.

Paramahansa Yogananda founded an organization called Self-Realization Fellowship (SRF). Following his death, divisions followed by lawsuits began immediately. Power exerts huge influence, and nobody shows more venom in protecting or gaining power than those who invoke religion to defend it. In a sense, this is understandable: Religion breeds convictions; money and power attract envy; conviction without love leads to heinous abuses justified by sacred talk. History is replete with examples of this from every religion. All major religions are guilty of this... Eastern spirituality is no exception.

The nemesis of SRF is another organization, simply called Ananda. Ananda was founded by Swami Kriyananda, a disciple of Yogananda. But SRF refuses to give Ananda rights to any of Yogananda's material. (I'm sure you've noticed *ananda* surfacing in all of these names. The word itself literally means "joy.") Each accuses the other of distortion, wrongdoing, and attempts at monopoly, and there is little joy apparent in these self-defeating charges. What it all means is that where there is religion, there is bound to be conflict. But where there is religion and money, there are bound to be lawsuits and bitterness, the very opposite of what true faith should engender.

Who was Paramahansa Yogananda? The following quotation is a sample of his teaching:

> Your religion is not your thoughts and beliefs in which you enclose yourself, but the garment of light you weave around your heart. Discover who you are, behind those outer trappings, and you will discover who Jesus was, and Buddha, and Krishna. For the masters come to earth for the purpose of holding up to every man a reflection of his deeper, eternal Self.[6]

Eckhart Tolle breathes out this identical stuff, almost verbatim.

Yogananda basically taught a blend of religious teaching called Kriya yoga, which is another slant on yoga. Though he wore a cross around his neck, he clearly believed in the divinity within each person and taught that each soul needed to probe that inner sanctum of the self and discover its oneness with the divine. The irony of the baser instincts that now characterize the turf war for his teaching shows that his own disciples never quite discovered the divine within themselves, instead evidencing a lot more of the ego within when confronted by the holdings without.

Yogananda was a contemporary of Vivekananda and was also from Calcutta. He was born Mukunda Lal Ghosh in 1893 and died in 1952. However, he chose a different guru than Ramakrishna and gave his yoga a different slant. Yoga has its roots in the idea of union with the divine and is not simply a physical discipline. Its metaphysical moorings make it technically a spiritual practice. When one sheds the spiritual side of it and focuses only on the physical aspects, it is no longer strictly yoga.

There are many analogies one can draw from this. It is ironic that Hindu apologists, who insist that yoga cannot be separated from its spiritual essence, are very comfortable with severing the text of Buddha's teaching from the context of his rejection of some of their own sacred texts, and very cleverly misuse the instructions of Jesus as well. They are adept at textual mangling by appearing to be very generous in their spirits. The cross Yogananda wore around his neck and his professed reverence for Jesus did not prevent him from blending the teachings of what he calls "the Masters," Indian spiritualizing at its best. Ironically, his disciples have each claimed the exclusive rights to teach his inclusive message.

Yogananda also traveled extensively in the United States and Europe, carrying his message across the Western world. He was honored wherever he went. He had a very distinctive appearance and a notable charm. His long, flowing locks of hair became the hallmark of how a swami should look. He, too, was well versed in many languages, as many Indians are.

Maharishi Mahesh Yogi

The Maharishi, with his Transcendental Meditation technique, is probably the best known of the three gurus. While Vivekananda and Yogananda did the groundwork of philosophical thought, it was the Maharishi who packaged it for the West. His fame was catapulted courtesy of the Beatles, and when he died in February 2008, the *Times* of London reported on his death and traced the Beatles' initial enchantment with him before their falling-out over his alleged inappropriate advances toward their friend Mia Farrow. (It was this that inspired John Lennon's song "Sexy Sadie" about a charlatan who "made a fool of everyone.") By the 1970s more than five million people were said to be practicing Transcendental Meditation, or TM, for twenty minutes every morning and evening. We have no data to tell us how many were practicing "yogic flying"—or bouncing in the air in the lotus position, also part of the Maharishi's teaching.

By the 1980s he had established schools across the world, founded the Natural Law Party, and built a multimillion-dollar business empire that included a property dealership and a company that sold Ayurvedic medicine and cosmetics, all primarily financed by donations and the $2,500 per-person fee to learn TM. He moved his headquarters to a former Franciscan monastery in the southern Dutch village of Vlodrop, from which he controlled his Global Country of World Peace movement as a recluse living in a pavilion, communicating by video link.

In 2002 the Maharishi announced that with $1 billion he could train forty thousand expert mediators and combat terrorism and war. For this, and for his plan to raise $10 trillion with which to end poverty by sponsoring organic farming in poor countries, he was roundly ridiculed.

Of course, the Maharishi is not the only New Age Spiritualist who has announced a cure for terrorism through meditation. On her blog on terrorism, New Age spiritualist Marianne Williamson said,

> With your thoughts, you can help build a system of spiritual quarantine for terrorists and would-be terrorists. You don't have to know who they are. The Creator does. Just do this. For a minimum of five minutes every day, meditate in the following way: Pray that anyone even thinking of committing a terrorist act...be surrounded by a huge golden egg. The eggshell is made of the spiritual equivalent of titanium...impenetrable. Any malevolent, hateful or violent thought that emanates from the mind of the terrorist cannot get past the confines of the eggshell. Before the violent thought can turn into violent action, it is stopped by the force of this meditative field. Energetically, the terrorist is quarantined. On the inside of the egg, see a shower of golden light pouring from the eggshell into the heart and mind of the terrorist. Pray for your lost brother. See him or her healed by the force of divine Love, wrapped in the arms of angels, reminded of who he truly is. Five minutes. Every day. Tell everyone you know.[7]

That aside, Deepak Chopra was quick to rise to the Maharishi's defense saying that he, Chopra, had once met Mia Farrow in an airport and she asked him to give the Maharishi her love. That supposedly puts to rest any accusation that he had made advances to her. The Maharishi made a great impact with his teaching. Businesses started to give their employees time off to do this training. One of those impacted by him was Deepak Chopra. Chopra's tribute following the Maharishi's death raises a lot of questions, and the response to it was not without variant claims on the part of some of the Maharishi's followers. On one occasion, Chopra claims, the Maharishi was declared clinically dead after an apparent heart attack but was kept on life support due to the intervention of Chopra's father and within thirty-six hours recovered sufficiently to be taken off life support. According to Chopra, the Maharishi exhibited at this time "both the all-too-human qualities found in every holy man and the other qualities one associates with the superhuman…It was easy to believe that other disciples in another time felt much the same in the presence of Jesus or Buddha."[8]

Chopra recounts that during his recovery the Maharishi required a blood transfusion and that Chopra was found to be the only one compatible. However, the Maharishi refused to accept Chopra's blood until Chopra assured him that his bad karma would not be transferred to the Maharishi in the blood transfusion because red blood cells contain no DNA and only hemoglobin would be transferred. Eventually the Maharishi accepted both Chopra's reassurances and his blood.[9]

Please do not miss the subtlety here. The pupil is instructing the guru on the transmission of karma. That little excursion into the makeup of the blood is intended once again to show the knowledge Chopra had that allowed him to even teach the teacher. This is Chopra at his double-entendre best.

Teachings and Beliefs

One can write ad nauseam on the teachings of these three gurus and their predecessors. Thick volumes adorn the bookstands and now are mainly available online. The most important thing is to know what lies at the heart of all these meditative techniques and how they actually end up perverting other religions to prove their point. Vedanta philosophy is based on Upanishadic philosophy and neo-Hindu reinterpretations and draws from the Upanishads, pulling together several important basic elements.

First and foremost is the ultimate essence of all things, encapsulated in the one impersonal absolute or deity called Brahman. The term often used to describe this state is *Sat-chit-ananda* (absolute existence-knowledge-bliss). The second is the existence of the transcendental Self, *atman*, as a microcosmic manifestation of Brahman. Atman is the core of each and every individual entity.

But just like a fruit leads to the seed and the seed leads to the invisible essence of the fruit, Vedantists believe the potential for divinity is within oneself, and when you reach that essence of "nothing" out of which first the seed, then the fruit, and finally the tree emerge, the famous affirmation, *Tat tvam asi*—"Thou art that!"—is discovered. When the self, or atman, attains *moksha*, or liberation, one has reached the point of "the atman is the Brahman."

According to Vedantists, there are four paths to liberation; *karma* yoga (the path of selfless service to work off your karma); *bhakti* yoga (the path of devotion); *jnana* yoga (the path of knowledge); and *raja* yoga (the path of formal meditation). In the early years of the movement, jnana yoga—the path of knowledge—was most popular among the educated followers. Bhakti yoga—the path of devotion or worship—was a popular means for the masses to achieve liberation; the irresistible tendency of the heart toward worship always draws a large following.

Through the adoption of *Shakti* (the power of consciousness and spiritual evolution that is usually associated with females), worship of female goddesses became quite prolific. One common position among the various exponents of these meditative techniques is stressing the acceptance of different religious faiths. Ramakrishna is seen as a Hindu reformer who syncretized all religions, even supposedly to the extent of becoming a Muslim for a few days. This attempt to accommodate all religions has, among other things, led to the redefinition of Christianity and the theory that Jesus was actually a young aspirant in search of nirvana, a theory very cleverly co-opted by Chopra.

Several years ago I saw a Dennis the Menace cartoon in which Dennis is seen standing beside a lemonade stand that he has set up. In big bold letters a sign reads, "All you can drink for 10 cents." In the next frame is a bewildered-looking boy holding a glass just a quarter filled with lemonade, and Dennis is saying to him, "*I* says that's all you can drink for ten cents, that's who says it."

When one realizes the philosophical underpinnings of Deepak Chopra's writings, one gets the same feeling. So, too, with the maharishis and the swamis who are bent upon making all religions one. Richard Niebuhr once said that in all these religious theories and expressions, what we are really looking for seems to be "a God without wrath who took Man without sin into a kingdom without righteousness through the ministrations

of a Christ without a cross." A different way to say the same thing
is that we have so deified man and humanized God that we can
scarcely tell the difference.

Here, for example, is a statement from Sri Sri Ravi Shankar:

Divinity is unmanifest, but man has an innate desire to
perceive the Divine in the manifest creation around him.
He creates idols, breathes faith into them and requests
the divinity to be present in the idols for a while so that
he can worship, express his love and lay with the divine.
At the end of his worship he requests Divinity to go back
into his heart from where he is manifested. This is in all
puja practices. People actually do not worship the idols
but instead worship the unmanifested Divinity which
has all the Divine qualities. So, the idol worshippers of
the East are not the same as those described in the Bible,
because they are not just worshipping different gods and
different idols, they are worshipping the one divinity in
many different forms.[10]

There are levels of verification and understanding here that
quite unwittingly reflect the quantum world. It is said of the
subatomic world that if you know what a particle is doing, you
don't know where it is, and if you know where it is, you don't
know what it is doing. That pretty well explains the epistemological hybrid of the Chopra-type argument. If a scientist pins
him on his inappropriate use of physics, he switches to medicine. If a medical practitioner questions his claims of medicine,
he switches to the Vedas or some mystery story that is unverifi-
able but supposedly true. So, in effect, regardless of any truth
claim, you are not sure what logic he is using to support it, and if

you understand the logic, you don't know what exactly is being claimed.

Chopra's debate with Mr. Shukla is a classic one. Shukla was clearly trying to pin him down on his jelly-like metaphysics that he refuses to brand Hindu. To settle for a pure term and at the same time use the Vedas to sustain his most rigorous mystical claims requires nothing short of a master with words who can rebaptize anything at will. All one needs to do is read Chopra's book *How to Know God*. Such name games can have serious consequences. But however we dissect it, the monistic base of Hindu pantheism is at the core of his teaching.

The New Spirituality, however, as it is practiced in the West, encompasses more than Hinduism. In the next chapter we will look at the other major Eastern influences on this movement.

CHAPTER 8

❧

SMILING YOUR WAY
THROUGH PUZZLES

The Buddhist Link

Hinduism and Buddhism are not identical teachings. But it is not possible to understand the New Spirituality without understanding a few of Buddhism's cardinal doctrines, as well. The links in the previous chapter are to the Neoplatonism of Greek thought and to Hindu pantheism, rebaptized Sanatan Dharma. While Chopra and his Hindu critics can debate whether or not what he is promoting to westerners is Hinduism, the rising and continuing interest in Buddhism gives the New Spirituality double strength, since all the methods of reasoning change. Buddhism is the main branch from which many of the underlying assumptions in the New Spirituality come, more specifically, the branch of Buddhism known as Zen.

Original Buddhism followed from six underlying principles. It would take a great deal of space to study the intricacies of Buddhism and its offshoots. The classic work on Zen was penned years ago by D. T. Suzuki. A more recent excellent text on Zen is by Heinrich Dumoulin, *Zen: Enlightenment: Origins and Meaning.*

Four noble truths—the truth of suffering, the cause of it, the end of it, and the eightfold path—are the most popular concepts of Buddhism and the most often discussed. But that is far from understanding its intensely complex system. From these basic precepts there developed huge bodies of teaching, especially in the law of causality, also called dependent origination, and the ultimate elimination of suffering. From conception to reflection to thought to action to appearances, there is the explanation of the illusionary idea of a self and its perceptions of the physical world, and the interconnectedness of causes, which makes it all both emergent and circular.

Once Buddhism left India and expanded into the rest of Asia, this religion broke down, and the number of sects and subsects that developed boggles the mind. When it entered China, the character of Buddhism changed dramatically, as it did even further when it spread into Japan. Buddha probably would never have recognized it. The main divisions began a short while after the death of Buddha, when his followers split into two sects, *Mahayana* (Great Vehicle) and *Hinayana* (Little Vehicle) Buddhism. The leaders of Mahayana Buddhism considered a shorter route to attain nirvana as they felt more people would be able to reach that state through Mahayana than through Hinayana. Mahayana then further divided into six branches—*Zen, Tian-Tai, Huayan, Fa-xiang, Clear Earth,* and *Mi.*

Hinayana Buddhism came into its own in the fourth century BC and then gradually declined. The Hinayanist School claimed that only a small number of people really understood and followed the true teaching of Buddha. Although they claimed him as their teacher, because of the fact that he attained nirvana they considered him no longer a mere man. From the implicit deification of Buddha to his three body states and thirty-two appearances, the numerous and varied teachings that are part of Hinayana are divided and subdivided and microdivided. Hinayana is dominant in Sri Lanka, Burma, Thailand, Cambodia, and Laos. But even within those regions there are divisions and subdivisions. The Thai version does not ordain women monks, so the first Thai woman monk went to Sri Lanka to be ordained and then returned as a monk to Thailand. I met with her shortly after her ordination and had an extended discussion with her in Bangkok. It was a fascinating time. Her answers to my questions were quite intriguing. I shall save that for another day and another discussion.

Let me just tackle one key idea contained in many of the Buddhist schools of thought. The two poems below from the renowned Nagarjuna indicate the heart of the teaching of four subbranches in Mahayana:

> *To causes and effects was born control,*
> *and to me there is nothing but emptiness,*
> *even though its name is righteousness,*
> *to me its name is false.*
> *They were not born;*
> *they were not dead.*
> *They did not appear often;*
> *Yet they do appear.*[1]

One can see where all this is headed by grasping the key words, *nothing, emptiness, appear,* and that "aha!" moment of discovery as the enlightened mind would catch ultimate reality.

The major exposition in Mahayana is of the word *rupa*, which literally means "a form" or "a body." Here is the key verse: "*Rupa* is emptiness; emptiness is *Rupa*." On that thought hinges everything else. So while for Solomon meaninglessness became a chasing after the wind, for Mahayanists anything physical became a chasing after the wind. Form and substance were two different things, so while we are preoccupied with form, in the end it is nothing more than mere appearance. Life in effect becomes as a crossword puzzle, where mystery, contradiction, clues, and answers posed as questions all play a part.

The most fascinating story of how questions of "what is real" are dealt with in Mahayana Buddhism comes from two episodes in the development of Chinese Buddhism. In one incident the emperor of the Qing dynasty, Shun-zi, asked a monk named Yu Lin, of the Zen branch, "Looking at my empire, my thoughts come. When I look at it again, my thoughts disappear. Do I have an empire or not?"

Yu Lin replied, "Sire, it is just like dreaming. It is there and it is not there."

How, then, is all this phenomenon around us explained in Mahayana Buddhism, if all is empty and ethereal, there and not there at the same time? What's the spinning top here? It is explained through the *heart* of human beings. This is actually called a "hearts-only" point of view in one of the sects of Buddhism. So much can be said here. Let me just sum it up with how this is translated in the transition of their successors. This is the second story.

The fifth ancestor, Hong-ren, of the Zen Buddhist subbranch, informed his disciples that he was going to choose his successor by means of a test. He asked his disciples to compete by writing a poem that they thought would please him the most. One of the disciples, Shen-xiu, who seemed the heir apparent, wrote:

The body is like a pipal tree.
The heart is like a mirror.
These have to be cleaned frequently
So dust will not cling to them.

Hong-ren looked at the poem and thought about it a moment and then said it was not good enough. A second disciple, Hui-neng, a worker who was just an orderly in the temple, took his shot at it. He wrote:

The pipal is actually not a tree,
The mirror also is a stand.
Everything is nothing but empty.
Where can the dust cling?

After reading this, Hong-ren selected Hui-neng as his successor. He had got it: If at its core everything is nothing, how can dust accumulate? As a sidebar, it is important to note that once Hui-neng was made successor, he hastily left for another town and changed his name, lest he be tracked down and the other disciples who were not chosen avenge his placement. His *rupa* had to escape, lest other *rupas* cornered his *rupa* and truly made what appeared to be, disappear.

But the story continues. Fifteen years later, Hui-neng, the sixth ancestor, went to Guangzhou, where he entered a temple. He turned his eyes and looked silently upon a banner that was blowing in the wind. Some claimed that the wind was moving and others claimed that it wasn't the wind, that the banner was actually moving on its own. Hui-neng corrected them by saying, "The wind is not moving. The banner is not moving either. The hearts of the people are moving."[2]

That lays the groundwork for determining what is real and what is merely apparent. It has everything to do with the filters of the person trying to perceive the difference and reality. It's really not the wind. Nor is it the banner. It is the stand in the heart that may only pragmatically be called the mirror. This is the path of reflection, introspection, intuition, and of ultimately minimizing the *rupa* world. "All solidity was ultimately nothing."

I cannot resist adding that if Mr. Chopra would like a word study, this is the place for it, not in the mangling that he does of biblical texts in his so-called word studies. As mentioned above, the word *rupa* means "a form" or "a body," something solid. But ultimately, all *rupa* is illusion and nonessential. Here is a curious point I would like to raise. The Indian currency is the *rupee*, or sometimes *rupaiyah*, which is what the currency is called in Indonesia. The etymology for something that is nothing but has been made into everything that defines value, all in the name of spiritual truth, would make a book of its own. I don't want to give away too much here, but you will see that propensity when Chopra comes to his study of some very profound texts in the Bible, while he seems to miss the obvious. But in this connection one can see with a smile that life has its material moments even when we pursue emptiness. Very interesting, indeed.

One very important link from Zen in "Weastern" Spirituality is the *koan*. What is a koan? American Buddhist Ruth Fuller Sasaki, who is married to a Japanese Zen master, says in the foreword to *The Zen Koan*,

The koan is not a conundrum to be solved by a nimble wit. It is not a verbal psychiatric device for shocking the disintegrated ego of a student into some kind of stability. Nor, in my opinion, is it ever a paradoxical statement except to those who view it from the outside. When the koan is resolved it is realized to be a simple and clear statement made from the state of consciousness which it has helped to awaken.[3]

Any time you see something very significant defined with a series of what it is not, you can be sure that the person defining it doesn't really know how to tell you what it is. Here is one illustration of a koan at work:

One day when Yuan-wu had taken the high seat in the lecture hall, he said: "A monk asked Yun-men, 'From whence come all the buddhas?' Yun-men answered, 'The East Mountain walks over the water.' But if I were asked, I would not answer that way. 'From whence come all the buddhas?' A fragrant breeze comes of itself from the south, and in the palace pavilion a refreshing coolness stirs."

Upon hearing these words, Ta-hui suddenly awakened to enlightenment. He became the Dharma successor to his master Yuan-wu.[4]

This is all so critical to understand if we are to fathom the very mystery and, yes, the numerous contradictions within the New Spirituality. These are the ideas that have helped to shape the present "Weastern" Spirituality. Here, for example, are the words of Elizabeth Lesser, a contemporary proponent of the New Spirituality:

> If the purpose of meditation is to accept the way things already are, then how do we justify any striving at all? When I was involved in Zen meditation I was very confused by this dilemma. The concept of reaching "enlightenment" is a big part of Zen Buddhism. But so is nonstriving. So, which is it?...The answer, and this is the answer to many of the Zen koans, is both. I eventually came up with a slogan that put the question to rest for me: "Not either-or, but both, and more."...And yes, the kind of work that it takes to reach enlightenment looks like a passionate form of doing nothing.[5]

When I read that, I couldn't help thinking of a friend of mine who has recently retired. He told me that he has enjoyed doing nothing. "When my wife asks me what I did that day, I say 'Nothing.' The next day when she asks me what my plans are for the day, I tell her it is to finish doing what I did yesterday."

Many years ago *Reader's Digest* published a little story from a contributor who had been taking flying lessons. The instructor described in detail the steps one takes to land a plane when the engines have lost power on a dark night, ending with "If you like what you see, land." The student asked what he should do in the event he did *not* like what he saw and after a pause was told, "Turn your lights off."

When you end up with a koan to explain what life is all about, it is not the landing strip you are hoping for; put aside your natural reasoning and celebrate obscurity until the light is turned on inside. How that will happen depends on which school of thought you belong to.

There's really something very sad about all of this. It is interesting that both Japanese and Chinese spirituality met the fates they did in their political climate. Horrific acts are committed when ethical religions provide only self-referencing points for conduct and koans to maintain the mysterious as dogma in order to obscure what is clear. Without the transcendent perspective, the mirror does distort the image. In fact, a hall of mirrors can wreak havoc with reality.

This Zen link of the koan and the main Buddhist link of rupa are woven into the fabric of the New Spirituality. Systemic contradictions hide under the guise of "both and more," appearances are equivocated upon to suit the koan, and the koan is leveraged to sustain contradiction. All of this effort is to define something as "nothing" and "nothing" as everything.

The Yin and the Yang

There is one final connection I want to make here. Many other systems of belief have been brought to bear that have influenced the body of thought in the New Spirituality and could be brought into the discussion, including the doctrine of dependent origination.[6] But I think that if we ignore the Taoist link, we do injustice to the total landscape of the New Spirituality.

Taoism really can and should be understood in the context of China's struggle to find harmony and moral reasoning. Between the extremes of using "law" and "love" and the political turmoil ever punctuating its history, it seemed that Confucianism would have the last word in Chinese ethical thought. Confucianism sought to place morality beyond a utilitarian and motive-driven base to doing things because they are right in and of themselves. That was key in Confucianism. What you do, you do because it is the *right* thing to do. It is almost Kantian in that sense of the ethical imperative and sense of duty. The debates regarding various descriptions of what is essentially good make up a significant part of Chinese philosophy.

Taoism was one of the major schools and differed from Confucianism significantly on how to get society back on an orderly track. There is much that can be said here about Taoism, but I want to just underscore a handful of Taoist ideas that have carried over to the New Spirituality.

One key idea of Taoism is that words do not have absolute meaning. They are considered to be misleading, limited, and, in fact, deceptive. Every word can be understood only in the context of other words, and every concept is understood only in the context of other concepts. In other words, words are word-related endlessly, cyclically. They cannot portray a comprehensive picture and are therefore relative. Language ends up as a game and can be a good side excursion but not the mainspring of communicating reality. (Of course, that very thought is expressed in words.) This is a little bit like what Nietzsche proposed but at the end had to concede that he, too, worshipped at the altar whose name is "Truth."

A second major concept of Taoism that has been added to the mix of the New Spirituality is that life does *not* have any clear purpose. Events may have causes, but they do not have immediate purpose. This has led to clever stories of whether man is the measure of all things or if there is some transcendent order behind it all. The food chain cycle reveals an endless cyclical nature. Man eats the beast, and then the beast eats the man, somewhat like what Voltaire opined when he said that the misery of each makes up the good of all. Self-realization, a skepticism of language, and the agnosticism of any final purpose made for a worldview that believed that finding the "Way" to interpret life, or the Tao, is like balancing on the trapeze rope of life.

Skepticism about language, morals, and government emerges from a view that the Way (the Tao) cannot be grasped by the intellect. The universe proceeds, it moves, it does what it does. But it cannot be grasped intellectually or expressed in words. It cannot be described. The way of nature, then, should be the model for proper living. Laws, government, and institutions are all unnatural creations that put unnatural demands upon people. The universe is not a machine; it is an organic whole.

The Tao Te Ching goes on to teach that the two forces that run the universe are the yin and the yang: Yin expresses itself through femininity and earthiness; yang through masculinity and activity. The yin is represented by water; the yang by fire.

When all is said and read, several conclusions are drawn:

1. There can be no absolute truth. Each idea borrows from its opposite.
2. All morality is relative. Everything gains only momentary explanation.
3. Purpose and meaning are vague and clouded.

There is a fascinating Taoist story that illustrates these conclusions. It is about a farmer whose horse bolted from the barn and took off. He went to his neighbor, who said, "Oh, that's too bad." The farmer stoically replied, "Who knows what's good or bad?"

But the next day, the horse returned and brought six wild

horses with it. The farmer went to his neighbor again, who said, "Oh, that's so good!" "Who knows what's good or bad?" the farmer drily responded.

The third day, the farmer's son tried to ride one of the wild horses and broke his leg in the process. The neighbor, hearing this, shook his head and muttered, "Oh, that's bad." The farmer shook his head and responded: "Who knows what's good or bad?"

The following day, soldiers of the landlord prince came around looking for able-bodied men to join their ranks. They ignored the farmer's son because of his broken leg. "That's so good," said the neighbor. "Who knows what is good or bad?" sighed the farmer.

Notice carefully that though none of these are moral events, they are given a moral value...good or bad. Here, too, there is a muddying of the waters and a confusion of categories. What moral reasoning caused the horse to run off? The events happened apart from any morality, but a moral explanation for them is demanded. It could have been put to just good fortune or a blessing. Instead, the events are given moral significance and demand a moral response.

Whatever answers are lacking are left to koans. What the spiritual books cannot explain, the poets are left to expound upon...When hard reason fails, leave it to the poets. Two poems sum up the resignation within Taoism toward whatever life brings; the first, from the Tao Te Ching, says it all:

First there was Tao
Then there was Yin and Yang.
And then there were words.
Oh that men would have left it alone.[7]

The other poem is from a former Confucian scholar who left the ranks of teaching to go and live in the countryside:

I pluck chrysanthemums from the eastern hedge,
Then I gaze long at the distant summer hills,
The mountain air is fresh at the dawn of day;
The flying birds two by two return.
In these things there lies deep meaning;
Yet when we would express it, words suddenly fail…
What folly to spend life like a dropped leaf
Snared under the dust of streets!
For a long time I have lived in a cage;
Now I have returned.
For one must return
To fulfill one's nature.[8]

One would think this was written in the sixties by a professor turned hippie in the United States. Or that it was the foreshadowing of books like *The Celestine Prophecy*. These ideas came into the melting pot of the New Spirituality. Terms like "yin and yang," meaningless ontic referents[9] in language, birds flying in a pattern as an omen, life itself harnessing the way of nature, fit well into the mix of "May the force be with you."

As the old adage goes, "and yet… and yet…" Somehow, while all these may provide an anesthetic for simpler situations, the complexities of life ride hard on the shoulders of reality. The average person knows he or she needs help with finding hope in the midst of the tragedies and disappointments of life, and these ideas provide no hope.

The Final Escape

I have told this story elsewhere, but it is worth repeating. I met a young woman who was poised, successful, and worked in a very public profession. Years before, she had fallen in love with a young man, but her parents denied her permission to marry him because he came from a lower caste. After much soul-searching, they eloped and moved to a different city where no one would know their castes. Both were disowned by their families.

A year or two went by, and by virtue of her job, she was transferred to another city and was able to go back to her husband only for visits. Gradually the visits home became fewer and fewer, and he feared that he was losing her. He traveled to the city she was working in and found out that she had developed a relationship with another man. Heartbroken, he pleaded with her to come home. He expressed how deeply he loved her and said that he wanted to make this marriage work. But regardless of what he said, she insisted that she had made the decision to leave him.

Finally, he stepped into the restroom for a few minutes, returned to her, and made one last request before leaving her. He said, "You know, I gave up everything for you because I love you. Will you do me one last favor? I promise not to lay a hand on you; I simply ask that you let me put my head on your lap and let me lie there for half an hour. Just that half hour to rest on your lap is all I ask, and I promise I will be out of your life forever." She felt sorry for him so she agreed. In only a matter of minutes, he started to convulse in her lap. Terrified, she called for help, but within moments he was dead. He had taken poison while in the restroom.

This completely shook her. Guilt, trauma, sleepless nights,

everything that you can imagine one would feel in such a situation. Finally, she visited a guru to help her sort this all out. After some time with her, studying her astrological chart and other signs that he used to look into her past, he arrived at a conclusion: In a previous life, he said, this man had raped her when she was a little girl. It was her karma that she had become the means for him to repay his karmic debt for the wrong he had previously done her, so she need feel no guilt.

This young, successful professional now boasted that she had been completely released from all previous guilt on the matter. The guru had done his job. Absolution had taken place. Her mind was rid of any negative thoughts. Karma had exonerated her because it was payback time for him. In effect, the man betrayed in love had poisoned himself in a triumph of good over evil, and the woman who had betrayed him was merely an instrument to set the balances straight.

King David says in Psalm 115:2–8:

Why do the nations say,
  "Where is their God?" ...
Their idols are silver and gold,
  made by human hands.
They have mouths, but cannot speak,
  eyes, but cannot see;
they have ears, but cannot hear,
  noses, but cannot smell;
they have hands, but cannot feel,
  feet, but cannot walk;
    nor can they utter a sound with their throats.
Those who make them will be like them,
  and so will all who trust in them. (NIV)

The tragedy of a worldview that is based on a blend of meta-physics, physics, spirituality, and medicine is that in the end, it violates those very disciplines to justify self-deification, which is the bottom line.

This is *becoming* the Absolute rather than *communing with* the Absolute. When you read Chopra and others of his stripe, you are told that God has a great plan for you. But the more you read Chopra, you realize that God is not visible in anything he has written. Chopra's conclusion is that you are he...the divine is in you. Ah! But here's the catch. To convince you of that, he has had to mutilate every other theory that holds to the contrary. How does he do that without seeming disrespectful of others? The bigger trick lies here. First, he takes their texts and strips them of their contexts. Next, he heavily quotes their own "authorities," as long as they don't actually believe their own texts. And finally, he dedicates his theory to all who lay claim to a different belief. This magical formula makes him look irenic and congenial, and then he can grace the talk shows as the ultimate glue that brings all religions together. He has provided spirituality without any absolutes and debunked any contrary claims at the same time. Anyone else may follow his lead and quote other texts out of context, but they dare not quote him out of context, unless they wish to meet him in a court of law.

This is truly the picture of the proverbial elephant being felt by four blind people; each one describes what he feels and gives his own perspective, to the exclusion of the other perspectives. If you shine the light on one chapter of the New Spirituality, it can almost look like Christianity. But when you shine the light on another chapter, you're sure it's Buddhism, then Hinduism, then Taoism. This is brilliance at work in a culture of spiritual hungers and an aversion for dogma.

If, when I am restless, I am wishing there were a God, why not trade that for a belief that tells me that when I am meditating, I *am* God, and that the momentary excursions into humanity are nothing more than illusion? It is quite ironic that many of the founders of these spiritual paths have found the West to be the ideal place for such frank and open discussion. One would risk his career, if not his life, in the hotbeds of some of those other worldviews these founders play with, were the same liberties taken there. Just as the charge of hypocrisy is the unintended compliment that vice pays to virtue, so is this a subtle compliment being paid to the worldview that allows them the privilege to attack the very foundations of belief that have made the freedom to believe and promote contradictory worldviews possible. Such is the glory of Christianity. Trying to redefine truth our way always results in redefining everything. The first temptation in the Garden of Eden was to play God with a different vocabulary, rather than taking God at his word. That is what the New Spirituality does best. But still hanging over our heads is the fact that relativism must eventually pay its dues in the currency of reality.

There is an old story about a man who proposed a bet with his friend. "First, I'll ask myself a question, and if I can answer it, you buy me a coke."

"What sort of bet is that?" countered his friend.

"But that's not all there is to it. After I have asked myself a question and answered it, you ask yourself a question, and if you can answer it, I'll buy you a coke. We will keep going till one of us asks a question we can't answer."

"Strange bet," said the friend, "but let's proceed."

So the man asked himself the first question. "How can a rabbit burrow a hole into the ground, without throwing mud out onto the outside? My answer is, it should start digging the hole from the inside."

"How can it do that?" came the immediate rejoinder.

"I don't know," said the man. "That's your question."

Between the koans and the subtleties, the obfuscations and the obscurities, there is a smile on the Buddha's face. It may not be the smile of enlightenment. It may well be that the questioner is trapped into believing that the questions are the answers.

CHAPTER 9

❦

DO YOU REALLY WANT TO LIVE?

"Would you kindly see her, Ravi? But be prepared for a shock." With those words, I was requested to meet a seventeen-year-old young woman whose story is tragic and in some ways terrifying. But it is at the same time a triumphant story of a human spirit that has conquered a sustained indignity. Her parents are European. She is a young Chinese girl, born with an extremely rare birth defect that is known by the medical name of harlequin ichthyosis.

Harlequin ichthyosis is a severe genetic skin disorder. Infants with this condition are born with very hard, thick skin covering most of their bodies. The skin forms large, diamond-shaped plates that are separated by deep cracks or fissures. These skin abnormalities affect the shape of the eyelids, nose, mouth, and ears, and limit movement of the arms and legs. As the name would suggest, the skin resembles the scales of a fish, and as the skin is produced at an abnormally high rate, the constant shedding gives it a pinkish-red hue. Combined with the disfigurement of the features, the sight can be quite terrifying.

As they came into the hotel lobby, I met the lovely couple

who adopted this little girl when she was only three. They are writing her story in a book. It is one of the most incredible situations I have ever seen with my own eyes. We all know that every life is a story. Sometimes the story takes on bizarre twists and turns. Seldom do we choose to make a tragic story part of our own lives. And when we do, we often underestimate how deep the anguish can be.

Our lives are shaped by others literally from birth, and even the best of intentions can result in the most unexpected of hurts. Each of us starts off with a minimum of understanding, needing a maximum of input. We gradually reach the middle stage of childhood when the input into our lives is both from others and from within ourselves. We process more intelligently all intimations of reality, both from our own promptings and from our experience. Finally we become adults, with a sovereign will and the awesome responsibility of making our own decisions. But every now and then a strange thought occurs to us: Are we really ever completely our own person or have we been conditioned in ways beyond our own imagination?

I have pondered long and hard the question of why people turn to God. I remember a woman from Romania telling me that she was raised in a staunchly atheistic environment. They were not allowed to even mention the name of God in their household, lest they be overheard and their entire education denied. After she came to the United States, I happened to be her patient when I was recovering from back surgery. When I had the privilege of praying with her one day, she said as she wiped away her tears, "Deep in my heart I have always believed there was a God. I just didn't know how to find him."

This sentiment is repeated scores of times. More recently, I had the great privilege of meeting with two very key people in an avowedly atheistic country. After I finished praying, one of them said, "I have never prayed in my entire life, and I have never heard anyone else pray. This is a first for me. Thank you for teaching me how to pray." It was a gripping moment in our three-hour evening, and it was obvious that even spiritual hungers that have been suppressed for an entire lifetime are in evidence when in a situation where there is possible fulfillment.

Although I agree that the problem of pain may be one of the greatest challenges to faith in God, I dare suggest that it is the problem of pleasure that more often drives us to think of spiritual things. Sexuality, greed, fame, and momentary thrills are actually the most precarious attractions in the world. Pain forces us to accept our finitude. It can breed cynicism, weariness, and fatigue in just living. Pain sends us in search of a greater power. Introspection, superstition, ceremony, and vows can all come as a result of pain. But disappointment in pleasure is a completely different thing. While pain can often be seen as a means to a greater end, pleasure is seen as an end in itself. And when pleasure has run its course, a sense of despondency can creep into one's soul that may often lead to self-destruction. Pain can often be temporary; but disappointment in pleasure gives rise to emptiness...not just for a moment, but for life. There can seem to be no reason to life, no preconfigured purpose, if even pleasure brings no lasting fulfillment. The truth is that I have known people who in the peak of their success have turned to God, and I have known others, drowning in pain and defeat, who seek God for an answer. Either extreme leaves haunting questions. God alone knows how we will respond to either.

This struggle between pain and pleasure, I believe, gives spirituality a more defined goal. People in pain may look for comfort and explanations. People disappointed in pleasure look for purpose. Dostoyevsky defines *hell* as "the inability to love." I think that is a pretty close description. But this is where, I believe, the West has lost its way and stumbled into the New Spirituality. We had what it took to experience pleasure, but in the end, what we experienced took from us what we had in terms of value. Pleasure disappointed in the West, and in our boredom, we went searching for an escape in the strange or the distorted, rather than looking to what God has clearly revealed in the underpinnings of the Christian faith that point to the person of Jesus Christ.

When we indulge in pleasure to the point that it destroys the value within us, the ends to which we will go, both spiritually and pragmatically, lead us into the quicksand of our own pursuits. Looking into the face of one born with a deformity may cause fear or revulsion within us and the desire to look away, but plundering pleasure to the point of creating spiritual deformity within the soul causes us to run from ourselves. We understand so little how to define life's purpose because we have chased pleasure for pleasure's sake and have come away empty.

The Core of the Christian Message

"Truth is stranger than fiction because we have made fiction to suit ourselves."[1] So said G. K. Chesterton. He went on to say, "What we need is not a religion that is right where we are right, but one that is right where we are wrong."[2] Those two cautions will stand us in good stead as we try to understand why we really search for spiritual answers.

In Psalm 8:4, David asks, "What is mankind that you are mindful of them, human beings that you care for them?" (NIV).

What is mankind? That question lies beneath all of our pursuits and hungers. If we do not have the answer to the question of what man is, we do not have the right to an answer to any other question. Are we at our core divine or nothing? Are these the only two options? There is a very moving Indian song that literally translates as: "I am not a God, nor am I Satan…I am but a human."

Isn't it fascinating how songs rip reality from the shroud of the sophistry we have tried to bury ourselves in? I want to take a look at how the issues of pain and pleasure point to the uniqueness of the Christian faith to the New Spirituality.

Sense Out of Essence

Nearly three millennia before John Lennon lived a man known for his wisdom. His name was Solomon. He wrote more songs and proverbs than any man before him, and probably more than most after him. I strongly suspect that if he had lived in our time, he would have owned most of the television stations. He loved the arts. He, too, imagined a world without heaven above or hell below. He just said it more obscurely in the book of Ecclesiastes when he used the phrase "under the sun," which literally means "with no input from above or below." He boasted that "under the sun" he had accomplished every dream and hope, every passion and indulgence, every aesthetic and intellectual pursuit known to man at his time. He lived as if there were no heaven to aspire to or hell to shun. And his conclusion was that everything became a chasing after the wind…meaningless.

Solomon was right. I cannot think of a more difficult subject to deal with than pleasure. Every culture exploits some segment of society in order to entertain hungers, either private or public. We are all pleasure seekers, and what gives us pleasure is a revelation of our values. It is not often that one hears the subject being addressed, except as a sociological phenomenon or a psychological description. In a society where pornography has become a multibillion-dollar industry, it is very evident that pleasure is both sought after and for sale. But deep within there always lurks that burning question: How does one define what is legitimate and what is illegitimate? A self-reflective, self-centered New Spirituality has no answers to give. Much of New Spirituality is actually based on psychological theory, and if psychology is all we have on which to base the answer to this question, we are in deep trouble.

Very recently, a professor from Yale, Paul Bloom, wrote a book on pleasure, *How Pleasure Works: The New Science of Why We Like What We Like,* in which he argues that there must be some underlying belief in the value of what one is doing or getting to experience pleasure. If one *believes* he is buying something once belonging to John F. Kennedy, then the pleasure quotient goes up. Of course, one doesn't need to have a degree in psychology to know that. But the argument Bloom derives removes pleasure from its sensory dimension and lifts it to its "essential" dimension. So far, so good. He actually has a point. The essence of an act is the determining factor. It's not just taste or sound or touch that should bring pleasure; the essence of the act should determine the intensity of the pleasure. More strictly speaking, the essence of an act as *believed* by the participant is the source of the pleasure. This takes us from the rationalist position of "I think, therefore I am," to "I think, therefore I feel." It is the utilitarian philosophy of pleasure à la Bentham and Mill (who developed a pleasure gauge) gone postmodern.

But as one reads this exposition on pleasure from a psycho-scientific point of view, what happens when matter dabbles in the spiritual and reserves the right to define the spiritual quickly becomes evident. This is a Copernican shift in the way we define our own senses and is, to me, precisely the trap that the New Spiritualists fall into, albeit for loftier goals and hopes. Ask yourself this question: *Who would I fear more, a person whose deformity sends me to science and faith to look for answers to their malady, or a person who uses science to advance sadomasochistic behavior to further deform humanity?* Academics often miss the larger point.

The reason we search for essence is neither psychological nor ancestral; rather, it is that we are hardwired and spiritually designed to probe into the ultimate nature of all that is real. It is a spiritual matter. We hunger for pleasure that goes beyond the physical because ultimately we are spiritual beings. This is the danger the New Spirituality risks; wresting quantum and physics and psychology to advantage in order to explain the spiritual leaves one vulnerable to the sadomasochist, who lays claim to essence and possibly blames his psyche for the way he thinks.

This is a very important point I am making. When strident atheists like Richard Dawkins vilify Christian belief as irrational, they do so because they do not agree with the metaphysics of those who defend it. When they mock the Deepak Chopras of this world for building a spiritual empire supposedly drawn from scientific jargon, they are refuting it because of the misuse, indeed, the abuse of physics.

Life is a search for the spiritual. Whether in the throes of pain or in the disappointments of pleasure, we strive for an essence that is beyond the physical. Let me give you an example. Suppose you were to raise a little child and give that child everything he needed...love, shelter, education, support, all the way to becoming an adult. Let's call him Jason. One day, there is a knock on Jason's door, and an older person standing outside asks to meet him. After a few moments of conversation, the visitor breaks the news to Jason that he is Jason's biological father. If this is the first time Jason has learned he is adopted, what do you think will happen? How do you think he will cope with it? His sensory emotions will tear him apart on the inside. "Why didn't you tell me this?" would be his question to his adoptive parents. "Where were you when I needed you?" he would ask the biological father. Essence is far more than belief. Essence is belief based on the intrinsic being of the person. This is the hunger of the spirit beyond mere sensory and belief components.

This is why I believe that the intertwining of pain with pleasure is at the root of the human dilemma. These extremes of feeling at either end of the spectrum that most of us wish to avoid, even as we are drawn into them, are the twin realities that help shape our search. We want to find happiness. We want to avoid pain. We want to know who we are. We want to know what we are. We care about our origin and our essence. Pleasure and pain become indicators along the way on the road that will lead us to our destiny, and they are rooted in the question of our origin.

It is not sufficient to say nice things such as "All religions say the same thing." Nobody, and I do mean nobody, really believes that. If they say they do, you can call their bluff in moments by exposing the preconceived sovereignty they have exercised in evaluating one religion over the other and by which they have arrived at the conclusion that all religions lead to the same destination, even though the religions all say different things. How can anyone make such an assertion? Even in broad categories they do not say the same thing. Buddha himself rejected Hinduism because of some of its dogmas. And literally just days after his death, Buddhism began to fragment into a series of different

Buddhist beliefs. Some even went into hiding, lest they be killed for the challenges they were making to the leadership. And only a short while after Muhammad died, blood was spilled over who his successor would be. The first three of the five caliphs in Islam were assassinated—varnishing such facts with niceties doesn't do anyone a favor.

Were these divisions for religious reasons? Oh yes, that is what is claimed. It was for reasons of essence, but the apologists of these faiths fail to come to terms with the essential nature of their beliefs themselves. Belief systems must justify themselves. If they cannot, the ever more bizarre will be required to bring the same degree of fulfillment.

We will pick this up again. For now, let me posit three things—relationship, stewardship, and worship—that must define life if the spiritual search as it relates to pleasure and pain is to be understood. Such definitions, then, build into a worldview.

CHAPTER 10

THE TIES THAT BIND

Relationship

In the Judeo-Christian worldview, all pleasure is ultimately seen from the perspective of what is of eternal value and definition. I often think of that day the astronauts became the first ones to go around the dark side of the moon. To them was given a beautiful glimpse of the "earthrise" over the horizon of the moon, draped in a beauteous mixture of blue and white and garlanded by the light of the sun against the black void of space. It was something human eyes had never witnessed before. Isn't it fascinating that no poem or lyric came to the commander's aid in lending him words to express that moment of awe? Instead, the words that came to his mind were the first words of the book of Genesis: "In the beginning, God..."

There are moments like that in our experience when nothing can take away from the miracle of human life. No amount of time can explain it. No pondering within can satisfy all that the moment declares. There is something extraordinary here. It is not just the miracle of life; it is the miracle of life imbued with particular worth. The identity of the child is as significant as the fact that it is. We all know that. The New Spirituality distributes life into the generality of "consciousness" and loses the particularity of personal relationship. So it is not merely time we are talking about here, or some pool of consciousness into which we all merge and from which we emerge. In the Judeo-Christian worldview, we believe that every "person" is actually created in God's image, in that God himself is a person, and that each person has *relational* priorities that are implicitly built in, not by nature but by God's design.

Consider again the tragedy of the earthquake and tsunami in Japan. Even in that stoic culture, where community rises above everything else, each one who wept was grieving the loss of their own loved ones: They were not grieving just for the total loss of life but also for their personal loss. This is real. It is not imaginary. We stand before the individual graves of the ones we love more often than we stand before a graveyard in general.

But there is more. Personhood transcends mere DNA. There is essential *worth* to each person.

Recently in a game show, a computer (named Watson after the founder of IBM) handily defeated two human contestants in a knowledge contest. This had happened before when the computer Deep Blue beat the world champion in chess, Garry Kasparov. Computers are faster and better at calculations and at chess. But what one article said is interesting: In this instance, where language was involved, Watson's victory over its two human competitors advanced IBM's master plan of making humanity obsolete. I would add that the ultimate revenge would be for Watson to deny that humans exist or that they created "him." You see, to create a computer to do what Watson did required brilliance. As David Ferrucci, the principal investigator of Watson's DeepQA technology at IBM Research, said,

> When we deal with language, things are very different. Language is ambiguous, it's contextual, it's implicit. Words are grounded really only in human cognition—and there's seemingly an infinite number of ways the same meaning can be expressed in language. It's an incredibly difficult problem for computers.[1]

It was precisely the coding of that "human-ness" into Watson that required the effort of twenty-five of IBM's top research scientists, and they accomplished it with a mishmash of algorithms and raw computing technology. "Watson is powered by 10 racks of IBM Power 750 servers with 2,880 processor cores and 15 terabytes of RAM; it's capable of operating at a galloping 80 teraflops. With that sort of computing power, Watson is able to...scour its roughly 200 million pages of stored content—about 1 million books worth—and find an answer with confidence in as little as 3 seconds."[2]

The question is, "What is Watson doing or thinking now?" The entire question is reduced to one issue: What does consciousness mean? It is not surprising that "consciousness" and "conscience" come from the same root word. When you put together terms like "consciousness," "conscience," "individual," "right," "wrong," "good," and "evil," you are on the path to spiritual thinking. Matter alone or resorting to quantum doesn't create spiritual thought. Chopra can write of an ageless body and a timeless mind all he wants, but when you lose your child, something has been lost that can never be replaced—even if you have another child—and can never be explained by his philosophy. Never.

What this means is that our essence is both shared and particular—a truth that is Judeo-Christian in its assumption. This leads me to see the critical and defining notion of essence and its connection to relationship. That must be defined first before pleasure can be derived legitimately or otherwise in concert with the essence of the thing enjoyed. So it is not merely the essence of the object that is being enjoyed that matters. It is the essence of the subject who is experiencing pleasure that legitimizes or delegitimizes the experience.

There is a clear and unequivocal assertion in the Judeo-Christian faith that God created us for his purpose: to fulfill life's sacred nature within the particularity of an individual life, in relationship with him and his indwelling presence. This particularity does not offset the fact of being part of the larger community of fellow human beings. It does not deify us, nor does it demean us. To be a human being is to be one who is fashioned in the image of God, who is the point of reference in all relationships. This is the difference between Islam and Christianity. In Islam, a person will kill to supposedly protect the honor of Allah. In the Christian faith, Jesus sacrificed his *own* life to honor the love of God as it is revealed for all humanity. In pantheism, the "I" dies the death of a thousand qualifications; hence that vacuous term "duty" in the Gita or even "dharma." For the Christian, the I is a person valued by God. This is a world of difference from all other religions.

In search of this relationship we pursue spiritual realities. And often we end up creating God in our own image when we have failed to see, or perhaps don't like, what it is that God intended to convey to us in his love. No, this is not the "relativity" of physics, special or general, or of quantum theory, or even of metaphysics. It is the relationship of a person within himself or herself. It is who we are, not fragmented, in the accretion of everything that makes us an individual. It is why we even refer to ourselves as "individuals"…indivisible…the underlying meaning being that we cannot be divided into parts.

Even in pantheism, one cannot be content with the Gnostic category of "knowledge." Nor in Zen can we merely mutter "*Rupa* is nothing." That is where the monists and Vedantists and Zen thinkers wish to leave us. Thus Hinduism has the Gita, the most beloved of Hindu texts (not the Vedas), in which questions of war, devotion, worship, and sacrifice are raised. These are relational issues. How can I go to war and kill my brothers? was the question Arjuna placed before Krishna. Only he didn't know who Krishna was, so reality and the nature of the source of the answers were veiled from him in the early stages of the text. What is good and what is evil? What is the *right* thing to do? That's what Arjuna wants to know. It came down to duty in a play called *Life*.

Buddhism raises the issues of poverty, pain, sickness, death, responsibility, and the causes of misery. All these were not just ideas, they were evidenced in persons or in how they impacted persons. Of all religions, Islam is the least focused on relationships, even though it gives the appearance of being a community. And the result is law, authority, and power over the community. These become the rationale for Islam. Thus, it is not surprising that the very word *Islam* means "to submit." And it's no wonder that it is sometimes called a "pantheism of force," where individuality is sacrificed at the altar of authority. Some Muslims I have spoken to admit this is what Islam is, but insist that it was not intended to be this way. How do you even debate such an issue when you are silenced if you disagree? This authoritarianism and submission become the means to the end of community.

Any community there is exists only in the narrow confines of faith, which often provides the adherents with justification to sacrifice their own for "their faith." The faith, in effect, negates the person.

I have two very special friends whose lives have been a blessing to countless children who have been deformed from birth. They have established an orphanage to give them a home and find medical help to correct what can be corrected. Then they look for families who will adopt them. One little boy had always been passed over for adoption because he has a particular brain malfunction that is very rare. He often doesn't connect thoughts. At about nine years of age, as I remember the story, he was becoming despondent as, one-by-one, he saw his housemates being selected by families and leaving. He began to ask those who were taking care of him why no one was adopting him. Why didn't anybody choose him?

Through an incredible series of events, a couple from Texas, who had already adopted one child from the same orphanage, called to ask if this boy was still there. Through the goodness of the parents' hearts, and the generosity of the couple who established the orphanage in agreeing to cover all the costs of his adoption, the day has been set for this little boy to be taken to his new home. The special part of the thrill for him is that he will be reunited with one of the little boys who was his housemate at one time.

His actual name is quite hard to pronounce, but it is quite a normal name in his native setting. His adoptive parents have sent him the name they want to give him—Anson Josiah, the initials of which are A.J. He now walks around that home, waiting for his new parents to come for him, telling everybody as he points to his chest, "You can call me A.J. My name is A.J." Is it not interesting that even with the debilitation of disconnected thoughts, he is able to pick up the redeeming thrill of relationship and particular worth evidenced in his new name?

One of the great epic poems of the Middle East is *Shahnama* (or *Shanameh*), written by the Persian poet and author Abu ol-Qasem Mansur Firdawsi (ca. 935–1020). In it he recounts the legendary history of the ancient kings and heroes of Persia. It is known to English readers principally through Matthew Arnold's version, written in the mid-nineteenth century: *Sohrab and Rustum*. I remember reading it as a young lad in Delhi. Rustum is a mighty warrior, second to none. War is his way of life and as the story unfolds, even though he has a family to take care of, Rustum is constantly far from home, taking on challenges. One day, he comes across a younger though equally well known warrior named Sohrab. Sohrab is reluctant to take him on because he knows that Rustum is actually his father. Years before when he was a small child, Sohrab had been sent away by his mother to spare him the lifestyle of his father, and Rustum has been misled into believing that the child who was sent away was a daughter, born while he was gone.

Sohrab and Rustum eventually meet in one-on-one combat. Twice, Sohrab could have fatally wounded Rustum, but he spares him. Finally, Rustum has Sohrab on his back, and victoriously plunges his sword into Sohrab's side. As the life is ebbing out of him, Sohrab tells Rustum who he is and, when challenged, proves it by producing a locket his mother had given him. The rest of the story is the grief and remorse that fill Rustum when he realizes he has killed his own son, who had spared him when he had the advantage.

I find utterly fascinating the stories of deep relationship that are woven into the histories of various cultures, stories that reveal the folly of succumbing to the lure of power and prestige.

What a tragedy to destroy our own children by denying the One who gave us life. Isn't that where we are today, in our geopolitical and religious wars?

The good and decent among us mourn broken homes. We mourn broken lives. We mourn shattered dreams. We celebrate reunions. We delight in long relationships that have withstood the test of time. This is a clue, a huge clue of how life is intended to be lived. We are designed, shaped, and conditioned to be in relationships of honor, and in our hearts we wish to see those relationships triumph over all other allurements. It has been nearly four decades since I lost my mother. I don't think a day goes by that I don't think of her. Is all this not an indication, given to us by the One who made us, that we are designed to live within relationship and to find our greatest sense of worth and fulfillment within relationship?

Relationships are multidirectional and multidimensional. For this, physics, chemistry, even psychology, for that matter, are all inadequate starting points. Relationship must begin with essence, not with the essence of others but rather with the essence of oneself. That is why pleasure and pain become critical. It is not psychologically necessary to teach somebody that their parents matter. We know that by intuition. My life has been replete with examples of meeting people who wish they could find that one friend or one relationship. It is not accidental that in the long bibliography at the end of her book on spirituality, which draws sparsely from Christian literature, Elizabeth Lesser still finds place to mention C. S. Lewis's *A Grief Observed*, a powerful book on the depth of his grief when he lost his wife, Joy.

How and why is this so? In Christianity, the essence of each and every person and the individual reality of each life is sacred. It is sacred because intrinsic value has been given to us by our

Creator. Atheism is the extreme form of placing ultimate worth in an accidental universe. For the atheist, the only real relationship is between each person and the universe. That is it. There is no outside voice or revelation. To attempt to mask the loneliness of this reality, we offer parallel universes, aliens or some other entities somewhere that will surely someday find us if we don't find them first. There was a play written some years ago called *Waiting for Godot*. The title was a play on words for the lonely inhabitants of the world in the play, waiting for a God who never shows up. The play to honor the sciences should be titled *Waiting for Logo*, which would mean waiting for a word from anybody out there.

In pantheism, which is the basis of much of the New Spirituality, the "I" is lost in the desired union with the ultimate impersonal Absolute; there is no more "I and you." In rebirth, all actual relationship with what has preceded is lost, and we are encouraged to believe there is an essential relationship only with the deeds of the past. No one in this cyclical framework ever answers what an individual was paying for in the first birth. After all, one cannot have an infinite number of lives to their credit: If there were an infinite number of births, one would never have reached this particular birth. So, going backward, what was the debt owed in the first life? As one of my Hindu friends once said after he came to know Jesus, "Even the banks are kinder to me. At least the bank tells me how much I owe and how much time I have to repay what I owe. In karma, I don't know what I owe or how long it will take me to repay it." For Deepak Chopra to bring relief to Maharishi Mahesh Yogi by telling him that his (Chopra's) blood would not carry his karma to the Maharishi borders on the pathetic…the pupil having to reassure the teacher that karma was not carried in the blood. Where is it carried, one might ask, in an ageless body and a timeless mind?

A *relationship* with God that is both individual and to be reflected to the rest of humanity in a shared birthright is God's gift to us.

Stewardship

It is in the area of stewardship that I think Christians have done an enormous amount but have also failed in a very serious way. The priority was right, but the reach was short. Let me explain.

The world is in great need. There is so much that needs to be done. Ask yourself this question: *Which worldview has reached out the most globally?* The numbers are staggeringly disproportionate. I remember in the early days of my travels walking into institutions for people with leprosy. You can go to the fringe of the Sahara desert or to the island of Molokai in Hawaii and see the footprints of Christian missionaries at work there. Look at the hospitals in many parts of the world, the orphanages, the rescue homes, the care for widows. Look way beyond the reach of one's own land. It is not enough to say that America has had much and therefore Americans ought to give. What about the wealth in the oil-rich nations of the world...how many hospitals and universities, orphanages and rescue homes have been built by that money? There is so much need in India that one just grows accustomed to it and walks by. Does Allah desire that billions of dollars be spent on a mosque while millions of people live in terrible need? Bangladesh, a Muslim country, is one of the poorest areas in the world, where hundreds of thousands live below the poverty line. In contrast go to Abu Dhabi, also a Muslim country, where the sheikh has spent more than $3 billion to build a mosque. Is this stewardship? Is this for God's glory, or is it for the glory of an earthly kingdom that forgets others of the same faith who are living on the edge?

But present-day Christians cannot rest on the actions of Christians of previous generations. Today, we would do well to also ask ourselves this same question as we build our church megaplexes that often border more on memorials to human icons than on anything that lifts the heart toward God.

Whatever one may say, only the blind and the antisocial can ignore the realities of a desperately needy world. Christopher Hitchens's cheap book attacking Mother Teresa showed a heart that was so hard he could not be touched even by the reach of a little woman with a big heart.

But I have to say that there is one area in which we as Christians have been negligent. We may have a good track record for reaching out to the hurting of the world...to building relationships with the world, but by and large we forget that there is a natural world out there to be protected as well. We have been negligent in matters of the environment, and just because the environment has no feelings we trample it underfoot. The pantheist deifies the impersonal and we ignore it. Both extremes are wrong. The created order was meant to be cared for.

If essence gave me the reason for relationships, existence gave me the mandate for *stewardship*. The world exists in real terms. It is not merely form. It is also substance.

Worship

In my study at home, I have an old Anglican prayer bench. It is my place of refuge. It is where I come on my knees before God and open my heart in its most deeply felt struggles and needs.

If you had told me as a young lad going to church that someday I would long for a prayer bench, I would have despaired even more than I already did. Kneeling in worship and being aware of others kneeling beside me was not exactly the highlight of my week. I would covertly glance out the corner of my eye to see what others were doing. *Worship* was nothing more than a word in my vocabulary. I saw prayer and the repetition of creeds as nothing more than a hypnotic effort at inducing some state of mind. It mattered little, except at examination time and in times of crisis. It was a sort of "God, if you are there, please help." Now, in my adult years, I have seen more happen during my time of prayer than any other time.

The hunger for worship is one of the greatest clues in life. In India, temples are full, and the whole cultic experience of priests, ceremonies, chants, blessings, fears, and superstitions is all part and parcel of the culture. You grow up knowing and accepting that "religion" is a vital part of a person's life. The interesting thing is that we seldom ask the questions that ought to be asked. Why? It seems that whatever ceremonies we are taught become part of our personal culture, a habit of the heart and an expression of our community. More often than not religious rites are performed out of fear or superstition. And they are seldom questioned or examined.

Growing up, I noticed many culturally meaningful things that several of my friends did. One was to touch the feet of the father of the family to show respect. This was a very admirable and beautiful act to watch. Each time the father would enter the room or the son or daughter would bid their father good-bye before heading on a journey, they would lean over and touch his feet as a sign of respect, and there would be a quick ceremonial blessing given by the father to his children. I had a very dear classmate who devoutly followed that practice. But I noticed something. The ceremony had become nothing more than that and did not reflect any true reality. In his private life, his values were anything but honoring to his father. What was even more tragic was a day that I remember well, when this young man doused himself with kerosene and lit a match to his body. When his parents came home, it was to find his charred body. What did this say to the parents? The son who had touched his father's feet in respect and the father who had given his blessing to his son really didn't know the other or what the other was thinking. All the formality and ceremony had amounted to nothing.

This is the ultimate violation of worship. All the ceremonies in the world, all the perfunctory reverence, do not make for worship. Worship that is properly understood and properly given is co-extensive with life...It informs all of life, everything we do and everything we say and think. At its core it is the sense and service of God. Worship brings into confluence all the questions and answers that we have and do not have. For the answers we do not have, a relationship with the One who does have them carries us through. It is the submission of our will, heart, and purpose to the sovereign will and the person of God who created us and loves us. Worship is a relationship from which all inspiration flows and the relationship through which all of our needs are met. It is knowing even partly the One who knows us fully.

Worship of the Supreme Being is what makes it possible to find unity in diversity in the world around me by enabling me to find unity and diversity within myself, first. *Worship* is the starting point.

Once you understand essence, existence, and reverence in the context of a relationship expressed in stewardship and worship, life's purpose becomes clear. From that come beneficence and the imperatives. Then *love* can be legitimately defined; otherwise, it is nothing more than a word that is open to each person's own interpretation and context. Then legitimate pleasure can be defined; otherwise, all pleasure is up for grabs.

The purpose of life given by my Creator is both general and specific. It is general in that we all are designed to have the sacred as a starting point in everything. This even means that the notion of truth is a sacred trust. It is specific in that love has its boundaries. When Oprah said that she couldn't conceive of God being jealous, she betrayed her warped definition of love. God is not jealous because he wants us to himself as a private possession, he is jealous because he wants us to have the supreme experience of love, which, contrary to the implications of the pluralistic religions, is exclusive. It is the nature of love to bind itself. Love is not free. Someone who truly loves another cannot be other than jealous for the object of their love.

Some time ago, I saw a special program on the progress that is being made in the development of artificial limbs. While I was awed by the incredible mechanical genius of giving a person arms and legs, there was something else that could have been easily missed. Two who had received these prosthetics and were able to stand up from their wheelchairs said something that was totally unexpected: "It is so wonderful to be able to hug and be hugged again." Who would have thought of that except someone who had been in a wheelchair and was unable to hug or be hugged because of the intrusion of the chair?

God embraces us with his love and has given us the extraordinary privilege of love and sexuality in a relationship from which God has exempted himself because he is "Spirit"; his love for us is so great that he has provided for us to have pleasure in our material finitude. And he makes that same body his dwelling place, his temple.

To be sure, the New Spirituality loves to talk of the sacred, or of purpose and meaning, but the starting point of an impersonal absolute without any of the attributes of God, except by negation, does not justify the New Spiritualists' participation in the categories they like to talk about. In doing away with God and deifying themselves, they have actually ended up losing the personal self as well. We are, in effect, amputated, because there is no one to embrace or to be embraced by. We are alone in a world where everything is nothing and we are part of the divine. From the Judeo-Christian perspective, humanity is the supreme creation of a personal, loving God. That starting point allows values and imperatives that find their definitions in a personal God.

Why So Much Pain?

If a relationship with God as a basis of pleasure forms the first component, the explanation of pain forms the next. The illogic of pain forms a thorny question on which volumes have been written. Why do the innocent suffer? Why do we face all these diseases? Why the suffering of millions because of natural disasters or the tyranny of demagogues? A loving God cannot exist in a wicked world. Among others, I have written much on this in previous books. But let me just underscore a few ideas that we can come to terms with:

- Pain is a fact of life.
- It is a universal fact of life.

- There are moral dimensions in the way we phrase our questions concerning pain.
- Every religion explicitly or implicitly attempts to explain pain.

The first thought is this: Why do we even ask these questions about suffering within the context of morality? Why have we blended the fact of physical pain with the demand for a moral explanation? Who decided that pain is immoral? Almost every atheist or skeptic you read names this as the main reason for his or her denial of God's existence. It is said that virtue in distress and vice in triumph have made atheists of mankind. New Testament scholar turned skeptic Bart Ehrman is one who states that this unanswered question precipitated his departure from faith in Christ. Charles Darwin said it was "the damnable doctrine of eternal damnation" that ended his faith in God. Many who survived the Holocaust state that when it was over, they found they had left their faith in God behind.

We know that in the Judeo-Christian framework, pain is connected to the reality of evil and to the choices made by mankind at the beginning of time. The problem of pain and the problem of evil are inextricably bound. However:

- When we assume evil, we assume good.
- When we assume good, we assume a moral law.
- When we assume a moral law, we assume a moral law-giver, but that's whom the skeptic or atheist is generally trying to disprove.

Why does assuming a moral law necessitate a moral law-giver? Because every time the question of evil is raised, it is either by a person or about a person. And that implicitly assumes that the question is a worthy one. But it is a worthy question only if people have intrinsic worth, and the only reason people have intrinsic worth is that they are the creations of One who is of ultimate worth. That person is God. So the question self-destructs for the naturalist or the pantheist. The question of the morality of evil or pain is valid only for a theist.

Only in Christian theism is love preexistent within the Trinity, which means that love precedes human life and becomes the absolute value for us. This absolute is ultimately found only in God, and in knowing and loving him we work our way through the struggles of pain, knowing of its ultimate connection to evil and its ultimate destruction by the One who is all-good and all-loving; who in fact has given us the very basis for the words *good* and *love* both in concept and in language.

Not far from my home lives a young woman who was born with a very rare disease called CIPA...congenital insensitivity to pain with anhydrosis. Imagine having a body that looks normal and acts normally, except for one thing: You cannot feel physical pain. That sounds as if it would be a blessing. But the reason it's a problem is that she lives under the constant threat of injuring herself without knowing it. If she steps on a rusty nail that could infect her bloodstream, she wouldn't even realize it by sensation. If she placed her hand on a burning stove, she would not know she had just burned her hand except by looking at it. She needs constant vigilance because she could sustain an injury that could take her life or cause serious debilitation. When her family was interviewed some years ago, the line I most remember is the closing statement by her mother. She said, "I pray every night for my daughter, that God would give her a sense of pain."

If that statement were read in a vacuum, we would wonder

what sort of mother she is. But because more than anyone else she understands the risks of this strange disease, there is no greater prayer she can pray than that her daughter feel pain and be able to recognize what it portends.

I ask you this simple question: If, in our finitude, we can appreciate the value of pain in even one single life, is it that difficult to grant the possibility that an infinite God can use pain to point us to a greater malady? We see through a glass darkly because all we want is to be comfortable. We cannot understand the great plan of an all-knowing God who brings us to himself through the value of pain or of disappointment with pleasure.

James Stewart of Scotland wrote a brilliant passage in one of his books to describe how, in Christ, we are able to conquer through the mystery of evil:

> It is a glorious phrase—"He led captivity captive." The very triumphs of his foes, it means, he used for their defeat. He compelled their dark achievements to subserve his ends not theirs. They nailed him to a tree, not knowing that by that very act they were bringing the world to his feet. They gave him a cross, not guessing that he would make it a throne. They flung him outside the city gates to die, not knowing that in that very moment they were lifting up the gates of the universe, to let the king come in. They thought to root out his doctrines, not understanding that they were implanting imperishably in the hearts of men the very name they intended to destroy. They thought they had God with his back to the wall, pinned helpless and defeated: they did not know that it was God himself who had tracked them down. He did

not conquer *in spite* of the dark mystery of evil. He conquered *through it.*[3]

The very thing that enslaves and traps us becomes the indicator of our need for God and the means to draw us to the recognition of our own finitude and to the rescuing grace of God. The pain of pain clasps the lifesaving hand of God and draws us into his arms.

In the New Spirituality, "pleasure" and "pain" become self-reflecting terms from a mirror that deceives and distorts. In the person of God, our Creator, revealed in Jesus Christ, we see what legitimate pleasure is and why evil inflicts pain. These real feelings/experiences point us to our essential worth and to our calling into an intimate relationship with God. That relationship has a reach that goes beyond us to others and enjoins a life of stewardship of all creation, culminating in worship.

We'll come back to the issue of pain before the end of the book.

CHAPTER 11

❧

THE SEARCH FOR JESUS

In the 1980s, I attended a lecture given jointly by Francis Schaeffer and C. Everett Koop, the former surgeon general of the United States. At that talk, Schaeffer made a comment that caught me by surprise. He said that the day was coming in the West when the name of Jesus would not be recognized by the average young person; and if it were recognized, not a single historical fact about him would be known. At the time I found his statement a bit hard to swallow and wondered if he had said it just to be provocative. But a generation later, it is appearing to be quite true. I find it rather amazing that the name of Jesus is used quite regularly in profanity not just in the West, but no one would dare use the name of Muhammad in the same way. And of course, no Hindu I know would use the name of any one of their deities with such disrespect.

Why has Jesus met with such response, especially in a culture that has benefited so much from his teaching and ought to know better? The sad reality is that there seems to be very little understanding today of who Jesus is and of what he taught. It is said to be better that a speaker not make an appearance at all than to show up and deliver a bad talk. So it is with knowledge: It is better to have none at all than to have a distortion or perversion of what is a fact. In this slippery slope of the New Spirituality, the numerous voices that have added to the cacophony have created more of a flea market than a reservoir of knowledge. Actually, if many of those within the movement who go under the same banner were to compare their beliefs, they would mutually destroy one another's assumptions. Odd, isn't it, that with all their stress in the power of the "now," they defend it with "ancient wisdom"?

In like manner, there are so many versions of Jesus being offered up that one has to marvel at the numerous possibilities. If one accepted all the plots and machinations of fiction writers creating stories about Mary Magdalene, she would have had to have been supernatural in order to be in all the locations she has been placed, all at the same time. The Jesus of the New Spiritualists is a Jesus of myth, not of fact.

Losing Him

The Jesus of history has suffered at the hands of critics who wished more than anything else to strip him of his uniqueness or make his name forgotten. Yet I maintain that the more I look at the Jesus of history, and the more I see the inspirational incentive he has been, there is no message as beautiful and powerful as his. If an honest seeker were to sit down face-to-face and ask Jesus the questions he or she would like to have answered, I am convinced that in Jesus' answers alone the seeker would find hope for the present and confidence in the future. At least Jesus offers answers; the New Spiritualists really don't have answers.

For the most part, they promote silence, literally and prescriptively.

I was recently listening to a group of mystics discussing how serene life is when we serve "Mother Earth." How ironic, I thought, that following the Japanese earthquake and tsunami nobody questioned "Mother Earth" or asked where she was in all this. After all, it was the earth that shook. Strange, is it not, that those who believe in Mother Earth blame Father God when Mother Earth misbehaves? Maybe this is the ultimate revenge for the gender exploitations of the past.

But maybe that is the key to New Age Spirituality. The answers supplied are only the feelings that one wants to generate, totally apart from any reasoning. That is not true of the Jesus of history and the same Jesus of experience. If one would only give his teaching a fair hearing…But in the volume of words offered today, history is being repeated.

There are at least three scenes I would like to draw our attention to in order to demonstrate how the Jesus of history and the Jesus who offers us life and hope has been lost in the least expected places. Understanding this will help lead us to how and where we might find him.

Easy to Happen

When you look back in the Old Testament, you see that in spite of all the instruction about worship, often repeated, an astounding loss nevertheless had occurred. All that the priests could control, they did. All that the ceremonies could control, they used to their advantage. And when a select or elect few control and sell salvation, the victim is always the common person. No religion is spared here. One would think that this New Spirituality has brought about a new Eden and that its rivers flow peacefully and calmly. But it is not so...In fact, it has never been so. Few arenas lend themselves to abuse and loss as that of religion.

In the enormous temple that Solomon built for the worship of the one true God, ceremonies were rife. All that glittered was gold. The largesse represented was almost unprecedented...the regal splendor of it was proverbial. Worshippers made pilgrimages to the temple and celebrated key moments in family life there. But Solomon lost his way, and before long, his people were like sheep without a shepherd. The temple remained busy; the ceremonies continued to be celebrated; but something crucial had been lost.

When Josiah became the king many years later, he ordered a thorough cleaning of the temple and, lo and behold! in the midst of that massive cleanup someone found the Book of the Law, God's written word to his people, buried in dust somewhere in a back room. The temple was the place where the Book of the Law had been valued and protected. But no one knew it was even there. And saddest of all, they hadn't missed it. This meant that people were still going to the temple to pray, but God was no longer in their midst and they didn't even know it. They were, in effect, talking to themselves. They went to listen, but the book was missing, so there was no one to speak to them. They were sitting in an echo chamber, listening only to themselves. There was no ear to hear them and no voice to speak to them. They lived their lives and carried out their ceremonies of worship in a vacuum.

It is hard to imagine how something like that could have happened. But it has happened repeatedly in history. Someone has said that the main thing in life is to keep the main thing, the main thing…because there are always multiple options vying to replace the main thing.

This is how the Bible describes the startling find in 2 Kings 22:8–10:

> Hilkiah the high priest said to Shaphan the secretary, "I have found the Book of the Law in the temple of the LORD." He gave it to Shaphan, who read it. Then Shaphan the secretary went to the king and reported to him: "Your officials have paid out the money that was in the temple of the LORD and have entrusted it to the workers and supervisors at the temple." Then Shaphan the secretary informed the king, "Hilkiah the priest has given me a book." And Shaphan read from it in the presence of the king. (NIV)

Imagine the scene. That which was the most sacred depository had been lost…lost in the very place that had been erected to guard that trust. The king was overcome with emotion at the find. He gathered an assembly of his people and read the book aloud to them. The long-lost treasure had been rediscovered, and there was a time of national repentance before God. It would have been one thing if they had lost the Book of the Law while traveling, or had hidden it someplace for "safekeeping" and the location of its hiding place had been forgotten over years. But to lose it in the temple itself?

The Word of God that was referred to as the Law had been the guiding light and wisdom for generation after generation. It had been a little over seven hundred years since the people had returned from captivity in Egypt. The same Book of the Law had been read to the people as they reentered their homeland in Joshua's time, and they were reminded to teach it to their children and to the generations that were to come so that they would never forget how they had been rescued by God against all odds and brought back from captivity. This Book of the Law contained God's instruction to them for life, following their redemption.

I cannot ignore the need to make an observation here: Look over the world today and observe how many wars are being fought because of border disputes. How interesting that we consider these wars over boundaries legitimate, but we do not wish to allow God the prerogative to establish boundaries for us.

When I was a child, I often played marbles with my friends. There was a set of rules for the game, but one of my friends introduced a new rule into the game, captured in two words: "Everything mine!" The rule was that whoever was the first to shout "Everything mine" became the determiner of what rules applied, and when. Even a game of marbles loses its fun when the rules apply only at one person's whim. Our world has rejected the transcendent law and is trying to play the game according to the rule of "everything mine." But when two "mines" collide, if one would pardon the pun, we find ourselves walking through a minefield of horror.

In the time following Solomon, each person began to do what was right in his own eyes. It was indeed a time of "everything mine." Gradually, the teaching of the Law was lost, and with society in total chaos, it took a massive cleaning of the temple, led by a young monarch, to even find this document.

I will never forget the first time I visited Russia during the days of the Cold War. I attended an old historic church in the city of Leningrad, which is now called St. Petersburg. I watched as people came in for the service, most of them quite elderly. When the pastor began to speak, my wife and I observed as one elderly woman carefully unfolded layers of old cloth in her lap until she finally held a Bible in her hands. She clasped it so tenderly, as one would the most precious and fragile treasure. She was one of very few people in the church who even had a Bible. That was more than twenty years ago.

A few short days ago, I addressed a packed auditorium in Moscow. The man introducing me said, "Not too long ago, if you had come to Moscow the only Bible you were likely to have seen would have been in the museum. Today, in this auditorium alone there are at least a thousand Bibles. What a great thing has happened in our country!" The audience broke into a thunderous applause.

I sat there and pondered what America would be like today if we had been without the Bible for ninety years. It has been the beautiful teaching of the Word of God across time that has given this nation its ethos. It was this Word of God that put a song into the hearts of slaves during their darkest days. It was this Word of God that gave William Wilberforce in England the conviction and the courage to speak out against slavery and sustained him in the long struggle to see it abolished in the British Commonwealth. It was this same Word of God that inspired Martin Luther King Jr. in his pursuit of civil liberty. It was from the sermon Jesus preached, recorded in this Word of God as the Sermon on the Mount, that Mahatma Gandhi often quoted. And this same Word of God has transformed the life of many a prisoner, and of many others I could tell of, from some of the darkest parts of the world where the light of God's Word has shone. The New Spiritualists would do well to read the Word of God again without prejudice and find in there the treasure that God has given to all of us.

Any nation that neglects teaching the sacredness of life and the family does so at its own peril. Any nation that sanctions the removal of God's boundaries will destroy its own.

I remember asking a Hindu and a Muslim in Canada why they sent their children to a Christian school rather than a public one. They both in effect answered the question the same way: "At least in the Christian school they will learn that values are something very sacred and will not be taught according to secular values." "We would rather point them to the God we believe in than have to prove to them that God exists," said one. What an interesting take on valueless, godless secularism! When the Word of God is lost, the basis of the sacred is lost and anything goes.

One of the all-time greatest books was written by John Bunyan. I believe that other than the Bible, it has been translated into more languages than any other book. I am referring, of course, to *The Pilgrim's Progress*. In it, Pilgrim struggles through life with his burden, going through the testing of Vanity Fair, the Slough of Despond, and so on. It is only when he reaches the foot of the cross at the top of the hill that his burden falls off him. But the journey doesn't end there. He is met by the "Three Shining Ones": The first is the Angel of the Dawn, who greets him with the words "Your sins are forgiven." The second is the Angel of the Daylight, who strips him of his rags and gives him a new set of clothes. The third is the Angel of the Dusk, who points the way for Pilgrim to the gate of the Celestial City. This third angel also puts a mark on his forehead and gives him a scroll so that he will have a map to guide him on his way. The first angel meets his spiritual need, the second addresses his physical needs, and the third engages his intellectual needs and gives him tools to help and instruct him along the journey.

The Christian's walk involves all three areas of life—the spiritual, the practical, and the intellectual. These are not mutually exclusive. God is an immensely practical Being, but he also guides us with reason and wisdom. God's Word is the scroll given to us to inform, enrich, teach, correct, and guide us to the celestial city. If we lose that Word, we have lost the light that guides us on the journey.

Incredible That It Happened

The second scene I want to bring before us is told in Luke's Gospel:

Every year Jesus' parents went to Jerusalem for the Festival of the Passover. When he was twelve years old, they went up to the festival, according to the custom. After the festival was over, while his parents were returning home, the boy Jesus stayed behind in Jerusalem, but they were unaware of it. Thinking he was in their company, they traveled on for a day. Then they began looking for him among their relatives and friends. When they did not find him, they went back to Jerusalem to look for him. After three days they found him in the temple courts, sitting among the teachers, listening to them and asking them questions. Everyone who heard him was amazed at his understanding and his answers. When his parents saw him, they were astonished. His mother said to him, "Son, why have you treated us like this? Your father and I have been anxiously searching for you."

"Why were you searching for me?" he asked. "Didn't you know I had to be in my Father's house?" But they did not understand what he was saying to them. (2:41–50 NIV)

His parents had gone through all the ceremonial requirements and were heading home. It is ironic to me that it was Passover time, the time when the lambs were sacrificed for the forgiveness of sin, the foreshadowing of the ultimate sacrifice of Jesus himself. I wonder what questions Jesus asked these intellectuals. We are told they were amazed. It wasn't until dusk on the first day of their journey home that his parents realized Jesus wasn't with them. This could easily have happened. These were times when family and friends traveled together in caravans, and it was a very festive time for the nation. One can only imagine how heartsick and frantic Mary and Joseph must have been as they hurried back to Jerusalem. Not until after three days of increasingly desperate searching did they finally find Jesus in the temple, which was actually where they had last seen him.

Their immediate reaction was to reprimand him...If you are a parent, I'm sure you can understand how they were feeling. "Why were you searching for me?" he asked them. "Didn't you know I had to be in my Father's house?" And the Scripture tells us they didn't understand why he said what he did and what exactly he meant by it.

This is an amazing question for him to have asked them: "Didn't you know I had to be in *my Father's house*?" Deepak Chopra's thesis that Jesus *attained* "God-consciousness" is just wishful thinking on his part. It is evident from this passage that Jesus early on knew who he was. Whether it was at his baptism by John the Baptist, at the wedding in Cana where he turned water into wine, or at the seashore where he called his disciples;

whether it was when he cleansed the temple of that which profaned it or when he stood before the high priests at his mock trial
or before Pontius Pilate; he knew who he was. In fact, when he
overturned the tables of hucksters and peddlers of religion who
were using the temple as a hangout for money-making crooks
exploiting those beguiled by mere ceremony, he used the same
expression: "my Father's house."

This is not a "higher consciousness" he is referring to. This
is a literal, physical place of prayer and worship that he uniquely
and assuredly calls "my Father's house." It is interesting that
when he taught his disciples to pray, he began with "*Our* Father,"
but when he cleansed the temple, he referred to it as "*my* Father's
House."

New Age Spirituality keeps losing Jesus because it reduces
him to just another voice and just another teacher or master. No
other claimant referred to the temple in the first person singular.
This was a house of prayer for all nations. But it was also the
place where God had said he would meet with them as a community. The boy Jesus was lost in the very place where he was found.
I shall say more on this later and on the fault of Christendom at
large for this great and costly loss.

It Happens All the Time

First, missing the Word; second, missing the Son. Now third,
missing the Truth.

There is a third scene. This of all scenarios takes place when
the three factors of religious authority, cultural practice, and
political power converge. In John's Gospel, chapter 18, once again
it is Passover time. Jesus is not a boy now. He is a full-grown man,

and his work is about to come to an end. The religious leaders are at their most powerful and most self-impressed at this nationally important time of the year as they lead the nation in their ceremonial worship. Cultural expressions come into play, including a custom that granted one prisoner special grace, someone guilty of petty crimes, practices that the culture deemed a violation of their convictions, or even a hard-core criminal.

It is during this time that Jesus is brought before Pilate, who is engaged in a tug-of-war between Caesar and the religious authorities in Judea who threatened Pilate with disloyalty to Caesar if he did not give them their way with Jesus. If they could persuade Pilate that Jesus was seditious and a religious extremist standing against Roman authority, they could accomplish their goals to do away with him, justifying his death with sound political reasoning.

At the end of John 18 we find Jesus standing bound before Pilate. Pilate tries to engage Jesus by asking him if he is indeed the king of the Jews (v. 33). Jesus very shrewdly asks him whether his question is genuine or he has been set up for it. I have said on numerous occasions that intent precedes content. Pilate, somewhat exasperated, tells him that though he has had nothing to do with Jesus' arrest, his future is now in Pilate's hands. Isn't this the arrogance with which political rulers and media pundits live? We see articles, especially around Christmas and Easter, asking, "Is there a future for God?" It is also the question Stalin and Mao asked and answered in the negative. They are both gone, and the Church in China is the strongest it has ever been, while much of the same is happening in Russia. The question should really be whether, apart from God, there is any future for humanity.

Jesus' response to Pilate's question is profound. "My kingdom is not of this world," he says (John 18:36 NIV).

"You *are* a king, then!" comes Pilate's triumphant response (v. 37 NIV). This is something he can wrest to his advantage.

Jesus replies, "In fact, the reason I was born and came into the world is to testify to the truth. Everyone on the side of truth listens to me." (v. 37 NIV).

"What is truth?" asks Pilate in disgust, and he walks away (v. 38 NIV).

I have to think that this is one of the most defining moments in the Bible. Pause and put this in context. In the prophecy of Isaiah, we read, "For to us a child is born, to us a son is given" (9:6 NIV). Note carefully that the Son is not born: The Son eternally existed.

Note now that Jesus says, "The reason I was born…" The incarnation of Jesus did not *create* him; it brought him down into the context of our human condition. He did not need to *attain* God-consciousness; he was God in the flesh, the incarnate expression of God. He did not reach a pinnacle by doing what he did; it was because of "who" he already was that he did what he did. In fact, in the book of Philippians we are told that although Jesus "existed in the form of God, [he] did not regard equality with God a thing to be grasped" (2: 6 NASB). The very thing the New Spiritualists make of him, a man who has attained God-consciousness (Chopra in particular), is specifically denied in the Scriptures. The Bible goes on to say in Hebrews 1 that in previous times God had spoken to us through his prophets, but now in the latter days, he has spoken to us through his Son: The "Word of God" had become "flesh" and lived among us.

The people to whom the Word and God's miracles were given lost him in the bustle of ceremony. His parents lost Jesus because they didn't completely understand who he was. Now we have lost him because we prefer to live a lie rather than the truth;

we prefer to believe that we are gods ourselves when, in truth, we are the glory of creation gone wrong. We have set up a context of rebellion within ourselves against him and are therefore no longer on the side of truth. Jesus makes a sweeping statement that our true intentions regarding truth or falsehood are revealed by what we do with him.

If there is any passage of Scripture that accurately describes our modern-day contempt for truth, our attachment to power, and our voluntary surrender to culture, it is this. It is not accidental that religious authorities, political appointees, and cultural symbols have come together to crucify him once again in our day. Barabbas was released…a cultural practice was fulfilled. "We have a law"…political correctness was enjoined. "He claims to be the Son of God…kill him"…all at the behest and with the blessing of religion. The irony is that he wanted to be owned by none of the three: culture, politics, or religion.

It is very easy to lose Jesus in the plethora of temple practices. It is easy to lose him in the busyness of our family lives. It is easy to limit him in the name of our laws. This is the strongest indictment I make against the New Spirituality. They have violated the true Jesus and formed him in their own image. While exalting themselves, they have denigrated him. Against the backdrop and the evolving ethics of a culture that is lost, the New Spirituality has manipulated the text of Scripture, ignored history with redefinitions of their own to leverage cultural desires to their own advantage. Consider the cultural hits they take at Christianity, which gain them a hearing from the same ones who would like to reject Christianity because of their own moral choices.

Not only did culture, politics, and religion or spirituality come together to kill Jesus, ironically, only in him do the Word, the flesh, and the absolute come together. John says in the first chapter of his Gospel, "In the beginning was the Word, and the Word was with God, and the Word was God…[And] the Word became flesh and made his dwelling among us. We have seen his glory, the glory of the one and only Son, who came from the Father, full of grace and truth" (vv. 1, 14 NIV).

In this one passage, the Gospel writer shatters the false beliefs of the Gnostics and the legalists. The incarnation of Jesus showed that the flesh was not corrupt, though it was corruptible. Jesus showed us that "in the flesh" we could see the glory of God. How wonderful it is that all that is lost can be found in him, through grace. Today we are a little more sophisticated than Jesus' parents. We do not lose him in places; we evict him from our lives and justify it with ideas.

CHAPTER 12

❧

RESHAPING JESUS TO SUIT OUR PREJUDICES

The Distorted Jesus

There is something very clever about the way the New Spiritualists deal with the Bible. A look at the extensive reading list on spirituality in Elizabeth Lesser's book betrays the prejudice. As I already noted, among the numerous books of Eastern authorship, C. S. Lewis is the only author listed who has a high view of the Bible. So when it comes to the Old and New Testaments, this amazing annotation comes from Lesser:

> Any modern traveler in the Landscape of the Soul will find the holy books of Judaism and Christianity helpful in two distinct ways. First, they explain the Western psyche and worldview; and second, they offer some of the most inspiring teachings and parables ever written.[1]

"First, they explain the Western psyche and worldview." What an incredible statement to make by one who supposedly displays scholarship. The Bible is an Eastern book about an Eastern people. Explaining Western psyche by reading the Bible, except as the Bible has influenced Western thought and culture, is to explain Eastern psyche by reading The Book of Mormon. This is the hermeneutical distortion that pervades so much of the New Spirituality. But there's a clue here. These are really psychologists masquerading as linguists and theologians. There are strains of William James and Carl Gustav Jung and others as well in what they say. This is precisely what Sri Sri Ravi Shankar does to a greater degree and Vivekananda does to a lesser degree. In one sense it is not fair to Vivekananda to put him in with this group. Vivekananda was a real scholar, but his forays into the explanation of Jesus give impetus to those of lesser credentials.

The Non-Crucified Jesus

The musings of Eckhart Tolle reveal the same word games when it comes to the historical Jesus. Tolle is the master of saying nothing while the masses sit and gaze at him in awe. I find it hard to believe that his pronouncements on life's deepest issues are actually taken with any seriousness by his readers. That is as kindly as I can state it. Here is his treatment of the phrase "the way of the cross":

> There are many accounts of people who say they have found God through their deep suffering, and there is the Christian expression "the way of the cross," which I suppose points to the same thing...Strictly speaking, they did not find God through their suffering...I don't call it

finding God, because how can you find that which was never lost, the very life that you are? The word God is limiting not only because of thousands of years of misperception and misuse, but also because it implies an entity other than you. God is Being itself, not a being. There can be no subject-object relationship here, no duality, no you *and* God...The worst thing in your life, your cross, turns into the best thing that ever happened to you, by forcing you into surrender, into "death," forcing you to become as nothing, to become as God—because God, too, is nothing.[2]

I remember in my teens listening to a sermon titled "Something About Nothing." As we walked out of the church, and everyone was secretly wondering what on earth that was about, one man leaned forward and whispered into my ear, "At least he warned us about the content." Tolle is the most verbose writer on "nothing" one can read. But he sure does it well. By the time you finish the book you are no longer in the same "now" as when you started, and, fascinatingly, you are no longer the same "you" who began it. Such discussions, once saved for comedian Bob Newhart in his comedy routine as a psychiatrist, now are mass-marketed as brilliance and enlightenment.

The Nonjudgmental Jesus

Of course, Neale Donald Walsch's *Conversations with God* could not possibly come in one volume: It required three volumes. Obviously, he wasn't just living in the now. He alerted us that there would be a "then." Can you figure out why? The answer is not hard. But Walsch claims to be speaking for God. This is probably the ultimate Screwtape scenario in its most seductive form. At least in Lewis's *Screwtape Letters* we knew who Screwtape was. In *Conversations with God*, we are given the ultimate lie that this is God or a surrogate for God, at best, speaking. Below is one conversation Walsch imagines:

> "Why did you create two sexes?…How should we deal with this incredible experience called sexuality?"
>
> [God's answer from Walsch's pen:] "Not with shame, that's for sure. And not with guilt, and not with fear…. Personal gratification has got a bad rap through the years, which is the main reason so much guilt is attached to sex…Practice saying this ten times each day: I LOVE SEX…I LOVE MONEY…I LOVE ME! Religion would have you take its word for it. That is why all religions ultimately fail! *Spirituality* on the other hand, will always succeed. *Self-denial is destruction.*"[3]

In a section where, in effect, Hitler is given a pass into heaven, the chapter ends with "God" speaking thus:

> Shall you then condemn Adam and Eve, or thank them? And what, say you, shall I do with Hitler? I tell you this: God's love and God's compassion, God's wisdom and God's forgiveness, God's intention and God's purpose, are large enough to include the most heinous crime and the most heinous criminal.
>
> You may not agree with this, but it does not matter. You have just learned what you came here to discover.[4]

There are other supposed discussions with God in Walsch's book that I would not even quote. It is the new brash, crude, and vulgar way of desensitizing us to the sacred and deforming our mind-set, all in the name of "God talk."

But then again, it is not quite original. When society ceases to think rationally, and when passions reign supreme to overthrow everything that stands in the way of our autonomy, then the more radical the teaching, the more coverage it gets. The more coverage it gets, the more famous the propagators become. The more famous they become, the less respect they have for anyone who doesn't agree with them. Their arrogance becomes self-deification. The "noble" stance of not judging anything or anyone has truly eradicated distinctions, and words are used to tell us there is really no particular meaning to anything. This line of reasoning also reflects their spiritual sources.

Let me end this section with a quote from the Gita, which reflects Donald Walsch's ideas, centuries ago:

Whatever happened is good.
Whatever is happening is also good.
Whatever will happen, that also will be good.
What did you lose that you are crying for?
What did you bring which you have lost?
What have you created that is destroyed?
Whatever you have taken is taken only from here.
Whatever you have given is given only from here.
Whatever is yours today will belong to somebody else
    tomorrow.
This inevitable change is the law of the universe and the object of
    my creation. (Krishna)

Disregard all the tenses, Tolle notwithstanding, and you have here the erosion of moral categories: In Tolle, you have the erosion of temporal categories; in Walsch, the erosion of essential categories; and in all the writers of the New Spirituality, ultimately the erosion of moral absolutes. This is a deadly word game at work. Morality, time, essence, absolutes—all are gone by the wayside in the name of spirituality. What is left but to deny anyone who still holds to those distinctions. So, refashion Jesus.

The Nonexclusive Jesus

Elizabeth Lesser writes from the perspective of her own spiritual journey that there's no need to limit your source of wisdom to one tradition or even to religion at all...that what resonates with your own experience is enough to spur you on to discovering "the vast and unified and fundamental consciousness" that she calls God.[5]

This is the ultimate knife put to the heart of transcendence. You are the transcendent one. You determine that there is no God out there. You are the ultimate alpha and omega. You select what suits you best. Says who? Not necessarily you, but "they."

Enlightened Jesus

I would have to say that if there is one book that most displays the distortion of the thinking behind the New Spirituality, it is Deepak Chopra's most unfortunate book *The Third Jesus*. It is a book that ought never to have been written. I will have to beg indulgence here because it is not often that I react as strongly to another's point of view, but it has been a long time since I have read such an ill-directed work on so lofty a theme. He is outside his league here. Frankly, time and again he betrays his ignorance of both the text and the context, and I dare say of the languages of the text. One has to wonder whether he had surrogate writers because the references often reveal more of how little he actually knows on the subject than of what he knows.

But before we even get into his text, I have some questions. First, the book is dedicated to "the Irish Christian Brothers in India who introduced me to Jesus when I was a little boy." Is the Jesus they introduced him to the Jesus of his text?

Next take a look at the endorsements in the book. There is not one author in that long list of names who actually believes the Bible is the Word of God. I may as well write a critique of Hinduism and ask Muslim scholars to endorse it. To have Bishop Spong endorsing a book on Jesus borders on comedy. And if Spong's endorsement of Chopra's Jesus means anything, then his own thesis on Jesus in the books he has written is wrong.

But all of this is part of the packaging of Chopra. So let's get on with the substance. Why does he title the book *The Third Jesus*? According to Chopra, "The historical Jesus has been lost... swept away by history." He says that "the first Jesus was a rabbi who wandered the shores of northern Galilee many centuries ago." According to Chopra, the first Jesus is less than consistent in his teachings, "as a closer reading of the gospels will show... And yet," he says, "the more contradictions we unearth, the less mythical this Jesus becomes. ...As one famous Indian spiritual teacher once said, 'The measurement of enlightenment is how comfortable you feel with your own contradictions.'"[6]

What is Chopra saying? He demeans the actions and sayings of Jesus by calling them "contradictory" while inferring that this is a positive attribute. The New Spiritualists are the ones who accuse those who are rationally driven of holding too narrow a view of life, but they are not slow to hurl the charge of contradiction at Christianity. And Chopra doesn't mean it to be something positive when he accuses Christianity of contradictions. But once again, he gives himself an escape hatch by throwing in the quote: "The measurement of enlightenment is how comfortable you feel with your own contradictions."

One can only shake one's head and ask how it is even possible to think in these terms. But this is vintage Deepak Chopra. And supposedly, he understands what he is talking about. So he continues:

> Millions of people worship another Jesus…who never existed, who doesn't even lay claim to the fleeting substance of the first Jesus. This is the Jesus built up over thousands of years by theologians and other scholars… the Holy Ghost, the Three-in-One Christ, the source of sacraments and prayers that were unknown to the rabbi Jesus when he walked the earth…the Prince of Peace over whom bloody wars have been fought. This second Jesus cannot be embraced without embracing theology first.
>
> The second Jesus leads us into the wilderness without a clear path out. He became the foundation of a religion that has proliferated into some twenty thousand sects [that] argue endlessly over every thread in the garments of a ghost.…Yet in his name Christianity pronounces on homosexuality, birth control, and abortion.[7]

I cannot resist a comment here. Such arrant nonsense from the pen of an educated man is unfathomable. It is actually deplorable and manipulative. "The Holy Ghost, the Three-in-One Christ." I am not at all sure what he is referring to. Who made Jesus the Holy Ghost? Christ never claimed to be three-in-one. Chopra doesn't seem to understand that they are distinct personages. I might add that if he is criticizing the Christian doctrine of the Trinity, as he seems to be, and he finds it difficult to believe in "three-in-one," how is it that he has no problem believing that all of humanity is One? And when he ran into problematic explanations of certain behaviors in the gurus, he tells us that each of them is actually three-in-one. (This is relayed in more detail in Chapter 13.)

Further, is it reasonable to suppose that Chopra, a medical doctor, an ethicist, and a person who believes every human has the spark of divinity within them, has no pronouncements on abortion? Coming from a country with such a huge population, he has nothing to say about birth control? You can be absolutely sure, without a shadow of a doubt, that Chopra knows exactly what he is appealing to here. Does he not know the difference between Catholic and Protestant doctrines? These comments are stabs in the backs of his "Irish Christian Brothers."

The intellectual side of his statement is empty. Mr. Chopra is blatantly resorting to cultural provocation while disguising irrational deductions in vacuous meaning. What has this theological Christ got to do with these issues? He knows exactly what. These are the issues that prompt those who do not want any view on sexuality or abortion brought to bear on their own private choices to despise Christianity. What better way can he find to make his thesis sound plausible to them than to introduce a caricature of that which is the source of their rejection? For a man positing Sanatan Dharma, there is a heavy dose of hate-provocation at work underlying his pronouncements. I would like to hear him instead respond to the famed Indian guru Swami Ramdev, who pronounced homosexuality as a mental illness and declared he can cure cancer through yoga. Interesting that these swamis and gurus get a pass on such pronouncements. Don't be fooled by Chopra's use of serene terminology. It is obvious what communication skill he is utilizing.

According to Chopra, these two versions of Jesus that he has invented, what he calls the "sketchy historical figure and the abstract theological creation," have stolen from the world "something precious: The Jesus who taught his followers how to reach God-consciousness."[8] It is appalling to even think that an honest scholar would denude the Christ of history of his authenticity and then complain that those who believe in that historical Christ have stolen something precious from him.

But in the introduction of his book he laid the groundwork for his deduction, categorically declaring that Jesus did not physically descend from God, nor did he return to heaven to sit at the right hand of God. He states that what made Jesus the Son of God was that he achieved God-consciousness, which, he says, Jesus himself affirmed over and over again by declaring that he and the Father are one.[9]

Such a thesis presented in the name of scholarship would never have been taken seriously in a school that respects the integrity of hermeneutics. Hermeneutics is the science of interpretation that seeks to wrestle honestly with the text from its history and grammar. Let me just posit three things for starters, to show how uninformed Dr. Chopra is.

First, Chopra comments that Jesus said "over and over, ... 'The Father and I are one.'" He uses this text to sustain his claim that Jesus "attained" God-consciousness. Really? Did Jesus use this phrase "over and over"?" He stated it once and only once, in the

Gospel of John. Not only that, the context in which he said it was that he (Jesus) is the only way to the Father.

Chopra's manipulation of these texts to make them say what he wants them to say is no different from his manipulation of Hinduism, borrowing from its underpinnings to make his Sanatan Dharma appear eclectic and uncategorized. But there is more. To sustain his thesis that this "third" Jesus attained enlightenment, he misuses scores of passages from the New Testament, the very source he has already disparaged by denying that we really know anything about the historic Jesus. So which is it? Are these passages true or not? If they are true enough for him to use as references for his theory, why does he insist their context is not true in what they say about Jesus? Let me put it differently. It would be like me saying that the Vedas are historically suspect and unreliable and then using those same Vedas to prove that Jesus is the truth.

His inaccuracies continue. His description of Jesus as the Son of Man betrays a total ignorance of the technical nature of that title. In short, the new Sanatan Dharma spirituality that he espouses by reducing the Jesus of history to his own distorted hermeneutical mold is reflective of a dishonest scholarship that cannot have it both ways. He cannot use the text to prove his point and reject the text in order to create his book.

Then he hides inside a universal solvent ideology that can't be stored anywhere. This is typical of the New Spirituality writers when they like to suggest that their teachings also incorporate the Bible. He begins his chapter on "Karma—Sowing and Reaping" by saying that finding out how much Jesus has to say about karma was a great surprise to him in writing this book. The primary tenet of karma, he says, is that every action works like a seed that sprouts and brings fruit in the form of a result.

Once again, Chopra plays with doctrines. That "primary" tenet of karma is not merely a connection between sowing and reaping, but is woven into the systemic belief that every birth is a rebirth. Into the belief that every birth is a rebirth, the karmic cycle is introduced. He ends his section on karma by first quoting Matthew 11:30: "For my yoke is easy, and my burden is light," and then saying that Jesus promised his followers there would be no work in heaven, the greater implication being that karma would no longer exist, based on his own experience in heaven, and on Chopra's belief that the English word *yoke* comes from the same root word as *yoga* … "union with God."[10]

This is such pathetic nonsense I'm surprised he didn't say that this is a demonstration that Jesus also believed in a weight-loss program, since his "burden is light."

Second, Chopra engages in a classic misuse of sources. He intermixes apocryphal writings with Gnostic writings, and, frankly, I'm not sure what some of his sources are for what he says. A quotation he claims is from the "Gospel of Thomas," which has 114 verses, he footnotes as "verse 144, 172 et al."; some of the other quotes he uses find no parallel in any translation. There are no such verses. Unless he has his own version, there is none that matches these quotes, even remotely. It could be, of course, that some research person gave him this information and Chopra didn't even know that there are only 114 verses in the so-called "Gospel of Thomas," which is actually not a Gospel and most certainly is not by Thomas.

Third, Chopra is most distorted in his interpretations when he comes to the hard passages. In John 14:6–7, Jesus says, "I am the way and the truth and the life. No one comes to the Father except through me. If you really know me, you will know my Father as well. From now on you do know him and have seen him" (NIV).

Jesus said these words in the context that he was preparing heaven for his followers and his followers for heaven. Chopra's comment on this verse is that the Gospel writer was trying to confirm Jesus as Messiah beyond dispute, as the resurrection was a fading memory after the destruction of the temple in Jerusalem.

Where does he get the idea that the resurrection was a fading memory? Does he not realize that the message of the resurrection was about to conquer Rome when this Gospel was written, to say nothing of its impact over the entire region? In effect, he is saying that Jesus never spoke these words, that John manufactured this verse. Chopra is all at sea here. It seems to matter nothing what Jesus says or affirms or declares; in Chopra's vocabulary, "higher consciousness" is the escape button, because that's where he wants to take us. He does the same thing again with the most familiar passages, such as John 3:16, which says, "For God so loved the world that he gave his one and only Son, that whoever believes in him shall not perish but have eternal life" (NIV). Chopra changes the context and makes it a pretext again to reduce the truth into something that can serve his intended ends.

I wonder if he would do such a thing with the Koran? Call it intellectual cowardice or hypocrisy or both, but his tactic of distorting the New Testament to prove his point is actually self-stultifying. Unfortunately, he attains his goal of deceiving those who don't know any better. His is not inductive or deductive reasoning. It is fuzzy logic garnered to suit an end in view.

Leveling (Actually, Tilting) the Playing Field

See the New Age Spirituality for what it is; a systemic methodology of appealing to a cultural mind-set that despises certain things and that follows a reductionistic approach that actually distorts any claimant to truth that differs from those the New Spirituality endorses in order to make them all say the same thing. This is the goal of the New Spirituality. Bring everything to the same level. There is a clear agenda. In their deep prejudice against Christianity, advocates of the New Spirituality malign the Christ of history in order to remake him into an image that is consistent with their ideas.

In his one-volume brief synopsis of spiritual writers, *50 Spiritual Classics*, English author Tom Butler-Bowdon reveals this prejudice even more clearly. From covering all kinds of extreme positions on spirituality, including that of Ram Dass, and giving them all a pass even in their dangerous recommendations, he nevertheless finds enough in his pen to cast in negative light any Christian writer who holds to salvation through Christ.

Some readers may remember that Ram Dass is actually Dr. Richard Alpert, former professor of psychology at Harvard. In the 1960s he became a drinking buddy of Timothy Leary and discovered getting high on the black mushrooms in Mexico. Alpert and Leary, along with Aldous Huxley, acquired a synthetic form of this "magic" mushroom, psilocybin, which they said produced within them visions and helped them experience the "I" behind the facade of knowledge, the "I" of timeless awareness. This was just what Alpert had been looking for. Leaving his position at Harvard, he backpacked through India and met up with another American, a guru named Bhagwan Dass. Bhagwan Dass (we are never given his American name) introduced Richard Alpert to the teaching of "the Now" in his pre-Tolle version, and Richard Alpert was "delivered" from his "sheer rationality based thinking" into a new consciousness and became Ram Dass. Ram Dass, whose name means "servant of Ram," the Hindu deity, came under the tutelage of Bhagwan Dass, whose name means "servant of God." He was moved, in his words, "beyond personality to consciousness" and "beyond rationality." Ram Dass went on to write a book titled *Be Here Now: A Cookbook for a Sacred Life,* in which he talks of the means of "awakening, from meditation to fasting to drugs."[11]

Many readers may not be aware that a vast majority of the men in India's holy city of Varanasi are knocked out on drugs during Shivratri, a euphoric celebration of the third member of the Hindu Trimurti, Shiva the Destroyer. The night is spent in a drug-indulging stupor, no doubt Ram Dass's kind of celebration. I mention this because Butler-Bowden goes on to say that Ram Dass's book is "one of the outstanding works of spiritual transformation" that "reminds us of Augustine."[12] It is really too bad that Augustine is not here to request that his name be removed from this list.

Regarding Rick Warren's *Purpose Driven Life,* Butler-Bowden's critique is that some readers will be offended by the Christian fundamentalist posture of the book. He finds Warren's statement that one is saved only through faith in Christ "a little threatening" and takes issue with Warren for not giving credence to other faiths or traditions. "Religious fervor is one thing," he says, "but denying the truth of other beliefs is what makes *The Purpose Driven Life* seem, in places, quite narrow." He also takes great offense at Warren's support of missions, or of taking the message of Christ to other people in other areas of the world.[13]

Butler-Bowdon's discussion of the meaning and application of C. S. Lewis's *Screwtape Letters* is very shallow, and he challenges the reader to lift it beyond its narrow confines into their own. One gets accustomed to seeing these comments reserved for Christian thinkers/writers and to laments that the Christ of history and experience is lost in their writings, and to the most pejorative words being reserved for those who follow Christ.

Here is the summary of it all: If you take all the religions of the world and all the claimants to divine or prophetic status and make them all equal (but the theistic ones less equal), then you have at work a false induction, which takes you through the seductive use of language and reduces spirituality to a pragmatic mysticism until it deduces that, after all, there is only One. And that One is you. The playing field is not level. It is tilted against any monotheistic faith and is pantheistic in its determined starting and ending points. Writers such as Butler-Bowdon are really not presenters of classics…they are ideologically driven and cannot resist reserving their sharpest barbs for Christianity.

But notice the genius. By wresting a cultural tension to their advantage, be it the environment or sexuality or gender conflict or political correctness, they engender a negative attitude toward anything that smacks of the "old authorities" (unless they are pantheistic) or of absolutes, and find then a heart ready to rebel into autonomy. The New Spirituality encourages a unified theory of God, which is actually a nondefined entity, a made-to-measure religion for each and every person. But don't be fooled by this "Let's get together" spiritual talk. The reason there are so many movements and voices and organizations and treatment centers and retreat places is that they do not believe their own communal theory of spirituality. It is truly a case of each one with his or her personal brand of spirituality, grabbing the newest ancient source to appear more esoteric than the next. What is lost, in the end, is any distinction between God, humanity, and the animal world. That is why all these definitions appeal to intuition gained through introspection. The New Spirituality will have its shelf life, and it, too, will someday suffer the same fate as Christianity when it became commercialized.

The apostle Paul summarized this ploy two thousand years ago in his letter to the Romans when he said:

> Since the creation of the world God's invisible qualities— his eternal power and divine nature—have been clearly seen, being understood from what has been made, so that people are without excuse. For although they knew God, they neither glorified him as God nor gave thanks to him, but their thinking became futile and their foolish hearts were darkened. Although they claimed to be wise, they became fools and exchanged the glory of the immortal God for images made to look like a mortal human being and birds and animals and reptiles. (1:20–23 NIV)

There Is a Reason

Before offering a brief critique of the New Spirituality, I must say there are some areas in which the Church must bear some of the blame for the discredit that has been brought to her by the New Spiritualists:

1. Churches that do justice to the message of Christ and his claim upon our lives are rare. "Churches," said one critic to me, "are country clubs for the nice people…they are really not so nice to everyone else." I have to admit that I've personally sat through some large gatherings of Christians after which I have walked out and wondered what I would have thought of Christianity if that was what I had heard before I came to Christ. For the most part there is

a huge gap between the preaching and worship of today and what faith in Christ and the worship of God were intended to be.

I am afraid that the forms and the programs have commandeered the message of Jesus into a kind of show and entertainment mold, where the congregants are merely spectators who have come to watch a show. I have friends who stand outside the churches they attend during the music because it is too deafening inside to endure. But they enjoy the preaching side of it and so step into the church at that time. Others tell me that they have stopped going to church because there is absolutely no substance to anything that is being taught. Still others tell me that after they had stumbled and fallen into a lifestyle or found themselves in a situation they had never wanted to be in, they ended up in a church. Hoping for healing and a chance to rebuild, they instead were pummeled with more and more guilt. "Stumble here and you've had it," said one to me. One said, "I know the Lord hates divorce. Every person who has experienced divorce hates it, too. But why does the church hate the divorced person?" A probing question that brings tears to the one who asks it and should to the one of whom it is asked.

The legalism of the Church has disenfranchised so many that the Church has found itself speaking to just the handful who still agree with its castigations and have lost the many who need its healing message of love. But let me add here that this is not so just in Christianity. In the culture in which I was raised, Hindu, Muslim, Buddhist, Christian, you name it, if you have a broken record, your name is sullied forever. So let's not just blame Christianity. Growing up in a predominantly Hindu culture, I was taught that if a woman was even seen with a man, her name would be tarnished permanently and no proposal of marriage would be forthcoming. This attitude, by the way, is the same basis for so-called honor-killings in Islam.

How does the Church maintain its teaching while at the same time love the fallen in this changing world of ours? Love does have its boundaries, but it must have a long reach. Those who are hurting and faltering need the strong arm of God to hold them. The Church has to provide those arms. Jesus himself said, "It is not the healthy who need a doctor, but the sick. But go and learn what this means: 'I desire mercy, not sacrifice.' For I have not come to call the righteous, but sinners" (Matthew 9:12 NIV). If we are to reflect Christ to the world around us, we need to "learn what this means," as Jesus said.

2. The Church has forgotten the teachings of quietness, solitude, and meditation that are part of our Judeo-Christian heritage and provide great strength to the soul. We have moved from silence to noise. We have moved from reflection to fast-moving programs. We have moved from quietness to the inability to remain focused on a thought for even a moment, so that the next item on the program has to begin as soon as the previous one has finished. There is no time in our services anymore for quietness and contemplation. We have moved from the progression of thought to a repetition of sounds. We have stolen the bridge between the head and the heart and gone to one of two extremes: either unable to engage the culture or reflecting the culture. Every need of the soul is met in the gospel, but like an intoxicated person, we swing between two walls without finding balance.

The New Spirituality compels us to examine how we do what we do. Our challenge is how to do it in form, without compromising the substance of what we believe. The need for community is a deep longing in the postmodern mind-set. How we build that community will shape the Church of the future. But while the New Spirituality points us to the weaknesses of the Church, the one thing in the Church's defense is that its violations are violations of its message. The flaw in the New Spirituality is in the message itself.

3. The institutionalization of Christianity made it vulnerable to all of the abuses we now see.

4. The problem of pain has not always been honestly and meaningfully dealt with by Christians. So the New Spiritualists hide behind illusion or koans.

5. The judgmental attitude of the Christian is often harsh and legalistic, forgetting the implications of what is being said. The backlash is that the New Spirituality almost implicitly subscribes to an antinomianism—implying that there really is no moral law.

At the same time, there are fundamental errors in the New Spirituality that I shall point out here before I move to the Christ of history and what he really taught:

1. New Spiritualists misunderstand or misuse the laws of logic. For them to say that they have transcended reason or rationality is to fail to understand the laws of logic. It is one thing to say that reason alone cannot point you to God. That is not new. Blaise Pascal and numerous others pointed that out. But logic does not merely point to the truth; more important, it points to error. Something that is systemically contradictory cannot be true. Yes, there can be paradoxes. Yes, you can have two poles of an argument. But systemic contradiction, where the laws of logic foundationally destroy the base on which the infrastructure stands, simply cannot be defended by "transcending reason." All spirituality has to transcend reason, but it dare not systemically violate it.

For example, Buddhism is atheistic. Some strands of Hinduism, but not all, are not: Which is it? God or no God? Judaism, Christianity, and Islam are monotheistic. To be consistent within itself, the New Spirituality will have to consider the monotheistic religions wrong. But in considering them wrong, they have to use the law of noncontradiction, which means they rely on logic to disavow another system of belief but "transcend logic" when they defend their own system. Gautama Buddha renounced some of the Vedas and the caste system. Was he right or wrong to do so? From the Hindu's point of view, to deny the caste system is to deny karma.

Keep asking. To argue for the "now" in a chronological isolation, while borrowing from "ancient" wisdom and looking to enlightenment in the future, is to toy with time-laden terminology where each term has died the death of a thousand qualifications. Maybe that is why Redfield of *The Celestine Prophecy* coined the term "the longer now" to appreciate humanity across the ages...a clever qualification.

2. Advocates of the New Spirituality falsely absorb two different questions into one. By denying the right of the Christian to legislate on morality, they deny the Christian belief that life and sexuality are sacred. But since they give legitimacy to the destruction of life in the womb while espousing that all life is sacred, their own belief that all life is "sacred" is illegitimate.

3. In personalizing spirituality, they actually end up snuffing out the person. That is an unaffirmable position. To say, in effect, that "I" do not exist is a self-stultifying proposition.

4. They are ultimately unable to define evil, and the core of spirituality is crushed by the wheel of time and human character.

5. They have no transcendent basis for love because spirit in self-reference cannot define love. Love is an "ought." Its prescription has to be from the very source of love. For that, only God is big enough as a person to define it. More to the point, love is not free. It has to have boundaries; otherwise, it is not love at all. It is the nature of love to bind itself.

6. In the process of exalting the individual and his or her right to make a spiritual choice, the New Spiritualists make individual

intuition the ultimate test rather than the objectivity of testing truth claims when examining conflicting worldviews. That test itself is not intuitively sustainable.

7. The notion of erasing time and Tolle's notion of the power of "now" play a dangerous game with the mind. Values past, present, and future are necessary to understand how we must think. I have often put it this way: The traditionalist lives for the past; the utopianist lives for the future; the existentialist lives for the present. When Jesus Christ took bread and broke it to share it with his disciples in what is called Holy Communion, he said, "Whenever you eat this bread and drink this cup [in the present], you proclaim the Lord's death [in the past] until he comes [in the future]" (1 Corinthians 11:26 NIV). The remarkable thing here is that he places importance on all three tenses of time, fusing them with meaning. It is so important that we invest value in time but live for eternity. Jesus and his Word constantly remind us to be delivered from the tyranny of the immediate.

8. No matter how loudly the New Spiritualists deny duality and try to argue for a monistic or single-entity framework, worship, prayer, and rituals all assume a distinction between the "I" and the "you." Advaita, the idea of nondualism, dies on the altar of human hungers and relationships.

Meeting Jesus Where We Need Him Most

Just as there were three key passages in which we saw where we have lost the real Jesus, let me move to three passages in which we find him in the most unexpected places.

The first is early in the Gospels when Jesus is on a journey and he passes through Samaria. To call a person a Samaritan was the meanest racial slur one could have cast in that day. The Samaritans were considered an impure race of an impure religion and were despised by the puritanical. The disciples had left Jesus and gone to fetch some food; it was lunchtime. Jesus saw a Samaritan woman coming to draw water and did a most extraordinary thing. He asked her for a drink. Quite taken aback, she asked him why he, a Jew, would bother to ask a Samaritan for a drink of water, especially a woman. She was shocked. And when his disciples returned to find him talking to her, they experienced their own dose of shock.

Jesus' answer to the woman has become a historic passage of Scripture, preached from for centuries. He told her that if she only knew who she was talking to, she would have asked *him* for a drink, because the water he offered was of a spiritual nature and would satisfy every hunger. Her immediate response was to deflect attention from herself and her hungers and focus on the divisions between the religious sects of her day in their methods of worship and debates over the appropriate holy places. But Jesus was a master at disclosing a person's heart, and he told her that her real problem was not the divisions between religious sects, but her own torn heart. "You have had five husbands," he said, "and the man you now have is not your husband" (John 4:18 NIV).

I ask you this question: Which religion in the world today would have chosen this woman as their first evangelist? Think about it. Not Islam, not a typical Hindu man, not even Christendom, the way religious power brokers have distorted it. But Jesus rescued her from herself, not from the wars within religion but from the war and rejection within herself. She ran back to her village and said, "Come, see a man who told me everything I ever did. Could this be the Messiah?" (4:29 NIV). The fascinating unstated line is, "And he didn't reject me!"

No one in that day would have expected Jesus to converse with this Samaritan woman of five shattered marriages. There are several surprising elements here. Christianity is often portrayed as being anti-woman. The gender wars that have raged over the years are not without reason. This painful subject of gender inequalities, often aided and abetted by institutions of power, has sent many thinking women into a gold mine of rescue in the Gnostic writings of feminine deities and worship. I often wonder if they are really aware of what some of those sources even contain.

Take again, for example, the so-called Gospel of Thomas, which is neither a Gospel nor written by Thomas, as I have already said. Gnostic writings are not Scripture but the writings of some spiritual sect that rejected the historic Christ in order to create their own privatized spirituality. Readers will remember the Jesus Seminar some years ago that attempted to debunk the gospel of Jesus, using the text called the Gospel of Thomas. Supposedly, that shed new light on Jesus' teaching and showed a better way. I would like to quote from the definitive Gnostic text about women, the Gospel of Thomas, Saying 114:

Simon Peter said to all the other disciples, "Let Mary Magdalene go out from among us because women are not worthy of life."

Jesus said, "See, behold, I will lead her so that I can make her a male; so that she, too, by becoming a male can become a living spirit resembling you males. For every women who makes herself a male will enter the Kingdom of Heaven."

Is this the Gnosticism that is supposed to rescue women? I would suggest just one counterperspective to this, but there are many more I could discuss. The most important moment for Christianity came at the resurrection scene of Jesus Christ. To whom did Jesus first reveal himself? In that society, the most important people would have been the high priest and his entourage. In fact, Jesus himself sent the lepers he had healed to the priests in Luke 17:14. The next would have been the disciples who followed him, most of whom were men. It is an incredible thing in that culture that he revealed himself first to the women, whose testimony at a court in that day would not even have been taken as reliable. And that is precisely the counterperspective of the gospel. To those who think Christianity has done a disservice to women, it is critical that they understand from whom the gospel first came. The standards of institutions, even those that claim to represent Jesus, ought not to be made synonymous with the person of Jesus.

There's another point to be made here. The apostle Paul is often made the scapegoat for a male-dominated church. In one of his final letters to his son in the faith, Timothy, Paul reminds Timothy that the Scriptures that were able to make him wise to salvation were taught to Timothy by his mother and his grandmother. That hardly smacks of chauvinism. A particular teaching is often taken out of its larger context and made into a pretext for attacking a system of truth. It is ironic that as humanism has come to the fore, life has been reduced to the essence of a game, and games have been elevated to become the essence of life.

Racial prejudice and gender discrimination are still strong realities in this world, yet race and gender are the only things one does not choose for oneself. In contrast, the opportunity to decide moral imperatives is being taken from us, while in fact, these are the things we *do* choose. That alone ought to tell us what happens when we choose to redefine good and evil, and morality is buried in spiritual or political talk with no transcendent source of authority. We victimize people for no culpable reason and exonerate people in spite of their culpability.

We end up with theories that put Hitler in heaven and consider the disciples fools for being willing to die for the truths of the gospel. But there will come a moment in which we will all stand before the ultimate Judge of the universe, a God who loves us and gave us the beautiful offer of salvation, and he will do that which is ultimately right. The Jesus who was lost where he should have been found, and who is found where we might not expect him to be, is the Jesus who is wantonly misplaced by the New Spirituality. As Alexander Pope suggested:

> *Snatch from his hand the balance and the rod;*
> *Rejudge his justice, be the god of God!*

The Alabaster Touch

This, again, is a story in which we would never expect to find a religious teacher. Jesus is at the home of a respected Pharisee named Simon when an uninvited and unwelcome woman of dubious reputation forces her way into the room and over to the table where the guests are reclining to eat, falling at Jesus' feet. She begins to weep so profusely that her tears fall on his feet and begin to soak them. She unties her long hair and uses it to dry her tears from his feet and then, before the silenced guests, she opens a small alabaster jar and pours the costly ointment, the aroma of which fills the room, over Jesus' feet.

The most interesting thing about the incident is that so little is said about her and who she was…just enough that her story would be told wherever the gospel was preached. The Pharisee, with his sense of self-righteousness, was convinced that Jesus obviously didn't know the character of the woman who dared to lay a hand on him or he would never have allowed such a thing.

But Jesus not only knew who she was, he knew what Simon, the Pharisee, was thinking and caught him off guard by asking him a question:

> "Two people owed money to a certain moneylender. One owed him five hundred [dollars], and the other fifty. Neither of them had the money to pay him back, so he forgave the debts of both. Now which of them will love him more?"
>
> Simon replied, "I suppose the one who had the bigger debt forgiven."
>
> "You have judged correctly," Jesus said…Then Jesus said to [the woman], "Your sins are forgiven…Your faith has saved you; go in peace." (Luke 7:41–50 NIV).

Jesus very subtly pointed out that it was not so much the extent of the debt that was important, but the sense of the indebtedness. The woman recognized something the Pharisee had not: that she needed forgiveness. This is so much at the core of the gospel. The worst effect of sin is that one may not even sense his or her sin. That is the ultimate pride. The woman gave her richest possession for her most impoverished self. Jesus did not respond to the monetary value of the ointment, but to her tears, which reflected the depths of her remorse for her sin and motivated her to part with the only thing she could have claimed as her treasure. This, again, is a story of contrasts. The one who was rejected is the one who was actually accepted by Jesus. The self-righteous Pharisee was far from him in spirit.

Childlike Beauty

The final story I want to mention where we might not expect to find Jesus is told in Luke 18. It is the story of the little children who came to Jesus to sit on his lap and play with him. The disciples were askance at their impudence and with their familiarity with him and rebuked them, sending them away. The idea was, "Don't you realize Jesus is too important to be spending his time with children? He's a famous man. And he's too busy to take time to play. Don't waste his time." They were clearing his calendar for the more important people he had to meet, and the more important conversations he had to have.

But Jesus surprised them. If there is one thing about children, it is their complete dependence on someone else. They simply cannot take care of themselves. Their entire existence is based on someone outside themselves. Jesus said, "Let the little children come to me, and do not hinder them, for the kingdom of God belongs to such as these. Truly I tell you, anyone who will not receive the kingdom of God like a little child will never enter it" (Luke 18:16–17 NIV).

Today, some would use children for suicide missions; others would use their exalted philosophical prowess or techniques to destroy the innocence and faith of children. Jesus pointed to the little ones as a reflection of his kingdom. He meant that it was only our total dependence on God and our trust in him for our salvation that secured us a place in heaven. Just as the children wanted to lean on Jesus, so do we need to lean on him for everything.

Look back for a moment: The Samaritan woman, an ethnic outcast; the woman with the alabaster ointment, the moral outcast; the children with their childlike trust, the intellectual outcasts. There are no breathing exercises necessary here. There is no highly developed philosophy of quantum or highbrow theorizing here. No priority is given to birth or ethnicity here. Of such is the kingdom of heaven…totally unexpected, totally unearned.

God meets us in the most unexpected places, just as we lose him in the least expected places. It was not the prodigal son who returned to the father who missed the gift of grace, it was the older brother who was confident in his own righteousness and believed he deserved to be celebrated who missed the feast. These are startling reminders that we are talking about a person and a relationship, not a place and an idea.

So, the next time you hold a little child in your arms, look into that sweet face and remind yourself, "Unless I become like this little one, trusting in the arms of God, I will never have the resources to live the life God intended." To know such dependence upon him, you can call on him anywhere.

Why Jesus? He is the Lord who makes reality beautiful and helps us to find him, even in the darkest corners of the world; not because of what we know or who we are or what we have accomplished, but because of who he is. He is truly the "Hound of Heaven" who says, "Thou dravest love from thee that dravest me."[14]

CHAPTER 13

~❧

THE GREATEST OF ALL

The most astounding thing about the following poem is not its pathos or its beauty, but that it was written by Oscar Wilde. He was incarcerated in Reading Gaol for a short period of time and one day witnessed the execution of a man who had brutally killed his wife. It is a very lengthy poem. What follows is just a fraction of it:

And every human heart that breaks,
*   In prison-cell or yard,*
Is as that broken box that gave
*   Its treasure to the Lord,*
And filled the unclean leper's house
*   With the scent of costliest nard.*

Ah! Happy day they whose hearts can break
*   And peace of pardon win!*
How else may man make straight his plan
*   And cleanse his soul from Sin?*

How else but through a broken heart
May Lord Christ enter in.[1]

    There's the reference to the woman with the alabaster ointment again. Wilde shows an amazing knowledge of Scripture. Actually, even on his grave in Paris, which has a giant phoenix as its mascot, are words from this poem, coupled with a verse from the book of Job. From the first time I read his story and some of his writings, it was impossible to miss his genius and his tragedy. Wilde died fairly young. It was at his deathbed that he called for a priest, telling his friend Robbie Ross that he wanted to make things right with God. The lines "The crimson stain that was of Cain / Became Christ's snow white seal" find a similar echo in his *Picture of Dorian Gray*. For Wilde to ask for the Eucharist on his deathbed signaled that he was serious about making it right, through Jesus.

    Let me switch scenes to several decades later. There lies a man in a hospital room. He was not an author, he is not renowned, he is just a man of high integrity, devout in his faith. He has spent many hours of his life in a temple, and everyone he knows describes him as a man of near impeccable character. The man is in his eighties and once held a high post in India's Finance Ministry. He has spent hours with us over the years, his son and I, speaking about spiritual matters, probing, questioning, challenging us, and reading heavily on spiritual themes. Stricken with cancer, he has been admitted to the hospital. At his request, all his friends have come to the hospital today, straight from the temple with their "Prasad," their sweet offerings, to give him their good wishes and a blessing from the priest. They mill around his bed, talking softly to one another. They do not know what awaits them.

Suddenly, he sits up in bed and speaks to them in clear terms. He says that he believes his moment to die has come and he wants to share with them, his family and friends, what he has just experienced. "I have lain here in bed asking myself the most important question," he says: "What or who is the way to God? I have pondered this for years...You know how faithful I have been in my service to the temple and to my belief. But I have come to this all-important moment and question: What is the way? Who is the way?"

He pauses as they lean forward to listen. "I have thought, reflected, and have finally concluded that there is only one way, and I want you to understand I am making that commitment." His voice lifts and his passion deepens. "That way is Jesus."

In the stunned silence that follows his declaration of faith in Christ he does something amazing, something only an Indian family could fully appreciate. He has lived a life of honor, married for more than fifty years through an arranged marriage, and has raised two sons. He turns now to his wife and says to her, "I have never told you that I love you. But I want you to know that I do love you and that you are my sweetheart." His wife is very embarrassed and dismayed by what he has said and doesn't quite know how to respond. He turns to his granddaughter and asks her to sing his favorite Christian hymn. With that, shortly thereafter he breathes his last breath. His friends are dumbfounded and stand in awkward silence around his bed, not knowing how to think about what he has said and done, what to say or what to do.[2]

As I write this, I think deeply. How is it that a man who had heard almost nothing of Jesus until he was well into his middle years came to this conclusion? How is it that a man so devout, whose house I visited frequently, where there was always an altar set aside to the pantheon of divinities in Hinduism, came to such a clear conviction of salvation through Jesus? How does one so totally consumed by his faith, and active in the temple, come to the end of his life and take a fork in the road?

This is something the New Spiritualists have to deal with honestly. How do they explain it? Did this honorable, devout man, and others like him, come to this intuitive conclusion wrongly? Did he make up a truth that was totally unsustained in his entire life prior to that point? From Oscar Wilde to thousands today in the Middle East and China, the same story is being repeated. These things are happening in lands where the name of Jesus has been maligned or evicted by political or cultural decree. Yet they have found him.

I have no doubt that many might well be offended by the challenges I have made to other beliefs in this book. I must expect that and will make every effort to defend my approach. Some might even consider the tone of this book too strong or harsh. That is not my intent. But it is hard not to get passionate when you read the bizarre twists of truth offered by proponents of the New Spirituality. I have been fairly blunt because I want readers to be brutally honest with themselves.

True spirituality is not a game we play. It is not merely a preference for some position over another. Nor is it at its core a search for some healing balm. It is an ultimate choice of ultimate definitions that require one's utmost commitment. One had dare not make a commitment to a belief for secondary or tertiary reasons or to "feel good." The issues of gender and sexuality are extremely important...I understand how important they are. But they are secondary to *why* we are living and *for whom* we are living. To be driven to adopt a combination of myth and mysticism because of blunders made by cultural exploiters in society is to run from the arms of a lion into the arms of a bear. There is little comfort in that.

In the beginning of this chapter, I highlighted two personalities to demonstrate that the pleasure-loving artist and the disciplined civil servant had each tried, in their own way, to find life's ultimate thrill. One, dying from a disease probably brought on by promiscuity; the other dying merely from the breakdown of the body in aging, who found out as all of us will that the body is not ageless, no matter how much we would like to believe otherwise. One lived a life of abandonment in the West; the other persisted in a morally and spiritually disciplined existence mainly in the East. One flirted with the law; the other upheld the law rigorously. One lived with multiple options and partners; the other was stoic in his commitment right to the end. One was a hedonist; the other devoutly spiritual. To both, the answer was in the same person: Jesus Christ. Why?

The Divine Conqueror

The words of Algernon Charles Swinburne (1837–1909) often come to my mind: "Thou hast conquered, oh pale Galilean. The world has grown grey from thy breath." These words were not originally stated by Swinburne; "Thou hast conquered, oh pale Galilean" was originally spoken by the Roman emperor Julian about the acceptance of Christianity under the emperor Constantine. I am reminded as well of the words of historian Will Durant, that Caesar and Christ had met in the arena and Christ had won.

Both of these statements are unfortunate. Jesus is not a

political conqueror, nor is he a gladiator. He did not teach a political theory as the superintending boundary for people. The aligning of politics with his name is a huge risk to both a political position and to the Christian faith. History is replete with such examples. Various nations have claimed that he walked there or have yearned to be the site of the New Jerusalem, as in the imaginings of William Blake.[3] These sentiments may be moving and powerful, but they bring fearsomeness to the scene. Making England the site of the New Jerusalem (or the seat of God) may be a noble idea, but throughout their history the English have certainly not behaved as citizens of a holy city. For that matter, neither have the inhabitants of Jerusalem, and now more recently the story is retold in America. A man recently made a strongly critical remark to me about America and added, "How can a Christian nation act like that?" I surprised him by asking, "Who told you it is a Christian nation?" It made for a fascinating discussion.

It is true that the unshakable principles and ideas on which America was founded are clearly Judeo-Christian. But with each succeeding generation there has increasingly come the desire to shake off the lessons and ideas from the past. America is rich in wealth but poverty-stricken in understanding the reasons for its wealth and has an abysmal ignorance of history, its own as well as anyone else's. In fact, aided and programmed by the news, anything a week old no longer holds any interest. We live with the remote control in our hands, changing scenes by the minute. I remember one politician telling me that most politicians don't even fear a scandal anymore because they know it will soon be swept away by the next day's news.

Our inability to focus or stay the course is reflected in our spirituality in America. It is amazing how jelly-like it is, how it shifts and shapes itself to the individual as truth is remade in his or her image. We would do well to remember the famed aphorism that anyone who refuses to learn from history is forced to repeat its mistakes.

To that end, the message of Jesus Christ is both timely and timeless. He continually contradicts us in the way we experience ourselves as alive and compels us to redefine what we mean by life. His answers are absolute because both love and truth are absolute, as is evil. These are the issues that ultimately haunt our souls. For Elizabeth Lesser to cavalierly say that twenty-first-century spirituality prides itself in being a dynamic blend of myth and beliefs is to say that the truth is only the truth today and may change into something else tomorrow. How can one build a life on such a foundation? She is right in admitting that the New Spirituality has myths within its scope. It sounds very magnanimous to present the cultures of some of these myths as unspoiled and worthy of being restored. But the truth of these cultures is often very different. The victimization of women and children was rampant and brutal in many pagan beliefs.

And Lesser has ignored that the most serious myth of the New Spirituality is that untruths can co-exist with truth without making the system toxic. She should know this is not possible from her own sad experiences that she herself points to. And she is not alone…We all have learned through personal tragedies and mistakes that mixing the truth with untruth creates a toxic environment. None of us are spared. A lie seldom comes in recognizable form. It is usually smuggled in as small grains that poison the whole. That is why Jesus referred to the enemy of our souls as the father of all lies.

I propose to explain in this chapter why Jesus is the Truth and why he dispels the myth of mere spirituality.

The Law Is Not an End in Itself

In the twelfth chapter of Matthew's Gospel, we are given three statements by Jesus that will give us profound insight into the distinctness of his teachings from the practices of established religion and from mere spirituality as well.

On a Sabbath day, Jesus and his disciples were walking through grainfields. Observation of the Sabbath was key in the religious practice of the day. It was part of the covenantal relationship between God and his people. The Sabbath was intended for two principal reasons—for worship and for rest. By inference, we can understand that it provided built-in family time and provision for physical, emotional, and spiritual replenishment from a hard week of work.

As they walked through the fields, some of the disciples who were hungry began to pluck the ears of corn and enjoy a little bite here and there. The Pharisees, legalistic guardians of the law, took note of it and immediately censured Jesus for allowing his followers to "work" on the Sabbath. One thing they should have learned very quickly in being around Jesus was that he knew the Scriptures better than they did and that he knew how to turn the question around to show how misguided those religious teachers really were. He knew that David was a big hero of theirs. So he borrowed from a chapter in David's life and asked them if David had violated the law when he allowed his soldiers who were hungry to enter the temple and eat the consecrated bread that had been set apart for the priests. Their response was silence. They knew they had stepped onto a religious minefield with their accusation and with Jesus' response to them.

Religion is a scaffolding for faith, but when it becomes the faith itself, it kills faith. We are often inclined to ignore the beauty of what is beneath and be distracted by the scaffolding. It was no different in Jesus' day; worshippers' attention to their religious ceremonies and customs had become so onerous that they had forgotten the purpose of their worship. Jesus not only drew their attention to their mistake, he shocked them further when he said, "I tell you that something greater than the temple is here. If you had known what these words mean, 'I desire mercy, not sacrifice,' you would not have condemned the innocent. For the Son of Man is Lord of the Sabbath" (Matthew 12:6–8 NIV).

These phrases he used in his answer—"greater than the temple," "Lord of the Sabbath," "mercy sacrifice"—are alone worthy of a whole study. Let's consider them briefly here. "Greater than the temple." Just imagine what the temple meant to the nation and what it had cost to build it. It was the quintessential definition of a people. It was where God had said he would meet with his people. In so being, it had become the power base for a few.

Wars have been fought over similar settings. In India today the religious buildings are showplaces, with each one trying to outdo the other in magnificence and artistry. Nobody visiting the Kali temple in Calcutta can come away without deep questions of the soul. The same applies to the great cathedrals of Europe, as well as the mosques. The Muslims recognized the importance of the "place," and when they conquered a city they almost always identified the most sacred space of the local people and either turned it into a mosque or built a mosque beside it and set stringent laws limiting where other holy places could be built and how high they could be. This has been carried through to today, in spite of the belief of some westerners that this is no longer true of

Islam. It is almost impossible to get permission to build a church anywhere in the Middle East, even a small place of worship.

And it is not accidental or innocent that the followers of the religion whose holy men coached those who uttered prayers to Allah as they turned the twin towers of the World Trade Center into an inferno, are determined to build a mosque in the same vicinity now. To the promoters of this project it is the ultimate slap in the face to the traditions of a nation whose founding beliefs are different from their own. Regardless of their smooth talk and reassurances, have no doubt that they know exactly what they are doing. I have Muslim friends who clearly condemn this effort because they know why it is being planned.

Some time ago, I was visiting the Grand Mosque in Casablanca, Morocco. It is magnificent. As we walked through the lower level, we noticed two rows of water fountains where men would do their ceremonial washings before entering to worship. I asked if the two rows of fountains were for men and women. "Oh, no," came the reply. "One is for the elderly and the other is for the younger ones. If we do not separate them, the young men will just elbow and push their way through and the older men would never get their turn."

How odd, I thought. Going in to worship without even common courtesy and decency? But that was not all. The whole group of us, men and women, were then ushered into the restroom area before we left. A naive American in the group asked if the facilities were normally used by both men and women. The Muslim guide was shocked. "Oh, no! The number of rapes would be unimaginable!" I was startled at his comment: A woman was not safe even in a mosque? But if you dare to profane the mosque or the religion by what you say or do in support of your own political or religious beliefs, blood will flow.

Mathura and Ayodhya, areas in India sacred to Hindus, are now occupied by Muslims and also the focus of many religious battles. The beautiful church built in Istanbul by the mother of Constantine has now been made a museum by Islamic forces, its Christian inscriptions defaced.

The tragedy is not just interreligious; it is also intrareligious. Many Christians will tell you that the biggest opposition to their mission in some countries comes not from those of other beliefs but from the mainline, so-called orthodox churches there. Probably the most incredible quarrel I have heard of is within the Church of the Holy Sepulcher in Jerusalem. Divided among five Christian sects, the parties do not even talk to one another. A few years ago, I personally went there and asked one of the archbishops to confirm that what I had heard was a fact. "Sad to say, it is," he said. This is the fanaticism that buildings and "holy sites" can engender. They have often been built by great political personalities as a reflection of their ego, and access to them is often restricted to a favored group.

Even modern religious edifices can be the targets of such perversions. Some years ago I was in a Buddhist country, and one night I heard a lot of noise and sirens outside my hotel window. The next morning I heard what had happened. A man had used an ax to deface some of the Buddhist statues. Another man rushed over to him, overpowered him, and with the same ax cut his body into pieces. When I heard that, I had a sick feeling in my stomach. Later, it was realized that the man had a history of mental illness. He paid for his actions by being mercilessly slaughtered himself. I ask you, if Gautama Buddha had been there, what would he have said? Shrines often become sacred beyond the very desires of the religious teacher. Buddha would never have endorsed or sanctioned the merciless action of the man defending his statue.

The New Spiritualists are no exception here.

But in the New Testament, God raises the question: "Who asked you to build these places?" That was an amazing question to a religious people who revered David and Solomon. This was not to indict them for something wrong they had done, but to ask them how something so noble could have gone so wrong.

Jesus said he was greater than the temple. In what way? The temple is a place; Jesus a person. The temple has a special authority and a hierarchy; all who wish to have equal access to Jesus. The temple was drowned in ceremony in an effort to attain intimacy with the Almighty; a relationship with Jesus is an intimacy that transcends ceremony. In a temple, you go to the place; Jesus comes to you. The temple is made of stone and mortar; the new temple Jesus spoke of, where he has promised to live and commune with each of us, is within the body of each believer. You can lie to a building; you cannot lie to a person with impunity.

In the book of Revelation, in the midst of John's description of the "New Jerusalem" he is startled and declares: "I did not see a temple in the city, because the Lord God Almighty and the Lamb are its temple" (21:22 NIV). Consummate worship requires no temple. Just as the sacrifices of the temple system pointed to the reality of Jesus on the cross, the temple itself foreshadowed ultimate communion with God, who is distinct from us and invites us into that intimate communion with him. There is no need for priests, no need for a temple, no power structure. Take note that this is not an absorption into an impersonal, absolute consciousness. This is not *union* with the divine: This is *communion* with the God of the universe. It is not Advaita (nondualistic). This is an I-You relationship with our Creator. There is all the difference in the world.

How sad that a truth as grand and beautiful as this is

reduced to spirituality and gender conflicts when it is intended to teach the transcending of both. Maybe this is the ultimate blinding of our eyes by our pride and prejudice toward one another: We make it all about us rather than all about God. He revealed himself in terms that had meanings by analogy so that we could relate to a concept, not be distracted by it. We still make the same mistakes the earlier religionists made. "Why are you violating our Sabbath laws?" Is it any different for us to raise our contemporary cultural or religious prejudices in asking the wrong questions?

Jesus said, "I desire mercy, not sacrifice." Think of the scene on the days of national sacrifice when thousands of lambs were sacrificed and the blood flowed out of the temple in rivers as new families poured into it to offer their own sacrifices. The same people could leave the temple and go back to exploiting the poor and the needy. The temple blinds us to the reality of our own hearts, making us think we have done all we need to do to be right with God. But the God who made us can see what is in our hearts beyond the sacrifices we have made and the laws we have kept in his name.

Age-Old Corruptions

The corruptions that blind religion are clearly shown in God's Word. In the passage in Matthew discussed above, we read that as Jesus was talking about being "greater than the temple," his mother and brothers came to see him. The crowd was so great around him that they couldn't gain access to him or find a place to sit down. Can you see what that meant in the culture of the day? Somebody came to him and told him they were there and trying to get to him through the crowd. Jesus reminded the person that those who were following him had equal access to him and were part of his larger family. There was no nepotism here.

Jude was the half brother of Jesus. Yet he begins his book with the following salutation: "Jude, a servant of Jesus Christ and a brother of James." I find this salutation utterly fascinating. By this time James had become the head of the Church in Jerusalem, and I would have thought that Jude would describe himself as "Jude, the brother of Jesus, serving under James." But no, he clearly recognized the lordship of Jesus, whom he was gladly willing to serve.

Jude then proceeds to warn his readers of three personalities in the Bible that he felt best represented the corruption of religion: Cain, Balaam, and Korah. Cain killed his brother out of jealousy because God saw Abel's heart and accepted his sacrifice, while he refused Cain's. Jude must have understood the temptation of sibling rivalry. Comparing oneself with another is the breeding ground for creating distinction in the very place where distinctions are supposed to cease. Jealousy in serving God has always been at the core of religious "one-upmanship." Jude warned of being jealous of another's service to God, of another's calling or station in life...an attitude like Cain's.

But he went further. The comparison to Balaam is more sinister. Balaam was a prophet known for his gift of making pronouncements that came true. Enemies of God's people came to him and offered him money if he would curse the people of God, "For I know that whoever you bless is blessed, and whoever you curse is cursed" (Numbers 22:6 NIV). The fascinating story of how Balaam struggled with the temptation, wishing he could do it and take the money, makes for an intriguing study of motives as people toy with their convictions. He never actually cursed

God's people, but in his heart he did, and he told their enemy how they could accomplish their goal to destroy them while still looking spiritual. There are Balaams in our ranks today for whom money and prestige are worth skirting the truth, all while still managing to look spiritual.

The third person Jude mentions is Korah. That name would have brought to mind for the reader the day of the rebellion Korah led against Moses, God's chosen servant. Korah was not willing to follow God's way through his servant. He believed his own ideas were better and wanted Moses' position as leader to exercise his own agenda. Cain, Balaam, and Korah—in the case of all three, the backdrop to their actions was religious zeal, which stood in the way of a godly relationship.

Cain—jealousy and hate; Balaam—greed and manipulation; Korah—power and sectarianism. Has anything really changed? That is why there will be no temple in heaven. God will be the object of all worship in consummate expression, in person. Jesus was greater than the temple.

The Prejudiced Prophet

On another occasion Jesus referred to himself as "greater than Jonah" (Matthew 12:41 NIV). There are two very important points here. We live in a world of hate and racial prejudice. It has always been so. More than twenty-five hundred years ago Jonah was commissioned by God to take his message of repentance and forgiveness to the Ninevites. The Ninevites were renowned for their cruelty and were feared and hated by all the surrounding peoples, including Jonah and his people. The last people in the world that Jonah would have felt burdened to reach with the love of God were the Ninevites. Just imagine the extent of his prejudice. He did not want to see them even extended an opportunity to receive the love of God. He wanted to see them punished by God and destroyed. Such is the extent of hate that even those called to preach can nurture. God had to do a deep work in Jonah to bring him to the place where he could understand and appreciate God's love for all mankind, even the most unworthy, and embrace the depth of his forgiveness.

There is a second aspect to Jonah's resistance. He was preserved from death for three days in the belly of a great fish in a supernatural way by God's protective power. Under natural circumstances, he would have died. His survival against all odds was a reminder to the people Jesus was talking to that God himself would conquer the grave and restore his Son, who would bring the message of forgiveness and demonstrate, by his resurrection, that he is the Son of God with power.

Jonah was called to love the people whom he hated, and the best expression of his love was to tell them of God's love for them. That, as Carlyle said, is the "greater miracle" in the story. People often misunderstand what this means. To question how God could ask us to love our enemies is to reduce love to a feeling and ignore the worth that God places on the object of his love. There is no such imperative within naturalism or pantheism.

Some years ago, it was my privilege to give the address at the Annual Prayer Breakfast that marks each new session of the United Nations. I had been asked to speak on "The Search for Absolutes in a Relativistic World" in twenty minutes, and to be cautious in talking about God. So in those few minutes I talked of the four areas in each of our experiences in which we search for absolutes: evil, justice, love, and forgiveness.

Try defining these from a pantheistic worldview, or any other worldview, for that matter. What is evil? How do we come to terms with what it is, as a reality? When you think about it, evil can be defined or understood only in a world where there is a duality and where purpose is clearly identified. How does one define evil in a world of one? As consciousness into which all other appearances merge? In Christian terms, evil is both a condition and an action. Our condition is that our default position is rebellion against God, and our actions are the outcome and demonstration of that rebellion. I have seen evil in the closest of proximities. All one needs to do is visit a war museum to see how much bloodshed humanity is responsible for.

But we have been seduced into thinking that evil is defined only in its cruelest form. That is categorically untrue. Or we think of evil in degrees, as in, how could *so much* evil be justified? But that again misses the heart of what evil is. How often in my own heart I have sensed desires and machinations that remind me of how vile the human heart can be. The escape doors here— that something is evil only when in its cruelest form or if there is an extreme expression of evil—make the New Spirituality look devoid of reality. Let me give you two examples of this.

When Maharishi Mahesh Yogi passed away, Deepak Chopra wrote an article attempting to defend his not-so-nice side. I will not go into the stories that had circulated about him. Chopra's article was called "The Three Maharishis." Why am I not surprised? He seems to love the triads for his explanations. There were three Jesus figures, according to him, so why not three Maharishis? Writing for the *Huffington Post* on February 6, 2008, after the Maharishi died, Chopra said the following. Read it carefully:

You could be walking down the hallway to his private apartments with the weight of the world on your shoulders and feel your worries drop away with every step, until by the time your hand touched the doorknob, by some magic you felt completely carefree. But if you were around him long enough, the older Maharishi in particular could be nettlesome and self-centered; he could get angry and dismissive. He was quick to assert his authority and yet could turn disarmingly child-like in the blink of an eye.

The Maharishi who was an Indian felt most comfortable around other Indians...He adhered to the vows of poverty and celibacy that belonged to his order of monks, despite the fact that he lived in luxury and amassed considerable wealth for the TM movement...In the end the movement's money went to preserve the spiritual heritage of India by opening pundit schools and building temples....

For good or ill, these two Maharishis are the only ones that the outside world knew. If you came under the power of his consciousness, however, Maharishi the guru completely overshadowed every other aspect.[4]

I have to wonder to what extent the mind can deceive itself with word games. Maybe that is part of the mystery of evil. So the darker side is explained away as not the real person, because there are really three of them: the not-so-nice side of him; the public side of him; and oh, when you came under the power of his consciousness, there was the divine and magical side of him. These are brilliant trisections to explain the human heart in its depravity. Actually, Chopra may have accidently blundered into the right. In a strange way there are three Chopras, too, and three of each one of us: There is who the *world* thinks we are, who *we* think we are, and who God knows us to be. Maharishi at his core was like all of us, as is Mr. Chopra. Verbal magic will not do here. Evil stalks us and we know it. To play word games is a ploy to escape the obvious.

The more we deny reality, the more mindless our solutions become. The story of Jonah is the story of both the preacher and the audience, if you'll pardon the pun, in the same boat. It is terrible to be the victim of hate, but it is even worse to be the possessor of it. Jonah simply despised his audience and wanted them to have no share in God's forgiveness. But through the storm and the story emerges the greatest miracle of all—a transformed heart, fresh with the hope beyond this life. Take a closer look at the implications of this story—love, forgiveness, and hope. This is the sum and substance of the gospel: love, forgiveness, and hope—because of Jesus Christ. He is greater than Jonah.

Supreme Wisdom

There is the third "greater than" that Jesus used to describe himself: "greater than Solomon" (Matthew 12:42 NIV). Proverbially, literally, and figuratively, the name Solomon is synonymous with wisdom. His name represents that even three thousand years after he lived. After visiting him, the queen of Sheba said that not even half of his greatness had been told. The Bible tells us that he was without peer in virtually every discipline. Yet he was his own liability. Knowledge without character is deadly. Solomon knew all the answers. He just did not live them. In the end, Solomon's is a sad story and a grim reminder that even the dispensers of wisdom have a breaking point. Highly gifted people are not gods, even if they think they act or speak for him.

Fyodor Dostoyevsky was a powerful writer in his day. When he died, thousands of people lined the streets of St. Petersburg to bid him farewell. His *Brothers Karamazov* and numerous other works were lofty in skill and far-reaching in impact. But Dostoyevsky was an inveterate gambler and went to the grave quite poor by virtue of that addiction.

Alexander the Great conquered the world but could not conquer his own thirst for alcohol. Dying a young man in his early thirties, he went to the grave a loser.

Michael Jackson—what an incredibly gifted entertainer and dancer, considered by those in the field almost superhuman in the scope of his gifts! But what a tragic end to a tragic personal lifestyle. He was almost a replica of Elvis Presley in his success and failures.

Stephen Hawking—one of the greatest minds to have ever lived. How enviable a capacity! But he lives in a wheelchair, communicating with the world by the movement of one finger.

We all have our breaking points. For some it will be moral or spiritual. For others, a physical malady of dreadful proportions. For still others, it will be the sudden stopping of their lives like an engine in midair. For all of us, life comes to an end in this world. All of us.

In giving the answers to our deepest struggles and breaking points, Jesus also embodied what character was intended to look like and what eternal life is. But there is more. He spoke it, lived it, and is able to empower those who seek to live that way. The temple, Jonah, and Solomon. All memories of what is real and transitory. Jesus Christ is greater than the temple, greater than Jonah, and greater than Solomon. He alone offers you and me the fulfillment and joy of walking with God. For that privilege we need a Savior.

As we look back upon history, we see dark spots of human behavior. Among them, few are as dark as the scourge of human slavery. The name that was most influential in bringing that horrific trade to an end is that of William Wilberforce. I have referred to him in a previous chapter. Wilberforce was converted to Christ at the age of twenty-six and was to give the rest of his life for the noble cause of breaking the chains of oppression and the demeaning of human beings in the massive phenomenon of slavery. Oddly enough, physically he was quite dwarfed. One writer said, "The hand that struck the shackles from the galled limbs of our British slaves was the hand of a hunchback." He was brilliant and extraordinarily gifted, a master of mimicry, a born actor, an accomplished singer, and a perfect elocutionist.

James Boswell said of him, "I saw a shrimp mount the table but as I listened he grew and grew, until the shrimp became a whale."[5] And "when he rose to address the House of Commons, he looked like the dwarf that had jumped out of a fairy tale; when he resumed his seat, he looked like the giant of the self-same story."[6]

As a member of Parliament, he fought his entire life to defeat this dreadful practice. So many discouraged him from the fight, saying that it would never be corrected. With more than a million souls in this dreadful traffic, some thought they would appease him by agreeing to a bill that made the fresh importing of slaves illegal. It took him twenty years just to get that bill passed. But he continued to work relentlessly to bring the whole practice to a halt and was literally on his deathbed when the word came to him that the bill illegalizing slavery had made it through the Parliament. Fifty years of his life had been dedicated to that cause. His words in response: "Thank God! I have lived to see the day."

I have often seen the dark scourge of human trafficking as a reflection of self-enslavement and plunder. We ourselves are in chains. This is at the root of all human discrimination.

There is an impact on the world when we ourselves are freed from our own enslavements. Those who would deny the Christian the privilege of sharing the Savior with others deny the Christian the beauty and power of Jesus Christ. Of all people, it was Bertrand Russell who attributed Gandhi's success in India to the fact that he was appealing to the conscience of a Christianized nation. That is quite a statement from an atheist, crediting the success of a pantheist to Christian theism.

CHAPTER 14

❦

FALSE ASSUMPTIONS AND MAGNIFICENT TRUTHS

There are clearly mistakes made both by the New Spiritualists and by Christians that are of deep significance. The New Spiritualist assumes that there is no mystical side to Christianity, or if it is acknowledged, it is eviscerated of any truth claims. The New Spiritualist sees in Christianity only hard doctrine that lays down rules for people and is ready to punish them when they break the rules, rather than drawing people in. And sometimes I fear that their caricatures of our heartless preaching and legalistic interpretation of the gospel are correct. The same mistake is often made by those of us who see in the New Spirituality nothing more than sitting in the lotus position with eyes shut and an inward look, with no dogma to proclaim. In this book we have come to see that neither of these generalities is a fair representation.

There is actually a rich and varied historical tradition among Christians who sought the path of mysticism to find tranquillity and serenity apart from the hustle and bustle of life. Unfortunately, more often than not, it became an escape from the real world. There are also legitimate criticisms from those in this movement toward the way Christianity is often presented or perceived.

Very recently, I was the guest of a leading figure from an old and historic Christian tradition in the Middle East. He had done his preparation work for Christian ministry in another Middle Eastern country. Just to be courteous, I asked him if he had enjoyed his seven years of preparation there. He managed a smile and said, "Enjoyed? That would be the one word that does *not* come to mind. We were in prayer or chanting all day. Then at six o'clock every evening the doors to the monastery were locked and we were not allowed to go out anywhere. The only diversion was an old television with no programming but religious programs. After seven years of that, I was ready to leave the ministry. I did, in fact," he said. "But my uncle persuaded me to return to the ministry and so here I am now, heading up this historic church." I shall say no more lest I reveal more than I should. But how sad it is when the lead voice in a historic church says *enjoyed* is the one word that doesn't come to his mind in the context of preparation for the Christian ministry.

Christian mysticism has gone to extremes and retreated from the world. It was a mistake. You do not win over life's struggles by hiding in rocks or barricading yourself from reality and from other people. Although Jesus said his followers were not *of* the world, as he was not *of* the world, they were *in* the world. In fact, he prayed to his Father, "My prayer is not that you take them out of the world but that you protect them from the evil one" (John 17:15 NIV). In Matthew 5:13–16, he commanded his followers to be salt and light to a deteriorating and dark world. How can one be salt and light when one has removed oneself from the world? This question can also be applied to modern Christians who remove themselves from society, associating only with those with whom they are in agreement.

Today on Mount Athos in Greece, there is a monastery where nothing female is allowed, not even chickens or cows. In fact, the ship we were on could not come closer than a prescribed distance because there were women on board. Readers may remember that the famed Cretan scholar Nikos Kazantzakis, author of the controversial *Last Temptation*, spent some protracted time on Athos in his search for communion with the divine. How sad that so many throughout Christian history have subjected themselves to such things in their efforts to commune with God, when Jesus stands simply before each of us and says, "Here I am! I stand at the door and knock. If anyone hears my voice and opens the door, I will come in and eat with that person, and they with me" (Revelation 3:20 NIV).

I actually thought of going to Mount Athos and staying there for a week, just for the experience, and I was told that it could be arranged. But with my very serious back problems I decided it could be a costly mistake, since one has to mount a donkey to even get to the last several hundred feet. Yes, that would have been my "monk for a week" experience.

The New Spiritualists make the same blunder, but from the opposite position. In their stress of quietude, retreat, and escape from the bustle, they act as if they have no doctrines. As if there are no rules. As if they have no authority except themselves. It is all about the mysticism and meditation. That is simply not true. The histories of the religions on which their beliefs are principally based have books and sects and rules ad nauseam. The metaphysical scaffolding of the authors they quote is based on a prior commitment to a very particular form of reasoning. Should

it not strike us as odd that those who live in "the now" nevertheless sign contracts for the future? That those who are so big on
the notions of silence and of emptying the mind of all thought
write big books on concepts intended to make you think? That
they say the world is illusionary and there is no I/you, and yet
they are obviously writing these books for "you"? That enlightenment comes from within in isolation, yet they use the mass
method of communication to their own advantage?

The Three All-Important Questions

All worldviews and religions need to take a hard look at themselves and at how they answer three inescapable questions:

1. How do they answer the question of exclusivity as it
   relates to their own belief?
2. What is the source of their authority?
3. How relevant is what they believe to the common experience; what difference does it really make?

Why are Christians so dogmatic? Why do they think their
way is the only way? These lines are repeated again and again and
reveal a prejudice on the part of the questioner. What else can
be expected but exclusivity when truth claims are expressed?
Growing up in India, it was always assumed that the predomi-
nant worldview was the only worldview. It was not uncommon
to have pictures of gurus and teachers or some verse from the
Gita or pronouncement of Krishna on the wall in every office and
school. Should it have occurred to us who held different beliefs
to question why they were being so exclusive? I do not ever recall

in all my school days a Christian coming to speak to the student body. I heard principally—exclusively—from Hindus. I accepted that fact because they formed the large majority and theirs was the prevailing worldview.

Anyone who thinks that the Hindu message is not being "propagated" is simply blind to reality. It subsumes the culture of a nation of more than a billion people and it is the logical out-working of prior commitments to belief. *Hindusthan*, which is the Hindi word for *India*, means "the land of the Hindus." And *Hindusthani*, or Hindi, as it is popularly called, means "the language of the Hindus." The religion and its worldview inform every aspect of society and culture. Hindus themselves do not see their religion as inclusive of other religions; otherwise, why would Buddha have felt the need to reject the defining tenets of Hinduism in his quest for truth? And why would the parents of young people who are brought up as Hindus but have become Christians—young people like my brother-in-law—mourn their decision as a death? Hinduism is propagated, and I would expect it to be if that is what is truly believed by the person.

It is clear, abundantly clear, that all religions without exception are exclusive. All religions ultimately collect cultural trappings and in turn become identified with culture. Buddhism is not Hinduism. Islam is not Christianity. Jainism is not Judaism. Each has its own uncompromising moorings. Each is distinct from the others.

When I was in Turkey recently, a Turkish man told me that one question is asked of him more often than any other. When he gives his name and identifies himself as a Christian, the person talking to him will say, "But aren't you Turkish?" "I am," he replies. "But you just said you were a Christian." He says, "I am Turkish and I am a Christian." The questioner always looks totally bewildered. I guess people don't remember anymore that most Turks were Christians until their country was conquered by Islamic forces and the people were forced to convert to Islam for economic reasons or for protection. But so go cultures everywhere. We have short memories.

When I became a committed Christian, a close Hindu friend said to me, "You have lost your originality." He loved that word. What he meant was that only if I believed as he did was I an original, or unique. By my decision to follow Jesus, I became, in his eyes, no longer unique…"nonoriginal." Before I became a Christian I actually believed very little about any spiritual matters. Is that what he would have preferred of me? The answer is yes. To believe nothing would actually be closer to his supposedly "believe all" faith.

Truth by definition excludes. We have to understand that by definition, truth excludes the denial of what it asserts. My ethnicity puts me in a certain category; my language puts me in a certain category; my education puts me in a certain category. All designations exclude something else. The problem with religious belief is that nobody wants anyone to preach a destiny that excludes anyone else, and so we reserve the description of evil for only the most heinous. And now some New Spiritualists would not even want that separation. Let's examine the notion of truth.

Some years ago, I was to address members of the Bar Association of a particular state. As I sat down at the lunch table, the president of the Bar Association commented to me that I had to be pretty bold to come and speak at an event where people made their living by working with words. I took note, because in a way, one can reduce my profession to that as well, if nothing else is taken into consideration. Anyhow, I just smiled and waited till the lunch was over and I had been introduced. There was a sense of discomfort in the air…any time you are before an audience for whom everything is relative and they know someone is going to introduce you as an absolutist or holding to a hierarchical position, the sense of unease is almost visible. How odd that those who argue for the law are the least trusted with the truth.

As it happened, my talk was during the days of the Clinton presidency, at the time that he was accused of some indiscreet behavior, which he had denied. You may recall that when he was asked, "Is it true?" he brilliantly answered, "It all depends on what 'is' means." That was the quintessential postmodern answer. We have gone one better now. The newest term for a lie is "I misspoke." I am not even sure how to spell that.

As I stood up to speak to this rather skeptical and jaded audience, I began this way: "I have just come here from watching the news in my hotel room. May I give you the first three items in the headlines? The first was from a reporter with his roving microphone, asking people on the street if words had any particular meaning or whether the speaker reserved the right to infuse his or her meaning into the words. In our 'salvation by survey' culture, the answer was predictable: 'The speaker has the right to assign any meaning he or she wishes to the words used.'

"The second item on the news was the roving reporter asking people whether morality has any point of reference or whether each person has the right to their own moral reasoning The answer was that each person has an individual right to determine their own morality.

"Those were the first two items on the news.

"Now let me tell you the third item: The United States has sent a warning to Saddam Hussein that if he doesn't stop playing his word games, we will start bombing his cities."

The facial expressions of those in the audience, dedicated to the practice of the law, suddenly changed. Isn't it ironic that as a culture we have reserved the right to define words and determine morality for ourselves, but when someone else plays word games with us or is morally duplicitous, we threaten to bomb them? This is the hidden menace masquerading as enlightenment: We tell people they are free to choose their own deities because there is no ultimate Authority, but when someone chooses to believe in an ultimate Authority, on the basis of truth, at best what they believe is distorted by society or their representatives, and at worst they become the objects of ridicule. What if what they believe came from a flash of insight in quiet reflection? Is belief in an ultimate Authority by definition a wrong insight? Suddenly democracy and diversity disappear. To deny the law of noncontradiction is to affirm it at the same time.

I want to be careful here. I realize that this kind of "rationalistic apologetic" is evicted in the thinking of the New Spirituality. But I must remind the critics that all of their links to thought and to philosophy actually originally subscribed to this basic law of logic: Sankara, Buddha, as well as the Greeks. The mistake in the spiritual journey was making logic the *only* test, thereby carrying something legitimate to an illegitimate extreme.

Building a Worldview

There are generally two tests for truth: the *correspondence* test, where assertions of fact can be tested against reality; and the *coherence* test, which ensures that all the assertions that make up a worldview cohere with one another, or are consistent with one another. Correspondence to fact and systemic coherence make for the test of any worldview.

Let me carry this a little further. How does one actually build a worldview? Invariably, give or take some minor points, a worldview is based on eight basic components:

1. A good worldview must have a strong basis in fact. This point alone has a two-edged reality: First, can the assertion being made be tested against reality? And second, is the assertion clearly false? If one assertion in the system is clearly false or cannot be tested against reality, there is a failure to meet the test of truth.

2. A good worldview must have a high degree of coherence or internal consistency. The New Spirituality fails miserably here. I shall demonstrate how as we come to the end of this section.

3. A good worldview must give a reasonable and logical explanation for the various undeniable realities that we sense all around us.

4. A good worldview will avoid the two extremes of either being too complex or two simplistic.

5. A good worldview is not explained by just one line of evidence.

6. A good worldview must explain contrary worldviews without compromising its own essential beliefs.

7. A good worldview cannot argue just on the basis of a private experience, but must have some objective standard of measurements.

8. A good worldview must justifiably explain the essential nature of good and evil, since those two alternatives

are the principal characteristics differentiating human beings from all other entities or quantities.

Once a worldview has been established, it becomes the grid for making particular judgments. To say that there are no moral absolutes and then castigate Christians for being hypocritical assumes that hypocrisy is a moral flaw and a contradictory position and, therefore, is to be vilified. To say that there is a spark of divinity in all of us and then treat the lower castes as "less divine"—to even create such a system that categorizes people like this—is again to run afoul of reason. Worldviews begin by definitions. Definitions create boundaries. Violations of those boundaries elicit condemnation. That condemnation itself excludes. It is impossible to sustain truth without excluding falsehood. All religions are exclusive.

Authority

This is a key issue with the New Spiritualist: What or who will be my authority? To move the final authority to a subjective, albeit an intuitive flash of enlightenment, an awful lot must be explained away. It is impossible to grant that right to each person.

One of my friends tells this story of a doctor trying to talk his patient in a psychiatric ward out of believing that he is Moses. But the patient is adamant that he is Moses. Finally, the doctor asks in frustration, "Who told you that you are Moses?"

"God did," comes the confident reply.

"I did not!" comes an indignant voice from the next bed.

Seriously, how does one know when people like Donald Walsch or Deepak Chopra speak with such authority whether they are speaking for God or whether they are themselves divine, or neither? Their own lives are clearly and indisputably flawed, by their own admission. So where does their moral authority come from? They have every right to debate, dialogue, dispute, argue, whatever. But when they speak with self-referencing conviction, as if they have the consummate answer, you have to ask, "Says who?" It is not enough to brush it off as one of them does by saying, "My children know that I'm a work in progress," or write it off by creating "Three Maharishis" in order to cover up the shortcomings of his mentor.

Jesus asks of his accusers, "Which of you convicts Me of sin?" (John 8:46 NKJV). Pilate said of him, "I find no fault in this Man" (Luke 23:4 NKJV). The dying thief on the cross next to him said, "This Man has done nothing wrong" (Luke 23:41 NKJV). The purity of Jesus' life and his unassailable example to us have won the adulation of millions, including Gandhi and Buddhist thinkers. The historian Lecky attested that he was unique and without parallel in history.[1]

Over the fifteen hundred years of recorded history in the Holy Bible, more than forty different authors either pointed to Jesus' coming or lived and walked with him, and speak of him as the One with authority. He warned against legalism that was content to administer harsh applications of the law. He showed the shortcomings of a religion that was empty, nothing but dogma. He avoided the political limelight. He never charged his audience for speaking. He lifted up the broken. He conversed with the rejects of society. He held the little ones in his arms and asked us to become like them in their propensity to trust him. In his defining conversation with another teacher who came to him with honest questions, he said that the answer to knowing God ultimately lay in a new birth that only the Holy Spirit of God could bring about. Mystified, the teacher asked how a grown man could enter the womb again. Jesus presented a "koan" of his own, if you will: "The wind blows wherever it pleases. You hear its sound, but you cannot tell where it comes from or where it is going. So it is with everyone born of the Spirit" (John 3:8 NIV).

This new birth that Jesus talked about is not self-caused or self-induced or self-engendered. Nor is it by the will of any human teacher or by anyone's recommendation. You can do nothing to earn it and nothing to make it happen. You cannot make yourself worthy of it or give yourself rights to it. New birth comes from God, who alone puts right what is ultimately wrong with the world—our broken souls. No amount of meditation or silence or retreat from the world will accomplish that. Only God in his grace is big enough. The only reasonable conclusion to any self-examination is that we cannot mend our world on our own, we cannot mend our broken spirits; we need someone from the outside to enter our world and our lives and set things right. We need a Savior.

The big question of authority is on the authority of the Scriptures. Many capable scholars have addressed this. I have included a bibliography at the end of this book for anyone who wants to do further reading on the authority of the Scriptures. One of the most capable critics of the Bible is Bart Ehrman, who studied under one of the most knowledgeable Greek scholars of recent times, Bruce Metzger, of Princeton. I would strongly recommend Ben Witherington's outstanding response to Ehrman, as well as the interaction on the subject between Ehrman and N. T. Wright.[2]

This is what I believe it boils down to: If you are determined to find flaws in the Bible, you will find them, especially in a book that has been around for so many centuries, was written by such

diverse authors over a great period of time, and has been translated into so many versions and languages. So it is with the texts
on almost any subject. It can be done. Ideas are easy to quibble
over, debate, dissect, and reject. One has to start by looking at
the big picture, at the overall truth that is being asserted. Then
one puts the main ideas of the argument to the tests that I mentioned earlier, and sees how they have been borne out in life, in
history, and in personal application.

When Deepak Chopra opines that John 14:6—where Jesus
says, "I am the way, the truth, and the life. No one comes to the
Father except through me"—is nothing more than Jesus attaining God-consciousness, one who is serious in the quest must
ask, "Really? Would the disciples have laid down their lives to
support Jesus' claim that he had attained a certain status if all
humanity can also attain such status on their own?" What would
be the reason for that? There would be nothing unique in that,
nothing worth dying for. Is this not a sham and a shame to make
such a pathetic distortion of the facts when it is clear why he died
and that his claim to be uniquely God was understood by his
persecutors? Did they all get it wrong—Jesus, his disciples, his
persecutors, Pilate, the millions throughout history who have
believed—and Chopra get it right? Is this not the ultimate hubris?
The big picture presented in the text within its context is indis-
putable.

The Big Picture and Particular Truths

There is nothing like the Bible in all of history, considering the
span of its writing and the varied writers. Nothing. The genre
of literature behind the New Spirituality doesn't compare. The

cumulative evidence for Jesus' claim to divinity and the prophetic specifics that had to congeal clearly make for a book with the power of the supernatural. That is why writers such as Peter, Paul, John, Jude, and Luke, from highly different backgrounds, nevertheless paint a similar picture of the Word of God who became flesh and dwelled among us, whose pure and impeccable life accompanied his teaching, and that he was the fulfillment of the prophetic voices from Moses to Malachi, who, over more than a thousand years, predicted his coming, his death, and his resurrection. From carpenters to fishermen to educators to theologians to civic leaders to a medical doctor—they all converge on the same truth. These don't sound like people who would make up a story and one by one go to an early death to support it! Take Paul alone—a Hebrew by birth who studied in Greece and was a citizen of Rome, a highly educated man and a leader in his community. There was nothing he wanted to do more than to disprove Jesus as the Messiah. Yet he ended up writing one-third of the New Testament and paid for his faith in Christ with his life. Why would he make up such a thing?

One of Ehrman's criticisms is that Jesus, he said, could not have been God because when he was asked when he was going to return from heaven, he answered that no one knows about that day, not even the angels in heaven, nor the Son, but only the Father. It is fascinating how colored one's glasses can be! I remember that the first time I read that passage of Scripture (Mark 13:32), I put the Bible down and shut my eyes, filled with awe at the beauty of this Savior. If he were a self-aggrandizing charlatan, why would he have answered the question that way? He wouldn't have. He would have answered it by saying, "I know the date, but I am not going to tell you." No one could have proven him wrong. He could have said, "About forty years from now," when he wouldn't have been around to face the embarrassment. Nothing would have been more Western than for him to have given an unfalsifiable date. Nothing would have been more Eastern than for him to have answered it in a riddle, and no one would have been able to discern whether he knew the date or didn't.

Instead, he said the most extraordinary thing…that he didn't know. So often he spoke of emptying himself of his divine prerogatives and of denying himself access to the power that was legitimately his in order to become the Word of God in the flesh. Paul says of him in Philippians 2:7 that "he made himself nothing" (NIV). In his self-denial, that knowledge was not his to demand as he humbled himself before his own creation, even to death. Is this any more a mystery than his agonizing prayer in the Garden of Gethsemane? Renouncing his rights as the Son of Man, he made it possible for the Son of God to be the sacrifice that he was. Everything about his story has the ring of authenticity to it.

After one gets the big picture, by all means the finer texts can be studied and the verbs parsed and the truths examined and the forms, the texts, and the extrabiblical sources studied. That is fair and expected. But so many critics take a pen and treat it as a penknife, coming to so many different conclusions that it evidences at the least that they themselves are at variance on what the variants really are. Maybe, just maybe, it is because whatever the cost, they want to find any way other than the one Jesus offers. Actually, he wished there were another way, too. But he committed himself to pay the ultimate price for us to be able to come to the Father. C. S. Lewis, who seldom replied to his critics, once made the comment that they were so wrong about certain sources attributed to him, some of which he had never even heard of, that he wondered how much more in error would they be in their critiques of a text two thousand years old.

Jesus said that the Word of God abides forever. His very life was the fulfillment of numerous verses of Scripture—an amazing confluence of hundreds of passages that would be almost impossible to design by collusion. When the tempter faced off with Jesus in the wilderness, he used Scripture texts to try to seduce Jesus. And in response to each temptation Jesus put those texts back into their contexts, which enabled him to resist Satan's schemings. Psalm 119 gives us scores of valuable insights into the Scriptures. It reminds us that it is a lamp for our feet and a light on our path. In the grim darkness of temptation, the light of Scripture shines upon the seduction and sends the seducers scampering. Truth will ever trump deceit when the text is applied within its context.

Relevance

Knowing Jesus and walking with him daily bring relevance to every thought and intent of the heart. I have walked with him nearly five decades now. Even as I say that, I find it almost impossible to believe. When I think of the self-rejection and alienation I felt before and the incredible worth God has placed upon my life, I am humbled by his call. When I think back to the things I hated then and love now, the contrast is unimaginable. I hated reading. Today I can hardly wait to get to the books I so dearly long to read, the history of thought, of philosophy of religion, but most of all, to those books that draw me nearer to God.

Indeed, the great mystics fascinate me as well. I recommend the finest volume I have read that pulls together the best-known

Christian mystics, a book titled *Water from a Deep Well* by Gerald L. Sittser. From Bernard of Clairvaux to John of the Cross, there is a gold mine here for thought, for reflection, for example, and for sensing God's near and dear presence. One statement in the book that caught my attention is: "The prayer of silence is not natural. Our attempts to pray this kind of prayer will expose how trivial and superficial our thoughts are, how noisy our world is, how inattentive we are to the reality of God's presence."[3]

The message of Jesus is totally relevant in connecting the greatest distance in life—the distance from the head to the heart—a journey that each one of us must take. The intellectual rigor of the gospel does not rob us of the mystical and mysterious depths of the very person of God. Charles Haddon Spurgeon said this:

> The proper study of the Christian is the God-head. The highest science, the loftiest speculation, the mightiest philosophy, which can engage the attention of a child of God, is the name, the nature, the person, the doings, and the existence of the great God which he calls his Father. There is something exceedingly improving to the mind in the contemplation of the Divinity. It is a subject so vast, that all our thoughts are lost in its immensity; so deep, that our pride is drowned in its infinity. Other subjects we can comprehend and grapple with; in them we feel a kind of self-content, and go on our way with the thought, "Behold I am wise." But when we come to this master science, finding that our plumb-line cannot sound its depth, amid that our eagle eye cannot see its height, we turn away with the thought, "I am but of yesterday and know nothing."[4]

Knowing this God and having him work in us is the difference between life and death.

What Difference Does It Make?

In a great church in Brooklyn, New York, where thousands gather weekly, I was introduced to a twelve-year-old girl. Some months ago, she was brought by somebody to meet the pastor because she was being courted by one of the roughest gangs in the area. The initiation into that gang involved taking a razor blade and slashing some random person's face. The pastor talked to her at length and, sensing an intense anger within her, finally asked, "Who are you angry at?" Gritting her teeth, she replied, "I'm angry at my father, I'm angry at my mother, I'm angry at God, I'm angry at Jesus..." The list went on and on. The pastor gently spoke to her, telling her that God could change her heart from hate and anger to love and peace, and finally he prayed with her.

Today she is at that church every day. She helps in the offices, in any way she can. She's a sweet little thing but could fight the toughest gangster because she has come from a rough background. One day recently, the pastor asked her how her week had gone. "Oh, fantastic, just fantastic," she said. "Jesus was so good...so good." Then she paused, raised her index finger, curled her lip and said, "Except on Thursday..." The pastor said it took everything he had to keep from bursting into laughter. "Jesus was good, except on Thursday." That's as transparent as one can be.

The Lord transforms us with extraordinary power and makes his truth relevant, even to the point of knowing that his own children can sometimes be disappointed in him until they realize and accept that his message does not mean an escape from the sharp edges of life. In this church there are so many nationalities that when I asked the question "How many?" the answer was, "It would be hard to think of any nationalities that are not here." They are people from disparate backgrounds, with hurts and fears and facing economic struggles, all finding Jesus' message relevant to their own particular need.

A few years ago, the noted English journalist Matthew Parris wrote an article that caught all of his readers by surprise. Parris is known as an avowed atheist. This is how he describes a recent visit to Malawi, the country of his birth:

> Before Christmas I returned, after 45 years, to the country that as a boy I knew was Nyasaland. Today it's Malawi…It inspired me, renewing my flagging faith in development charities. But traveling in Malawi refreshed another belief, too: one I've been trying to banish all my life…It confounds my ideological beliefs, stubbornly refuses to fit my world view, and has embarrassed my growing belief that there is no God. Now a confirmed atheist, I've become convinced of the enormous contribution that Christian evangelism makes in Africa: sharply distinct from the secular NGOs…Education and training alone will not do. In Africa Christianity changes people's hearts. It brings a spiritual transformation. The rebirth is real. The change is good.[5]

He continues that he wished he could conclude that the answer for Africa is to be found in enough aid and in education, but that does not fit the facts he saw. The missionaries' faith in God and the character of their lives had been transferred to the people, bringing an enormous change in their ethos and in their way of thinking and acting…the smiles of confidence that put them on equal footing, shaking off a servile and servant look. So much change within them was impossible to explain away. He takes issue with the long-held belief among Western academic sociologists that tribal value systems developed over centuries by tribes are "best" for them and are intrinsically equal or of equal worth to ours, observing that tribal belief is no more peaceable than ours and in fact, suppresses individuality. People are forced to think collectively, which feeds into the gangster politics of the African city, an exaggerated respect for the leader, and a literal inability to understand the concept of a "loyal opposition." The whole structure of rural African thought is weighed down, he says, by anxiety, fear of spirits, ancestors, nature, and the wild, and it is a weight that grinds down the spirit.

Acknowledging the heartache and destruction that have come to Africans as a result of this, he ends with these staggering paragraphs:

> Christianity…with its teaching of a direct, personal, two-way link between the individual and God, unmediated by the collective, and unsubordinate to any other human being, smashes straight through the philosophical/spiritual framework I've just described…
>
> Those who want Africa to walk tall amid 21st-century global competition must not kid themselves that providing the material means or even the know-how that accompanies what we call development will make the change. A whole belief system must first be supplanted. And I'm afraid it has to be supplanted by another. Removing Christian evangelism from the African equation may leave the continent at the mercy of a malign

fusion of Nike, the witch doctor, the mobile phone and the machete.[6]

This is an incredible acknowledgment, by an avowed atheist, that mere spiritual or altruistic ideas are not enough; it is only the message of Jesus to change the heart that will change a continent. I admire Mr. Parris's bold recognition of this. If Christians would live out their faith with confidence and in love, I suspect he would say this is true not just for Africa, but for the world as well...perhaps even for Mr. Parris.

G. K. Chesterton was right: The problem with Christianity is not that it has been tried and found wanting, but that it has been found difficult and left untried. The message of Jesus is beautiful and magnificent and life-changing. If you have not already discovered that for yourself, may you discover it now. Spirituality is not good enough.

Jesus proclaims the truth—that is why it must exclude all that is contrary to it. He lived and spoke with authority—that is why what he said applies to each of us. His message bridges the greatest gulf within us—that is why it is relevant even today, two thousand years later.

Picture This Scene

In Luke 4:14–21, we are told of this incident:

Jesus returned to Galilee in the power of the Spirit, and news about him spread through the whole countryside. He was teaching in their synagogues, and everyone praised him.

He went to Nazareth, where he had been brought up, and on the Sabbath day he went into the synagogue, as was his custom. He stood up to read, and the scroll of the prophet Isaiah was handed to him. Unrolling it, he found the place where it is written: "The Spirit of the Lord is on me, because he has anointed me to proclaim good news to the poor. He has sent me to proclaim freedom for the prisoners and recovery of sight for the blind, to set the oppressed free, to proclaim the year of the Lord's favor."

Then he rolled up the scroll, gave it back to the attendant and sat down. The eyes of everyone in the synagogue were fastened on him. He began by saying to them, "Today this scripture is fulfilled in your hearing." (NIV)

This is the message of freedom for those in bondage, a message that will open the eyes of our darkened spirituality to the bright light of his grace, that will convince a Church to live the love of God by taking care of the poor and taking up the cause of the oppressed, that assures us there is an end of time where eternity awaits, and that all who long for his presence will live in the fulfillment of their faith to the grand consummation of seeing the Ultimate One, face-to-face.

The Christian believes, too, in justice and liberation and in caring for the neediest among us. The Christian believes, too, that the mind will suddenly grasp the Ultimate. The Christian believes, too, in the ultimate synchronicity of all that is true and good and beautiful. The Christian believes, too, in moments of deep reflection and meditation and in God's self-disclosure to the one who truly seeks after him. The Christian believes, too, that the harmony of the soul that is longed for is to be sought. But the Christian believes all that is foreshadowed in the now is consummated in the divine presence of God when we are called to be with him. It is not in *us*. It is in *him* that we find it all.

The songwriter captured this well:

Seated one day at the organ,
I was weary and ill at ease,
And my fingers wandered idly
Over the noisy keys;
I know not what I was playing,
Nor what I was dreaming then,
But I touched one chord of music
Like the sound of a great amen.
It flooded the crimson twilight
Like the close of an angel psalm;
It lay o'er my feeble spirit
Like the touch of infinite calm;
It quieted pain and sorrow—
Like love overcoming strife;
It seemed a harmonious echo
From our discordant life;
It linked all perplexed meanings
Into one perfect peace,
And trembled away into silence,
As if it were loath to cease.
I have sought and I seek it vainly—
That one lost chord divine—
Which came from the soul of the organ
And entered into mine.

It may be that death's bright angel
Will speak in that chord again,
It may be that only in heav'n
I shall hear that grand Amen![7]

That will be the sound of ultimate harmony and the silence of ultimate awe.

APPENDIX

❧

SUGGESTED BIBLIOGRAPHY ON THE AUTHORITY OF THE SCRIPTURES

Bauckham, Richard. *Jesus and the Eyewitnesses: The Gospels as Eyewitness Testimony*. Grand Rapids, MI: Eerdmans, 2008. A seminal work on the Gospel writers' use of original eyewitness testimony, with an updated examination of the role of oral tradition in biblical times.

Blomberg, Craig. *The Historical Reliability of the Gospels*. 2nd ed. Downers Grove, IL: InterVarsity Press Academic, 2007. For more on this book and Blomberg's response to supposed Bible errors, see also http://thegospelcoalition.org/blogs/justintaylor/2008/03/26/interview-with-craig-blomberg/.

Dickson, John. *Life of Jesus: Who He Is and Why He Matters*. Grand Rapids, MI: Zondervan, 2010. An engaging look at the life of Jesus in his first-century environment from a historian of ancient history.

Ehrman, Bart, and N. T. Wright. "'Dialogue Between Bart Ehrman and N. T. Wright: Is Our Pain, God's Problem?'" Available online at http://bit.ly/bundles/ehrmanproject/3.

Ehrman Project. Various biblical scholars respond to Bart

Ehrman's challenge to the credibility of Christianity and reliability of the Scriptures. Available online at http://ehrmanproject.com/index.

Evans, Craig A. *Fabricating Jesus: How Modern Scholars Distort the Gospels.* Downers Grove, IL: InterVarsity Press, 2008. New Testament scholar Evans looks at the biblical and ancient sources that provide a portrait of Jesus and the arguments made by *The Da Vinci Code* and the Jesus Seminar.

Kitchen, K. A. *On the Reliability of the Old Testament.* Annotated ed. Grand Rapids, MI: Eerdmans, 2006. An examination of the correspondence between archaeology and the text of the Old Testament by an emeritus professor of Egyptology and archaeology at the University of Liverpool.

Lennox, John. *Seven Days That Divide the World: The Beginning According to Genesis and Science.* Grand Rapids, MI: Zondervan, 2011. Although the focus of this work looks at the origins of the universe from scientific and biblical data, Lennox, professor of mathematics at Greens College, Oxford, provides great insight for approaching biblical literature and scientist theories and evidence.

Witherington, Ben. "Review of Forged (by Bart Ehrman)." Available online at http://bit.ly/bundles/ehrmanproject/4. See also his lecture "Will the Real Jesus Please Stand Up," available online at http://www.patheos.com/community/bibleandculture/2011/02/28/will-the-real-jesus-please-stand-up-a-vertical-jesus-in-a-world-of-horizontal-analysis/.

Notes

Chapter 1: Movie Making or Soul Making

1. Marilyn Ferguson, *The Aquarian Conspiracy: Personal and Social Transformation in Our Time* (New York: Tarcher, 1987), 296.

Chapter 2: How the West Was Lost Through Its Gains

1. William Blake, "The Everlasting Gospel," in *The Oxford Book of English Mystical Verse*, ed. D. H. S. Nicholson and A. H. E. Lee (Oxford: Clarendon Press, 1917), emphasis added.
2. Steve Turner, *The Gospel According to the Beatles* (Philadelphia: Westminster John Knox Press, 2006), 188–89.
3. Sri Ravi Shankar, "The Ancient New Age," as addressed online at http://www.parauniversal.com/2007/10/the-ancient-new -age-august-1996-santamonica-california/_.
4. Sri Ravi Shankar, *Hinduism and Christianity: A Talk* (Kendra, India: Vyakti Vikas, 1998), 70–71.
5. The choice of taking either that which has been offered or nothing at all. This term is named after Thomas Hobson of Cambridge, England (1544–1630), who rented horses and gave his customers only one choice: the horse nearest the stable door.

Chapter 3: Exhaling the Old, Inhaling the New

1. Elaine Woo, "Writer Was Pivotal Figure in New Age Movement," *Los Angeles Times*, November 2, 2008, accessed online at http://articles.latimes.com/2008/nov/02/local/me-ferguson2.

2. Ibid.

3. Ibid.

4. Ibid.

5. Ibid.

6. Elizabeth Lesser, *The New American Spirituality: A Seeker's Guide* (New York: Villard Books, 1999), 31.

7. Elizabeth Lesser, "Insider's Guide to 21st Century Spirituality," *Spirituality and Health*, Spring 2000, accessed online at http://www.spirituality-health.com/NMagazine/articles.php?id-738.

8. Ibid.

9. Ted Turner, quoted in David Friend and *Life* magazine, *The Meaning of Life: Reflections in Words and Pictures on Why We Are Here* (New York: Little, Brown, 1991), 73.

Chapter 4: From Oprah to Chopra

1. Bill Adler, ed., *The Uncommon Wisdom of Oprah Winfrey: A Portrait in Her Own Words* (New York: Carol Publishing, 1997), 3.

2. Janet Lowe, *Oprah Winfrey Speaks: Insight from the World's Most Influential Voice* (New York: Wiley, 1998), 37.

3. Ibid., 38–39.

4. Adler, *The Uncommon Wisdom of Oprah Winfrey*, 4.

5. Ibid., 7.

6. Ibid., 28.

7. Marcia Z. Nelson, "Oprah on a Mission: Dispensing a Gospel of Health and Happiness," *Christian Century*, September 25, 2002, 24–25. Used by permission.

8. Kitty Kelley, *Oprah: A Biography* (New York: Crown Archetype, 2010), 97.

9. Ibid., 419.

10. Ibid., 49.

11. Ibid., 54.

12. Ibid., 87.

13. Ibid., 86–87.

14. Ibid., 337.

15. Ibid., 73.

Chapter 5: The Religion of Quantum

1. Deepak Chopra in "Quantum Healing," interview by Daniel Redwood, accessed online at http://www.healthy.net/asp/templates/interview.asp?PageType=Interview&Id=167.
2. "Deepak Chopra," in *The Skeptics Dictionary,* accessed online at http://www.skepdic.com/chopra.html.
3. Ibid.
4. Ibid.
5. Ibid.
6. See also "Alternative Health Practices," in *The Skeptics Dictionary,* at http://skepdic.com/althelth.html; "Faith Healing," at http://www.skepdic.com/faithhealing.html; and "Readers Comments: Ayurvedic Medicine & Deepak Chopra," at http://www.skepdic.com/comments/chopracom.html. For further reading, see John Ankerberg and John Weldon, *Encyclopedia of New Age Beliefs* (Eugene, OR: Harvest House, 1996); Kurt Butler, *A Consumer's Guide to "Alternative Medicine": A Close Look at Homeopathy, Acupuncture, Faith-Healing, and Other Unconventional Treatments* (Buffalo, NY: Prometheus Books, 1992); Heinz R. Pagels, *The Cosmic Code: Quantum Physics as the Language of Nature* (New York: Simon & Schuster, 1982); and Douglas Stalker and Clark Glymour, eds., *Examining Holistic Medicine* (Buffalo: Prometheus Books, 1989).
7. Deepak Chopra, *The Seven Spiritual Laws of Success: A Practical Guide to the Fulfillment of Your Dreams* (San Rafael, CA: Amber-Allen Publishing, 1994), iv, v.
8. "Deepak Chopra," in *The Skeptics Dictionary.*

Chapter 6: Go West, Young Man

1. Aseem Shukla, "Dr. Chopra: Honor Thy Heritage," *Washington Post,* April 28, 2010, accessed online at http://onfaith.washingtonpost.com/onfaith/panelists/aseem_shukla/2010/04/dr_chopra_honor_thy_heritage.html.
2. Plotinus, quoted in Michael Cox, *Handbook of Christian Spirituality* (San Francisco: Harper and Row, 1983), 39.

3. Albert B. Simpson, "Himself," in *Hymns of the Christian Life* (Harrisburg, PA: Christian Publications, 1962), 237. Public domain.

Chapter 7: The Three Gurus

1. Swami Vivekananda, *The Complete Works of Swami Vive-kananda*, accessed online at http://en.wikisource.org/wiki/ The_Complete_Works_of_Swami_Vivekananda/Volume_4/ Lectures_and_Discourses/My_Master.
2. "Swami Vivekananda," Wikipedia, http://en.wikipedia.org/ wiki/Swami_Vivekananda.
3. Bhupendranath Datta, *Swami Vivekananda, Patriot Prophet: A Study* (Calcutta, India: Nababharat Publishers, 1954), 212.
4. Vivekananda, *The Complete Works of Swami Vivekananda*.
5. Swami Vivekananda as reported by the *Chicago Tribune*, September 20, 1893, quoted by David L. Johnson, *A Reasoned Look at Asian Religions* (Minneapolis: Bethany, 1995), 106.
6. Paramahansa Yogananda, accessed online at http://www .anandapaloalto.org/joy/gurus.html.
7. Marianne Williamson, "A Spiritual Response to Terrorism," December 17, 2008, http://blog.marianne.com/journal/ archives/2008/12/a_spiritual_res.php.
8. Deepak Chopra, "The Maharishi Years: The Untold Story," *Huffington Post*, February 13, 2008, accessed online at http:// www.huffintonpost.com/deepak-chopra/the-maharishi-years -the-u-b-86412.html.
9. Ibid.
10. H. H. Sri Sri Ravi Shankar, *Celebrating Love* (Udaypura, Bangalore: Sri Sri Publications Trust, 2005), 35.

Chapter 8: Smiling Your Way Through Puzzles

1. Quoted in Li Cheng, *Song of a Wanderer: Beckoned by Eternity* (Cincinnati, OH: Foundation for Chinese Christian Authors, 2002), 88.
2. For further details of all these stories, see E. F. Wu et al., *The Five Great Religions of the World* (Hong Kong: Holy Literatures, 1989).

3. Isshu Miura and Ruth Fuller Sasaki, *The Zen Koan: Its History and Use in Rinzai Zen* (New York: Harcourt, Brace, 1965), xl.

4. Heinrich Dumoulin, *Zen: Enlightenment, Origins and Meaning*, trans. from the German by John C. Maraldo (Boston: Shambhala, 2007), 67.

5. Elizabeth Lesser, *The New American Spirituality: A Seeker's Guide* (New York: Villard Books, 1999), 113.

6. A crucial Buddhist doctrine of the cyclical cause and effect of suffering. Also used as a way to approach problems in daily life or forms of collective suffering.

7. David L. Johnson, *A Reasoned Look at Asian Religions* (Minneapolis: Bethany, 1995), 50–51.

8. Ibid., 53–54.

9. An ontic referent is that which in and of itself is objectively real, apart from anything anyone can contribute to it.

Chapter 9: Do You Really Want to Live?

1. G. K. Chesterton, *Heretics*, accessed online at http://www.gutenberg.org/files/470/470-h/470-h.htm.

2. Quoted in Dale Ahlquist, *G. K. Chesterton: The Apostle of Common Sense* (San Francisco: Ignatius Press, 2003), 63.

Chapter 10: The Ties That Bind

1. Alec Liu, "IBM's Watson Computer Wallops 'Jeopardy!' Champs in Trial Run" (January 13, 2011), accessed online at http://www.foxnews.com/scitech/2011/01/13/ibm-watson-takes-jeopardy-champs/.

2. Ibid.

3. James Stewart, *The Strong Name* (Grand Rapids, MI: Baker, 1972), 55, italics mine.

Chapter 12: Reshaping Jesus to Suit Our Prejudices

1. Elizabeth Lesser, *The New American Spirituality: A Seeker's Guide* (New York: Villard Books, 1999), 410.

2. Eckhart Tolle, *The Power of Now: A Guide to Spiritual Enlightenment* (Novato, CA: New World Library, 1999), 223, 225.

3. Neale Donald Walsch, *Conversations with God: An Uncommon Dialogue*, book 2 (Newburyport, MA: Hampton Roads Publishing, 1997), 74, 75, 80.
4. Ibid., 57.
5. Lesser, *The New American Spirituality*.
6. Deepak Chopra, *The Third Jesus: The Christ We Cannot Ignore* (New York: Random House), 8, 9.
7. Ibid., 9–10.
8. Ibid., 9.
9. Ibid., 3–4.
10. Ibid., 111, 112.
11. See Tom Butler-Bowdon, *50 Spiritual Classics* (Boston: Nicholas Brealey, 2005), 76.
12. Ibid.
13. Ibid., 286.
14. Francis Thompson, "The Hound of Heaven."

Chapter 13: The Greatest of All

1. Oscar Wilde, "The Ballad of Reading Gaol," accessed online at http://www.gutenberg.org/files/301/301-h/301-h.htm.
2. Story used by permission.
3. See William Blake's poem "And Did Those Feet in Ancient Time" (ca. 1804–1810), in M. H. Abrams, *The Norton Anthology of English Literature*, 3rd ed. (New York: W.W. Norton, 1975), 1,342.
4. Deepak Chopra, "The Three Maharishis," *Huffington Post*, February 6, 2008, accessed online at http://www.huffingtonpost.com/deepak-chopra/the-three-maharishis_b_85432.html.
5. As quoted in EricMetaxas, *Amazing Grace: William Wilberforce and the Heroic Campaign to End Slavery* (New York: HarperOne, 2007), 37.
6. F. W. Boreham's comments on "Wilberforce" as excerpted in "29 July: Boreham on William Wilberforce," accessed online at http://thisdaywithfwboreham.blogspot.com/2006/08/29-july-boreham-william-wilberforce.html.

Chapter 14: False Assumptions and Magnificent Truths

1. See W. E. H. Lecky, *History of European Morals from Augustus to Charlemagne,* vol. 2 (New York: D. Appleton and Company, 1890), 8.
2. See the appendix: "Suggested Bibliography on the Authority of the Scriptures," for these and other excellent resources.
3. Gerald L. Sittser, *Water from a Deep Well: Christian Spirituality from Early Martyrs to Modern Missionaries* (Downers Grove, IL: InterVarsity Press, 1997), 185.
4. Charles Haddon Spurgeon, quoted in A. W. Pink, *The Attributes of God* (Grand Rapids, MI: Baker, 1975), 88.
5. Matthew Parris, "As an Atheist, I Truly Believe Africa Needs God," *Times,* December 27, 2008, accessed online at http://www.timesonline.co.uk/tol/comment/columnists/matthew_parris/article5400568.ece.
6. Ibid.
7. "The Lost Chord," lyrics: Adelaide Anne Proctor (1825–1864); music: Arthur Sullivan (1842–1900). Public domain.